Well-Being and Success for University Students

Well-Being and Success for University Students: Applying PERMA+4 is grounded in the science of well-being and positive psychology and teaches students how to strengthen their health and well-being, as well as to make their study journey more enjoyable and successful. Higher education has changed dramatically during the last few years, and given the massive growth of mental health challenges among students, universities and faculty have recognized the need to help students strive, not only survive. Universities have great potential and responsibility to promote the well-being of their students. This book provides students with information, motivation, and skills to build their own unique well-being and helps colleges to produce more well-being in the university culture.

Students and faculty will be introduced to PERMA+4, an evidence-based framework for enhancing well-being and positive functioning, including academic performance. This book emphasizes practical applications of findings from the best available research to have students learn several steps they can take to strengthen their well-being and academic performance. Individual chapters talk about popular topics of positive psychology such as positive emotions, engagement, relationships, meaning, achievement, physical health, mindset, environment, and economic security. Each chapter summarizes the knowledge on specific topics, invites students to assess their well-being in the particular life domain, and encourages them to explore and try activities and evidence-based interventions to learn how to care for their own mental and overall health.

This book not only serves as a guide for students but also as a useful tool for professors seeking to enhance their courses and programs with well-being promotion and student wellness centers across the world.

Jana Koci, PhD, is an Assistant Professor of Health and Well-Being Education at Charles University in Prague, Czech Republic, and she is a leading researcher and educator on building academic well-being in her country. She teaches a popular Students' Well-being class for Charles University and 4EU+ Alliance students, and she wrote this book based on her deep care for all young adults she works with.

Stewart I. Donaldson, PhD, is Distinguished University Professor and Executive Director of the Claremont Evaluation Center at Claremont Graduate University. He is deeply committed to improving lives through positive psychology research and education. He is Co-Founder of the first PhD and research-focused master's programs in positive psychology at Claremont Graduate University and mentors many graduate students specializing in positive psychology and evaluation science.

Well-Being and Success for University Students

Applying PERMA+4

Jana Koci and Stewart I. Donaldson

Routledge
Taylor & Francis Group

NEW YORK AND LONDON

First published 2024
by Routledge
605 Third Avenue, New York, NY 10158

and by Routledge
4 Park Square, Milton Park, Abingdon, Oxon, OX14 4RN

Routledge is an imprint of the Taylor & Francis Group, an informa business

ISBN: 9781032457185 (hbk)
ISBN: 9781032457208 (pbk)
ISBN: 9781003378365 (ebk)

DOI: 10.4324/9781003378365

Typeset in Times New Roman
by codeMantra

I would like to thank my beautiful family for their infinite love and support, and to all my students and colleagues for reminding me of how much goodness and beauty is in people every day. I would love to humbly dedicate this book written from my heart to students from all around the world.

Jana

Contents

Preface   *viii*
Acknowledgments   *x*
About the Authors   *xi*

Introduction   1

 1 Caring for Your Well-Being   5

 2 Building Your Positive Emotions   32

 3 Building Your Engagement   53

 4 Building Your Relationships   76

 5 Building Your Meaning   97

 6 Building Your Achievement   115

 7 Building Your Physical Health   140

 8 Building Your Mindset   172

 9 Building Your Environment   193

10 Building Your Economic Security   215

Conclusion   232

Index   *235*

Preface

When I was 17 years old, circumstances gave me the passion of my life – positive psychology. Something that spoke to my heart with the energy of a thunderbolt and something that caught my attention like nothing ever before. Since there was no opportunity to study positive psychology at the university yet, at the age of 18, I chose to study Health Education, and I started my academic journey. I always loved being a student. My university years were not only the most joyful, but also the most stressful years in my life. I feared failure and I struggled with perfectionism as a result of my low self-esteem. I used to be nervous to speak in front of the class, I did not sleep well, and even though I studied well-being, my overall lifestyle was not very healthy. I spent almost all of my time with excessive studying that made me feel exhausted, followed by self-educating on how to help myself feel better. Right after I passed my master's state final examination, closing an important chapter of my life, my professors asked me if I would like to teach in our university. "You mean like me?" I asked. "Yes, you." They replied. "And what would I teach?" I got scared. "Exactly what you just told us." I got their answer.

I would never believe that someone like me, with such a deep fear of public speaking, could ever teach other people. But I loved health and well-being education so deeply, so while reminding myself of what my dad taught me (that if you decide to do something, you can always figure out how to do it) I said, "All right, I will do it." Another great chapter just opened in front of my eyes and my life gifted me with another passion of mine: the opportunity to work with wonderful, witty, brilliant, cheerful, and spontaneous students like you. I still get nervous speaking in front of people sometimes. But I am also passionate about well-being topics like never before, studying and researching them every day. And being able to work with my students has been the best thing that has ever happened to my well-being.

This book is a result of my almost 20 years in academia, my love for the field of positive psychology, my desire to learn how to live authentically, and my deepest appreciation for students like you. I hope this book will help you to get to know your beautiful self better and to build your well-being in the way that is right for you. You will learn how to take care of important areas of your life, you will have many opportunities to try on different activities and tools supporting your well-being, and you will be invited to use tips and strategies to maintain your health backed up by science. May this book help you enjoy your studies as much as possible and be successful in living the way you desire. Enjoy building your good life and know that you can do anything you want. It is all already within you! And I hope this book will help you to embrace it. I am excited that I can stay connected to you through these lines. Be well and have fun reading the pages!

Jana Koci
Prague, Czech Republic

More than two decades of positive psychology research and practice have provided us with a new understanding of well-being and positive functioning. This book will introduce you to the new evidence-based framework, PERMA+4, and provide you with new tools and ideas for improving your well-being and success on a daily basis. Professor Koci's passion, leadership, and many years of health and well-being education experience have enabled us to translate the latest peer-reviewed well-being science into a very practical resource. This book specifically aims to provide university students, faculty, and staff with new strategies and tools for enhancing students' well-being and success across the world. I wish you much engagement and success as you explore the following chapters intended to help you improve your university experience and your life for many years to come.

Stewart I. Donaldson
Claremont, CA, USA

Acknowledgments

I would like to personally thank my family. Thank you for being supportive, loving, and such an important part of my life. I would like to thank my current, previous, and future students for letting me witness their awesomeness, and my special thank you goes to all my students attending our well-being classes for the love, kindness, and support they show towards each other in every class. You have a special place in my heart. My heartfelt thank you belongs to you, Stewart, for all your wonderful research on PERMA+4, for sharing your views on life with me in our endless discussions, and for our friendship that means a lot to me.

Jana

We would first like to thank all of Professor Koci's students who have given her feedback on her design of the flower well-being assessment; suggested activities, pictures and figures; and the suggested sources she has provided. Thanks also to those students and colleagues who have read the draft sections and improved the book. Special thanks to Natalie Bílková, Carrie Blakely, Lena Beck, and Petra Koldová for providing editing services, and to Jaroslav Artemov for helping with the graphical illustration of our well-being wheels. Finally, we would like to thank the team Adam Woods, Nivedita Menon, and Alison Macfarlane at Routledge who believed in this project from the start and who have helped us every step of the way to publish this resource for you.

Jana and Stewart

About the Authors

Jana Koci, PhD, is an Assistant Professor of Health and Well-Being Education at Charles University in Prague, Czech Republic. She is a leading researcher and educator on building academic well-being in her country and she wrote this book based on her deep care for university students. She teaches a popular student well-being class for Charles University students and also for students from European universities from the 4EU+ alliance, based on the content of the book you hold in your hands. She organizes research on students' well-being at her university, and her sincere care for her students is reflected in her excellent student evaluations. Jana graduated with honors for her outstanding academic achievements and she was honored for her contribution as an outstanding young researcher by the EFSA European Food Safety Authority committee in 2015. Jana is a visiting professor at Claremont Graduate University in California where she works on independent research in positive psychology, and she has also spent several semesters at the University of Nebraska – Lincoln designing a nutrition education program for Czech students. She earned her PhD in Pedagogy with an emphasis on Health Education, and she focuses her research on the application of positive psychology within the academic environment through the fostering of well-being for university students, professors, and university employees. Jana appreciates discussions with her dear colleagues while teaching a course for professors on How to Build the Well-Being of University Students, and she also strives to support the well-being of teachers, professors, and all academic personnel in her Well-Being for Academics course. She is a member of the Positive Education Consortium, and she also enjoys writing books on well-being care for middle schools and high schools. She is a co-active well-being coach and the founder of Uniwellsity. She deeply respects and appreciates the science of well-being; she enjoys working with her students and she cares for the well-being of the whole academic community. And you are her main motivation to write this book in one breath.

Jana can be reached out at jana@uniwellsity.com.

Stewart I. Donaldson, PhD, is Distinguished University Professor and Executive Director of the Claremont Evaluation Center and The Evaluators Institute at Claremont Graduate University. He is deeply committed to improving lives through positive psychology research and education. He is Co-Founder of the first PhD and research-focused master's programs in positive psychology at Claremont Graduate University, and he mentors many graduate students specializing in positive psychology and evaluation science. Professor Donaldson serves on the Council of Advisors for the International Positive Psychology Association (IPPA), is Faculty Advisor for the Student Division of IPPA (SIPPA), served on the IPPA Board of Directors (2013–2017), and was Chair of IPPA's World Congress of Positive Psychology in Los Angeles (2013). He has published numerous articles, chapters, and books on the science of positive psychology and has been honored with many career achievement awards for his research and evaluation contributions including the 2021 IPPA Fellow Award, 2019 IPPA Work and Organizations Division Exemplary Research to Practice Award, and the 2019 SIPPA Inspiring Mentor Award.

Authors' contributions

Jana Koci has written this book and invented the content, designed the flower tool as a well-being assessment, built suggested activities, produced the pictures, and suggested the sources of where to learn more. Stewart I. Donaldson has edited this book and helped with the publishing process.

Introduction

Hello beautiful student! How are you doing?

I can't help being curious about how you are doing and feeling, as I start every class by asking my students this question. Whether you are doing well or less well, there is no right or wrong answer. Everything gets to be here, and all emotions and states of our well-being are welcome. We all come to reading this book, as well as my students come to our well-being classes, with different emotions, various moods, and unique experiences we are trying to process in our lives. But we all also come here jointly to enjoy the process of learning about how to build our own good lives. It is beautiful how much we can learn from the science of well-being today. But we can also reflect on our current well-being state regularly and decide whether we want to pick and try some fun activities to maintain our well-being or not. In this book, you will learn about the positive functioning of university and college students and about the building blocks that generate your well-being. You will find a brief theory on each area of your life that puzzles your good life, you will have an opportunity to self-assess (download your free self-assessment workbook by scanning the QR code below or at https://www.uniwellsity.eu/workbook) and reflect on your current well-being regularly, and you will be presented with fun, engaging, and easily applicable well-being activities backed by science.

But the purpose of this book is not to tell you what to do. Rather than a cookbook for well-being, this book can be seen as a menu you can choose from. It is to provide you with several possible ways, strategies, and activities you can pick from, try, and embrace. To gain information, to get motivated, and become skilled. It is to show you that there are many researchers in this beautiful world who care for your well-being. And there are fields of positive psychology and positive education that create an effort to provide you with theory and practices to help you build your own unique, well-lived life. The purpose of this book is to show you that your professors and teachers want you to be well and that your universities and colleges care about you. Your classmates do too, as well as your friends and your family. And I do as well. I care for you deeply. Keep in mind that this book is your personal companion on your unique well-being journey, and it is here for you anytime you decide to come back to it. Always. Enjoy your journey to self-discovery and self-care. I will be there with you on every page.

Jana

DOI: 10.4324/9781003378365-1

How to Work with This Book?

As you will learn, we all experience well-being our unique, slightly different ways. We all have different needs and different things help us to fulfill them. After reading this book, you will understand the theory behind various areas of our lives that help us generate our well-being. You will reflect and learn, for example, not only about your relationships and your physical health but also about your mindset, positive emotions, or economic security. And you will have a chance to self-reflect on where you currently stand in all those and many more so-called building blocks of well-being. But what if you would like to grow and cultivate any of those life domains? As mentioned in the introduction, the book will provide you with a number of activities, interventions, and tips where to learn more. Science-based tools and activities will be marked with this icon 🔵 and you can find suggestions on where to learn more on websites, in other books, or even through videos online under this icon 💡. And you will sometimes see both icons together in case there is an activity including the suggestion where to learn more at the same time. So what can you expect after your first well-being assessment looking deeper into the individual life domains in Chapter 1? Some of you will be interested in going straight to the chapter discussing the building block of well-being that you might feel like need your attention (e.g., you will be interested in looking at your meaning in life deeper, because you struggle with seeing it clearly). Some of you will, on the other hand, be more interested in cultivating the building block you already do good at (e.g., your engagement is already high, but you seek some inspiration to engage with your life in new ways). And some of you will simply go straight to the chapter talking about the building block of well-being that interests you the most regardless of how you are doing in that particular life domain. There is no right or wrong way to work with this book. Follow your gut and do what feels good for you. Choose the tips and activities that will fit you the best. But how to pick and choose the right ones? If you feel like you experience well-being as something outside of you, you will probably benefit from activities including other people and your environment. You might enjoy learning and practicing activities such as active constructive responding and spending more time in nature, but journaling might not be the most suitable activity for you at the moment. Or vice versa. If you experience well-being mainly through the lance of pleasant emotions, journaling about what went well or processing unpleasant emotions can work wonders for you. Or you might gravitate toward activities cultivating your character strengths if you experience well-being dominantly from the inside. Listen to yourself and what feels right. And if you feel overworked, and needing to rest from activities, do it. Even just reading the book and learning about them with no intention to try them will expand your well-being literacy, and it will provide you with ideas that might come in handy in the future. So please relax, take your time, and enjoy your well-being journey in your own way and speed.

Your Well-being Care Strategy

To create the right approach to your well-being care, you might find it helpful to look at the upcoming picture. I would like to invite you to always **choose what fits you**. Remember, one size does not fit all. If some recommendation does not feel right for you or some activity does not interest you, skip it and move to something that fits better. You might also find it helpful to be creative and to **tailor tips, recommendations, and activities to your lifestyle**. If you are a morning person, you might enjoy stretching your body first thing in the morning. But if you feel like you hardly get through your mornings and you feel more energized in your afternoons, you can enjoy stretching your body after school or before your bedtime better. Another thing to consider is your commitment. Many interventions such as journaling about an event to vent your emotions, mind mapping your values, or investing 10 minutes to deeply relax your body will provide you with an immediate effect, but there is also a lot of evidence supporting the strategy of sustaining with your interventions to generate the long-term impact. So, **give it time** please, and make the chosen interventions a part of your everyday life to enjoy the benefits. Science also embraces the idea that we support our health and well-being the best when we focus on our health and well-being care holistically. Thus, feel free to focus primarily on the area of your life that needs your attention the most (e.g., to care for your relationships). But don't forget that your physical health, meaning in life, and a good mindset also deserve your time, please. If possible, **focus on more than one building block of your well-being**. You might also find it helpful to **choose mutually reinforcing activities**. What does that mean? Pair-up activities that go hand in hand. Buying a gym membership to brisk walk on a treadmill will support your physical health but the extra cost won't be aligned with your effort to save money on making your coffee at home. Choose smart but play with it as well. Experiment, innovate, and make it fun. You are the one who holds the steering wheel. **You choose and decide** where you want to invest your time and energy and what you want to focus on. You are also in charge of the rhythm of your well-being care. Whether you can try new things or you choose to slow down while feeling like resting. What will also make your strategy effective is to make your well-being care **as accessible to you** as possible. Thus, let me invite you to prioritize actions that you have time for, feel energized enough to do, and are also financially available to you at the moment. If you need to save money to be able to buy a new phone, you might consider focusing on your needs rather than wants for some time. If you feel chronically tired and out of energy, you might consider stopping running and choosing to do yoga or some comfy lazy stretching at home. And if you feel pressured by lack of time over your examination period, you might prefer some short activities such as writing three good things down each evening that will only ask for 5 minutes of your time. This leads us to adjustability. **Make your well-being care flexible** enough to sustain. It is all right to adapt to your current schedule by cooking yourself a healthy lunch one day and a balanced dinner another day. By going home one weekend to connect with your family and staying in dorms the next one, saving it only for yourself. Or to reschedule your swimming session while feeling out of energy. Give yourself the freedom to be flexible. And finally, to make sure you don't forget, **remind yourself** by adding the planned activities to your calendar. Write your intentions down on a sticky note and place it somewhere visible. Or if you function like I do, write your plan of action down on the back of your hand. Whatever strategy you use, I hope it works the best for you, so you can enjoy your well-being journey to the fullest.

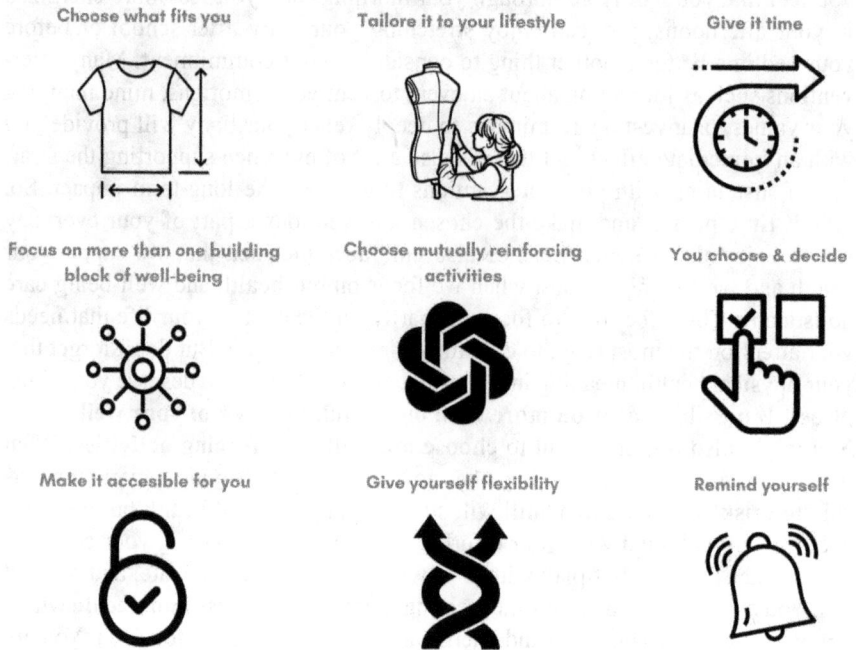

Figure 0.1 My well-being care strategy.

1 Caring for Your Well-Being

Being well starts with caring for yourself.

— Jana Koci

What Is Well-Being?

To better understand well-being, let's start with a few questions that help us grasp its meaning. First off, let me ask you what is well-being to you? How would you define **a good life** and how do you feel while **being well**? Do you feel joyful? Balanced, complete, and confident? Or do you feel safe, relaxed, and peaceful? Do you smile? Laugh and even joke? Or do you prefer being authentic no matter the feelings you are experiencing at a certain time? What about where you are and who you are with? Do you feel well at home? In the city or in nature? Do you like the company of those who love you? Or do you also enjoy being alone? Think for a minute about what and who contributes to your health and life satisfaction and what being well actually means to you.

We use a beautiful portfolio of terms to describe what being well might be. So, it is understandable that we still don't have one general definition of well-being. But for now, let's zoom out a little bit and let's look at an even broader term – **health**.

The World Health Organization (2022) defines health as *a state of complete physical, mental and social well-being and not merely the absence of disease or infirmity.* The enjoyment of the highest attainable standard of health is, according to the World Health Organization, one of the fundamental rights of every human being without the distinction of race, religion, political belief, economic, or social conditions.

How can we understand this? Well, for example, not having our leg broken or not being diagnosed with any illness does not necessarily mean that we consider ourselves healthy, and vice versa. Any objective diagnosis (let's stay with the example of one's broken leg) does not reflect our subjective state and does not necessarily have to be a limitation for us to feel healthy.

Mental health is defined by the World Health Organization as *a state of well-being in which an individual realizes their abilities, can cope with the normal*

DOI: 10.4324/9781003378365-2

stresses of life, can work productively and is able to make a contribution to their community.

Again, well-being is characterized not only by the absence of illness but also mainly by the presence of **resilience, strengths,** and **positive qualities** that allow us to **flourish** and **thrive**. Therefore, being well can be seen as having the capability to maintain your physical vitality, prosper mentally, and express your care for society, and have the capacity to love and be loved.

The Centers for Disease Control and Prevention (2018) states that even though there is no consensus on a single definition of well-being, there is a general agreement that, at minimum, a state of well-being includes *the presence of positive emotions and moods* (e.g., contentment and happiness), *the absence of negative emotions* (e.g., depression and anxiety), *satisfaction with life, fulfillment, and positive functioning*. Thus, well-being can be described as *judging life positively and feeling good.*

The bottom line is, despite the complications of clearly defining what well-being is, we know what well-being includes as well as what it excludes. We can find the words that allow us to subjectively describe what being well feels like to us and what, in the long run, represents a good life. Well-being is measurable, and even though it fluctuates over time, there are certain areas of our lives that generate it, too. Such areas of our lives can be **built** and **cared for**.

Figure 1.1 State of well-being.

Measuring Well-Being

Is well-being measurable? And how can we measure something we can barely define? Who is the judge of concluding that one is being well while another is not? The answer is simple. **You**. You are the one who decides what the phrase "good life" means to you and what being well *actually* feels like. And you are the one who judges where you stand, looking at your current well-being.

You might wonder whether we measure how well we are **doing in our lives** in general or how well we are **feeling at a certain moment**. Do we feel well *about* our lives, or do we feel well *in* our lives? Feeling well about our lives is an evaluation of our lives as a whole, while feeling well in our lives reflects our day-to-day joy, whether we believe we live a good life or not.

The UN World Happiness Report searches for answers as to whether we feel satisfied in our lives as a whole and Gallup's *Global Emotional Report* strives to answer how joyful our previous day was. It might not surprise you that each measure brings different results.

Both (the UN World Happiness Report and Gallup in its Global Emotional Report) use a scale from 0 to 10 to rate their respondents' present lives. How does the scale work? **Imagine a ladder with steps numbered from 0 at the bottom to 10 at the top.** The top of the ladder represents the best result, while the bottom of the ladder represents the worst. This simple but accurate evaluation lets us measure national well-being and even compare individual countries to each other. In 2021, there were 137 countries measured in the World Happiness Report, ranging from low as 1.86 in Afghanistan up to 7.80 in Finland, with an average of 5.53 among all measured countries for the particular year.

Are you curious about how the world is actually doing in terms of happiness and life satisfaction? Look at the top highest-ranking nations in terms of *how we are doing in our lives* (the first chart) and *how we feel about our lives* (the second chart):

Top 10 Nations according to the World Happiness Report in 2021

(OurWorldInData.org, 2023)

1 Finland (7.80)
2 Denmark (7.59)
3 Iceland (7.53)
4 Israel (7.47)
5 The Netherlands (7.40)
6 Sweden (7.40)
7 Norway (7.32)
8 Switzerland (7.24)
9 Luxembourg (7.23)
10 New Zealand (7.12)

Gallup's Positive and Negative Experience Indexes measure life's intangibles — feelings and emotions. The 2022 Global Emotions Report offers a snapshot of Gallup's latest measurements of people's positive and negative daily experiences as the second year of the COVID-19 pandemic continued. The findings are based on nearly 127,000 interviews with adults in 122 countries and areas in 2021 and early 2022, and Country Level Index Scores range from 0 to 100.

Top 10 countries leading in positive experience due to Global Emotions Report in 2021

(Gallup World Poll in Global Emotions Report, 2022)

1   Panama (85)
2   Indonesia (84)
3   Paraguay (84)
4   El Salvador (82)
5   Honduras (82)
6   Nicaragua (82)
7   Iceland (81)
8   Philippines (81)
9   Senegal (81)
10 Denmark (80)

So, what creates our well-being? To get a sense of what people find important in their lives, here is a list of what made us happy in 2020 (World Economic Forum, 2020). Can you relate?

- our health and physical well-being
- our relationship with our partner or spouse
- our children
- feeling that our lives have meaning
- our living conditions
- our personal safety and security
- feeling in control of our lives
- having a meaningful job and employment
- satisfaction with the direction our lives is going
- having more money
- our personal financial situation
- our friends
- our hobbies and interests
- finding someone to be with
- the amount of free time we have
- well-being of our country

The Science of Well-Being and Positive Psychology

Psychologists and researchers have expanded their focus from helping to eliminate what might be going "wrong in life" to also building what goes "well in life" within the last few decades. When elected as a president of the American Psychological Association in 1998, Professor Martin E. P. Seligman proposed Positive Psychology as a new subfield of psychology. As the name might tell us, he intended Positive Psychology to focus on what is life-giving rather than life-depleting with the first foundational article published in 2000 (Seligman & Csikszentmihalyi). Professor Peterson (2008) defined positive psychology as:

> a scientific approach to studying human thoughts, feelings, and behavior, with a focus on strengths instead of weaknesses, building the good in life instead of repairing the bad, and taking the lives of average people up to "great" instead of focusing solely on moving those who are struggling up to "normal."

Let me share a personal story with you. I will never forget the moment I first learned about positive psychology. I was a 17-year-old girl, and I devoted all my Saturdays in my senior year in of high school to a psychology course to get prepared for the university. In the middle of one long Saturday at school, our young and beautiful teacher, who was still a college student in psychology, mentioned the name of Professor Martin Seligman. She introduced him as the founder of positive psychology, the youngest applied psychology discipline that focuses on what can be done in our lives to make us happy. The Earth stopped spinning under my feet at that moment, and I asked myself, astonished, *"Can we really study what to do to be happier?"* I fell in love with positive psychology at first sight (or at first hearing?) and my life has been forever changed. I started university a few months later and have never left that environment since then. I studied health and well-being and started to teach it at the university right after my graduation. In that time, I was rewarded with the greatest gift of all: the opportunity to work with you, college students, day in and day out. Learning, teaching, and discussing health and well-being to make our lives a bit happier together. And this book I wrote for you from my heart will be all about that. While knowing that we all have bad days, we are all working on getting back to normal after traumatic or stressful events, knowing that asking for help can be the most courageous thing to do, or knowing that having flaws and weaknesses is a perfectly natural part of our life experiences, you will be guided to focus on your personal strengths, to explore what to do to really be happier, and to learn how to deepen your human skills. Skills of your emotion awareness and emotion regulation, of your communication, your ability to build relationships, empathy, skill of giving and receiving help, skill of showing respect, but also setting your goals, making decisions and solving your problems, taking new and different perspectives, building your self-efficacy, optimism, and a sense of purpose or meaning to make your everyday lives healthier and more well.

Well-Being of University Students

As you all might have experienced, being a college student is fulfilling, exciting, and fun, but also stressful and oftentimes exhausting. Studies show (2006) that there is a greater strain placed on your well-being, especially once you start university. The levels of your well-being do not return to their pre-university state, at least not during the first year of your studies, and this emotional strain also gets stronger throughout your semesters. Students often start their academic year enthusiastic and energized, but as the semester goes on, it leaves them feeling more and more stressed and less and less happy. Students report the biggest dropdown in positive emotions around exams, but it all comes back again with the beginning of the new semester (or the summer break, of course :-)

Working with students on a daily basis and observing my students over the years, I can sense how the years spent at university are times of **heightened stress**, **anxiety**, and even **depression** for them. Research shows that as life goes on, nearly every college student, like any other human being, feels restless, experiences a lack of sleep, and turns to unhealthy habits more frequently. Some students report having a lack of confidence and low self-esteem and notice their own inability to be assertive. Such feelings can be related to higher competitiveness, comparing yourself to others, or even doubting your abilities – nowadays called "imposter syndrome." Some students struggle with perfectionism, procrastination, or improper time management that increases their stress levels as a result. We all sometimes deal with our past or recent traumas. Some may experience abuse and eating disorders, and sexuality or gender identity questions also arise often. Nearly everyone feels under pressure to live up to family expectations and deals with family and relationship issues. In other words, if any of the above applies to you, **you are not alone**. We all experience distress in our personal ways, even during our college years.

But to be fair to our university years, students also often say that the best years are those spent at college! We often experience our first love, build lifelong friendships, receive deep inspiration, build a strong foundation for our personal identity, and create memories for life. Life has its ups and downs, even in college. The truth is that every student can practice **their resilience-building skills** and **care for their well-being**. And it is so worth it.

We know from evidence that students who **feel** and **do well** (compared to students with low well-being) have fewer:

- sick days at school and are less ill
- stress-related problems and have lower levels of burnout
- sleep-related problems

Students with **higher levels of well-being** also have better:

- overall physical health and experience higher levels of wellness
- stress management and better coping abilities and are more resilient
- have higher school attendance
- perform better at school
- have higher academic achievement
- are more prosocial and cooperative with classmates
- have more satisfying relationships at school and in personal life
- have greater self-control and have better self-regulation

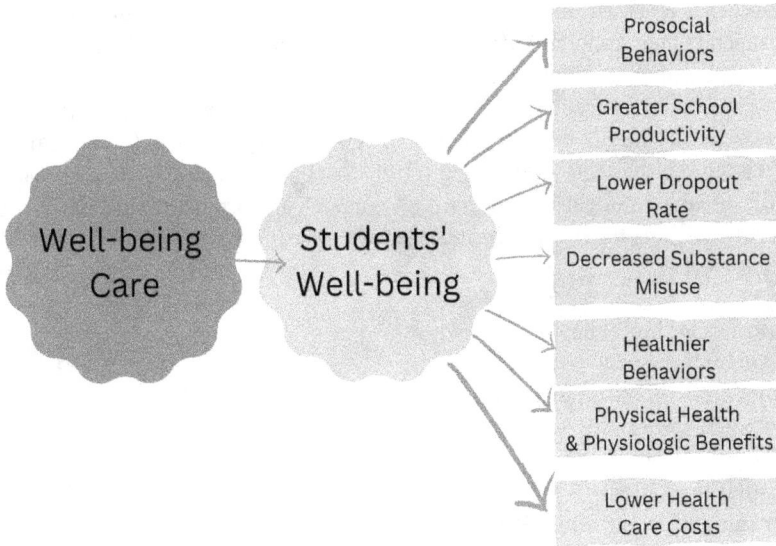

Figure 1.2 What well-being care generates for college students.

We recently asked (Koci, 2023) our seniors in their graduation year (from 17 different schools at Charles University in Prague, Czech Republic) what well-being means to them and what is the magic behind their success. We assessed their life satisfaction, and we had them rate their well-being building blocks across 78 different well-being subsections (life domains). And these are the answers we got from 600 of our students.

The most common words used by students to express **what well-being is to them** were:

- peace
- no stress
- satisfaction
- balance
- feeling good
- health and mental health

The "magic" behind our students' success was most commonly expressed by the words:

- my perseverance
- social support from family
- support from my friends and significant others
- my willpower
- my fear of failure

Our students assessed their life conditions as exceptional, and they believe they have reached their important life goals so far. They are very satisfied with their lives overall. But only half of our students agreed that their lives are close to their ideals, and they were strongly convinced that they would change almost nothing if they had a chance to live their lives over again (they mostly disagreed with this statement).

Viewing our students' well-being more closely (Koci, 2023), we were able to identify areas of students' lives that they generally feel need some improvement and growth. Using the 0–10 Cantril ladder (0 = worst; 10 = best), our students scale **at the lowest**:

- satisfactory investments
- good body posture
- enjoyment of what they do at school
- faith and spirituality
- engagement in school activities
- regular relaxation
- meaning in school activities
- ability to focus
- satisfactory savings
- good income

On the contrary, our students often feel confident about and rate **the best** their:

- high-quality relationships with animals and pets
- taking responsibility for their actions
- high-quality relationships with significant other(s)
- serving others with no expectation of getting anything back
- high-quality relationship with nature
- access to quality health care*
- shared positivity and enjoyed seeing other people being happy
- engagement in their hobbies
- responsibility
- recognition and enjoyment of others' achievements

We are learning that students appear to agree on some specific areas of their lives as "better" and some as "worse." Those assessments of individual areas of students' lives will fluctuate over time, and my research team also hypothesizes differences will be found from country to country, university from university, and even major from major as we continue measuring the well-being determinants more. Stepping a little bit back and looking at the bigger picture, Charles University students in our studies (Koci, 2023) as students in general struggle with economic security and would like to have better body posture, and they would like to increase joy, meaning, and ability to focus at school. But they also struggle with finding time to relax,

---

* The Czech Republic has a universal health care system with fee-for-service care funded by mandatory employment-related insurance plans

and many students don't have faith nor find themselves spiritual. Conversely, our students report overall good relationships with animals, pets, significant other(s), and nature, and they are responsible, giving, and enjoy others being happy and successful. They believe they have good access to good health care, and they are highly engaged when spending time doing their hobbies. Do you relate? Or do you not? And do you wonder how you would rate your well-being determinants? If yes, great! You will have many opportunities to do so across this whole book, and I would like to invite you to do this as often as you would like to. Learning about your well-being strengths and current weak spots can help you tremendously to become aware of **what works well** in your life and what you might want **to focus on to strengthen**. Enjoy the assessments that were created just for you in this book and play with your lifestyle to feel good and to be successful.

Figure 1.3 Well students, well universities!

Universities and college students themselves seek well-being support like never before. As we know the world today, we are witnessing a growing field of Positive Education, *an approach that brings together the science of positive psychology with best-practice teaching and learning to encourage and support schools and individuals within their communities to flourish* (Geelong Grammar School, 2011). Colleges as well as elementary, secondary, and higher schools have a great potential and responsibility to promote the well-being of their students (Koci & Koptikova, 2022a, 2022b). Research has identified two main ways to do that. Students can learn specific skills that contribute to their well-being, and the university environment (all physical, social, and psychological elements) can be structured in ways that promote well-being. Thus, university education can focus on both academic learning delivering the traditional outcomes of schooling (such as knowledge, critical thinking, communication, and other personal skills) and building students' well-being by teaching them skills and by building a good environment for them. This book can serve not only as a fun and entertaining guide for you, students, but it can also serve as a useful tool for professors seeking to enhance their courses and programs with positive education, and universities and colleges with well-being promotion, as well as for Student Wellness Centers across the world.

Positive Education

Skills of
Achievement

Skills of
Well-being

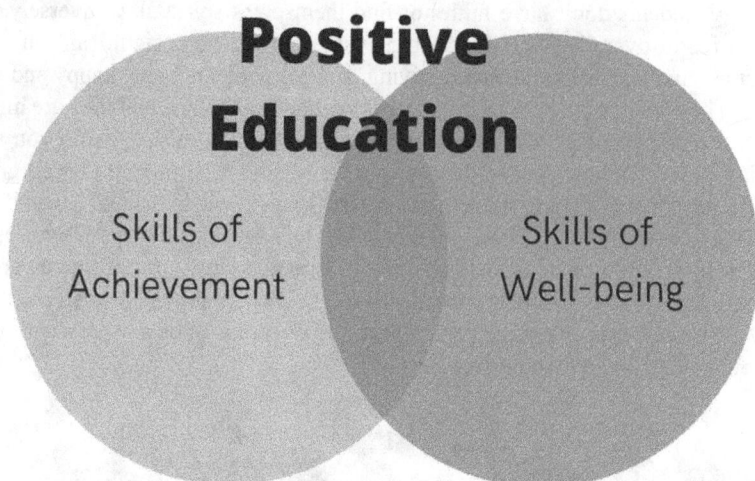

Figure 1.4 Positive Education, where skills of achievement meet skills of well-being.

Success and Academic Achievement

The word "success" might mean different things to different people. Some say success starts with good education that leads to a good career generating a good income. But some also say that success means being less stressed, less worried, more peaceful, and happier. Oxford Languages defines success as the **accomplishment of an aim or purpose**. In other words, success can be our graduation, finding our dream job, or being promoted at work, as well as being healthy, having close friends, enjoying life, learning, and feeling free.

We all dream about different things, especially during our college years. We dream about writing our first book, about being a professional athlete, about starting our company, being madly in love, living in a foreign country, or about our financial freedom. All we have to do is not let our dreams stay only dreams. Turn your dreams into visions and visions into specific plans.

Imagine a vision of what you want to achieve in your life – what you see as an important goal at the moment. What is your dream? Do you know what it is that **you** want from life? What do you want in the near future or what would be the way **you** want to live after college? If yes, make a plan on how to make your visions come true. What are the main goals you would like to reach along the way and what are the steps to be taken? It is worth it to work on our dreams. And so it is to persist. There is a process of making your dreams come true. And the activity is the real key to all success. Step by step, continue toward the goal you set for yourself. Trust the process, get back up when you fall down and persist. Sooner or later, you will get anywhere you want.

Success Success

what people think
it looks like

what it really
looks like

Figure 1.5 What does the way to success really look like?

Well-Being and Success

The evidence accumulated by positive psychology over the past two decades strongly supports the link between well-being and students' academic performance. We know today that students' success at school could be effectively supported through interventions promoting students' well-being (Koci, 2022; Koci & Donaldson, 2022). Still, students' mental health issues, poor academic achievement, and frequent school dropouts are becoming more and more prevalent. For this and many other reasons, academic well-being has garnered increased attention. Thus, many universities call for effective positive psychology interventions supporting well-being in students' everyday lives.

From Academic Well-Being to Success in School and Beyond

For a successful university student's life, it is healthy to find **harmony** between one's study responsibilities and private life. To be able to make time for yourself and to enjoy after-school activities. So, one could say, establishing the right **school-life balance**. Furthermore, the social aspect of student life was often mentioned as establishing new relationships and maintaining a collective, which plays an essential role. The current knowledge also shows that a student who wants to be successful should not focus solely on studies; they should also try some part-time jobs **to gain experience** and, mainly, find moments to **enjoy student life**. At the same time, let me emphasize that school does not only deliver knowledge. Students who learn to relax after a work day under pressure and students who take good care of their bodies and environment they live in also manage to stay focused and engaged. Students who see meaning in the activities they do and students who consciously work on their mindset by taking time to celebrate their achievements report better well-being compared to those who don't.

It is also important to learn how to find time to maintain healthy relationships, to set priorities, to make practical use of your knowledge, and even to manage finances to get the most out of your studies. **Habits you learn in your student years will grow with you, becoming a part of your work and family life afterwards** (Koci, 2022).

Academic Success

Academic success can be defined as the sum of **academic achievement, attainment of learning objectives, acquisition of desired skills, competencies, satisfaction, persistence, and post-college performance** (Koci, 2022; Koci & Donaldson, 2022; York et al., 2015). But your success as a student also includes all the friendships and good relationships you develop during your school years, all the lifestyle changes you make, and all the personal development you go through as a result of your college experience. Finding time for **your hobbies in the middle of the stressful finals to regenerate, making time for your family and friends, and building your personal life is success as well.**

But who defines your academic success? Others do, as well as you do. There are two dimensions to your success evaluation: **the subjective dimension** (what you perceive) and **the objective dimension** (what others perceive and where you stand in objective comparison to others or to set norms). And the two of these don't necessarily have to be (and aren't always) in line. Sometimes, we fail objectively, but subjectively, it can still feel like a win, or vice versa. Even though we get the best grade possible and we objectively really did perform great, we often cannot get over the little things that did not go as we expected, and we let the feeling of failure invade our success.

So, what really defines your academic success and how do you see it? There are many external and internal factors. One of the most influential external factors is, for example, our family. Beliefs and values of our caregivers, their support, and the skills they have helped us build until now. What has also been proven to be important is the support and positive approach of your peers, friends, your close social circle, and then the school itself: the school norms, emotional climate, or expectations of the school personnel we work with. The internal factors determining our success are also variegated. Our academic success is influenced not only by our intelligence, biology, and central nervous system but also by our character, values, motivation, experiences, and beliefs, as well as perceived self-efficacy. Self-efficacy sums up our individual beliefs about whether we have the capacity to reach our chosen goal and whether we believe in ourselves. Albert Bandura, the author of self-efficacy theory, used to say that believing that we can make it gets us halfway to the desired outcome. And I cannot agree more. But there is one more strong determinant that can help you reach your goals and dreams. And that is **your well-being**. Nowadays, we know that supporting students in building their well-being during their university studies and within the university environment positively influences their academic success.

This book aims to walk you through ideas on how to build and care for your individualized way of living as a university student in order to fulfill the potential of your academic success while also experiencing happiness and life satisfaction through your well-being care. Thus, the way of living is when you express your enthusiasm for what you are interested in, what fulfills you, and what brings you joy. To do activities that meet your needs and make you feel alive. To create and care for relationships, helping you meet your necessity to feel safe, stable, and secure, capable and cared for. To take adequate care of your physical health and to be genuinely interested in the environment you live in.

The Bottom Line

We have learned so far that well-being can be measured and built. But I would like you to learn more about particular areas of your life that actually help you to generate your well-being now. You will be introduced to a new framework for caring for your well-being in the upcoming sub-chapter, and this whole book will lead you, chapter by chapter, through the specific areas of your life that research finds essential for your flourishing. You will be invited to learn about the building blocks of well-being that generate a good life for us. Each chapter will introduce a particular building block that facilitates your flourishing. You will be guided step by step through your well-being assessment in each chapter to see how you are standing in that particular area of your life and you will be provided opportunities to reflect on your current situation and ideal state. You will also be kindly invited to try different evidence-based practices for building the skills of well-being, and you will be provided tips on how to practice hands-on well-being activities and techniques to increase all your building blocks in your everyday life. All to generate well-being, support your positive functioning, and your eventual success will come along!

Building Your Well-Being

Martin Seligman, the founder of positive psychology, in his very popular book called *Authentic Happiness* (2002), concluded that authentic happiness is evolved from three major sets of experiences in our life. Specifically from:

- experiencing pleasantness and positive emotions regularly (**living the pleasant life**)
- experiencing a high level of engagement in satisfying activities (**living the engaged life**)
- experiencing meaning and a sense of connectedness to a greater whole (**living the meaningful life**)

Following on his theory, in his other well-known book *Flourishing* (2011), Professor Seligman presents five building blocks of well-being that enable flourishing in our life. They are:

- positive emotions
- engagement
- relationships
- meaning
- achievement

He referred to all five elements of well-being above with the acronym PERMA, where each building block can help you increase your well-being by focusing on combinations of feeling good, being fully engaged with life, building high-quality relationships, living meaningfully, and accomplishing your goals.

Professor Seligman's framework of well-being has been expanded by Professor Stewart I. Donaldson's research by adding four more evidence-based building blocks in 2019 (Donaldson, 2019; Donaldson et al., 2021b, 2022) with the acronym PERMA+4. The newest building blocks of well-being are:

- physical health
- mindset
- environment
- economic security

PERMA+4 represents the nine building blocks of well-being as we know them today. And you can get excited, because each of those building blocks will be discussed chapter by chapter throughout this book you are holding in your hands!

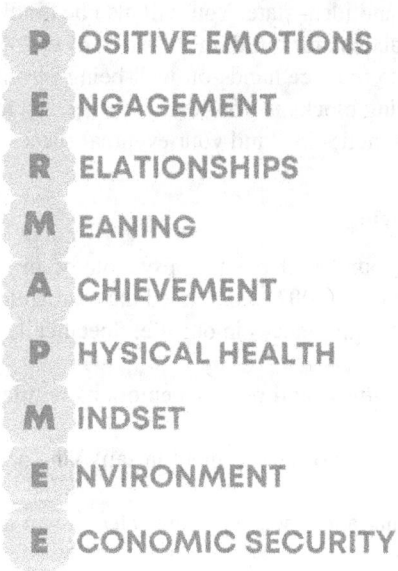

P OSITIVE EMOTIONS

E NGAGEMENT

R ELATIONSHIPS

M EANING

A CHIEVEMENT

P HYSICAL HEALTH

M INDSET

E NVIRONMENT

E CONOMIC SECURITY

Figure 1.6 PERMA+4: The nine building blocks of well-being.

Throughout this book, you will be introduced to the nine different building blocks of well-being with the acronym PERMA+4 and many possible ways to strengthen them in your everyday life. Each upcoming chapter covers one specific building block and I will do my best to help you develop your building blocks of well-being in **your unique** and **powerful way**. Caring for your well-being means deciding to **pay attention** to the nine different areas of your life, **reflecting** on the strength of your building blocks, and **choosing** thoughts and behaviors that help you to be your best and have the best PERMA+4 (Cabrera & Donaldson, 2023; Donaldson et al., 2021a, 2021b, 2022, 2023).

What Is (not) PERMA+4

- PERMA+4 is a well-being tool that helps you to **care** for your own well-being and the well-being of others rather than a destination.
- PERMA+4 is a **way to think about living**. It is an inspirational lifestyle rather than a solution for all our problems. Ask yourself: How do I want to live? What do I want to focus on? What do I want to develop in my life and what do I want to develop in the lives of others? How can I build it? This book will help you with all that!
- PERMA+4 is an **assessment tool** that gives you a sense of what your well-being looks like. It gives you a sense of how you stand, and it provides you with a space for reflection, rather than judgment of yourself or even others.
- PERMA+4 is **a map** of what your PERMA+4 can look like. Your PERMA+4 is constantly changing and developing. It helps you to become aware of what you want to avoid. Or you can only look at your assessment with no urge to do anything with it. It gives you space to decide what your well-being will or won't look like.
- PERMA+4 **helps you grow and develop your potential.** It helps you to be the best version of yourself and to be caring with people in your community.
- PERMA+4 is a tool that helps to develop your skill of **understanding others better** as you become more aware and have a better understanding of your own strengths. The more you develop your PERMA+4, the more you see and support the well-being strengths of others.

Activities Building Well-Being

There are many ways to care for your well-being and it can be beneficial to start building your well-being by making small changes in your daily lifestyle. I would like to kindly invite you to start incorporating evidence-based well-being-building activities into your everyday life.

Inspecting current knowledge closely, some activities seem to **benefit students' well-being more than others**. This book will encourage you to try as many activities as you would like to find the ones that will suit you and will prove helpful when building your well-being strengths. It is up to you, what activities will you decide to try and what activities will you skip. One size does not fit all, and the aim of this book is to make you more sensitive toward your needs and wants and to teach you to decide what is best for you on your own.

Let's have a look at the trends across the most promising positive psychology interventions for generating well-being.

Studies show (Hendriks et al., 2020; Tejada-Gallardo et al., 2020; van Agteren et al., 2021 in Donaldson et al., 2021a) that many of the most effective positive psychology interventions raising well-being are **long term,** ranging from 4 to 12 weeks. They also consist of **multiple components** and address several building blocks of well-being and positive psychology topics.

The most popular topics are:

- strengths
- gratitude
- positive relationships
- positive emotions
- mindfulness

In a nutshell, to strengthen your well-being, it can be beneficial to learn from several reasonably **well-validated intervention practices such as:**

- using multiple components
- tailoring
- using evidence-based curriculum
- flexibility
- using mutually reinforcing activities
- long term
- providing an option for self-selection
- possibility of using reminders
- accessibility

It is often through a series of knowledge and skill-building exercises that you can improve your well-being or even reduce negative outcomes such as stress, anxiety, and depression.

To support your well-being effectively:

- pick and choose from a variety of activities in this book and give them a try
- all the activities were chosen or designed to be tailored to the specific needs and lifestyles of college students
- this book presents evidence-based interventions and tips that were made based on current recommendations and guidelines
- activities that can be flexibly incorporated into your schedule
- activities that often relate to and support each other
- try to stick with them for at least a few days or weeks ideally
- reflect on whether the chosen activity is suitable and enjoyable for you or not
- work with your calendar and set reminders on your phone
- activities were designed to be financially, time, and materially accessible for students

Seligman and Adler (2018) created a list of well-validated interventions in the Positive Education field that became an inspiration for interventions and activities you will be invited to practice. To make them the best fit for you, these interventions were explored in the context of college students. Thus, you will be introduced to interventions from the college environment and activities supporting the well-being of university students throughout this whole book. Please, upon reading about those in the upcoming chapters, feel free to practice them and use any or all of them in your everyday life. Among many others, you will be presented with the activities below as an opportunity to try to see if they will sound like a good fit for you.

- *What Went Well* (Seligman et al., 2006)
    This is an intervention where you will have a chance to learn how to record (typically three) events that went well in your day and why they went well.
- *Gratitude Visit* (Emmons, 2007)
    You will be invited to write a letter of gratitude to someone who has done something meaningful for you and was perhaps not thanked enough. You will also have the chance to read it to the person themselves if you feel like doing so.
- *Active Constructive Responding* (Gable et al., 2004)
    You will learn about different responding styles and how to practice responding constructively to another person's victories to deepen your connection.
- *Character Strengths* (Peterson & Seligman, 2004)
    You will learn about the good character traits we all have and you will be asked to identify your specific signature strengths. You might find it especially valuable to learn how to use those in your everyday student life!
- *Best Self* (Roberts et al., 2005)
    You will have a chance to write about your best self and reflect on your proudest moments.
- *Meditation and Mindfulness* (Davidson et al., 2003)
    You will have the opportunity to practice one or more of the various mediation and mindfulness techniques throughout different chapters.
- *Empathy Training* (Bryant, 1982)
    You will learn about empathy and use empathy techniques in your everyday life to care for your own well-being and the well-being of others.
- *Coping with Emotions* (Deci & Ryan, 2010)
    This book will help you to identify, understand, and manage your emotions – the unpleasant ones, but particularly the pleasant ones.
- *Decision-making* (Albert & Steinberg, 2011)
    You will learn to process any desired situation and to choose the best action plan from the options available.
- *Problem-solving* (Steinberg, 2014)
    You will be invited to use effective strategies to solve theoretical and practical problems beyond your school life.
- *Critical Thinking* (Marin & Halpern, 2011)
    You will learn about critical thinking and how it relates to problem-solving and decision-making.

Practicing some of these (and many more) evidence-based well-being activities regularly can help you build your well-being strengths and develop your resilience, so that you can bounce back faster when you find yourself down or when you experience sad feelings. To make your journey successful, let's have a look at what rigorous experimental research (Donaldson et al., 2021a) suggests regarding our self-care interventions to grow our well-being:

- learn
- practice
- reflect
- relate
- plan

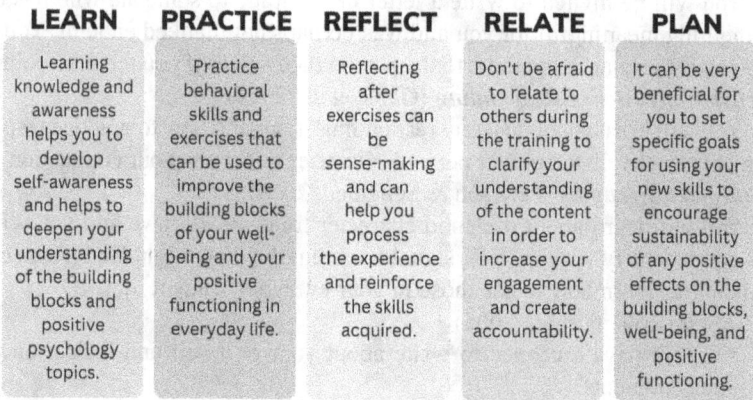

LEARN	**PRACTICE**	**REFLECT**	**RELATE**	**PLAN**
Learning knowledge and awareness helps you to develop self-awareness and helps to deepen your understanding of the building blocks and positive psychology topics.	Practice behavioral skills and exercises that can be used to improve the building blocks of your well-being and your positive functioning in everyday life.	Reflecting after exercises can be sense-making and can help you process the experience and reinforce the skills acquired.	Don't be afraid to relate to others during the training to clarify your understanding of the content in order to increase your engagement and create accountability.	It can be very beneficial for you to set specific goals for using your new skills to encourage sustainability of any positive effects on the building blocks, well-being, and positive functioning.

Figure 1.7 The process of effective strengthening of your well-being.

And my personal goal for this book is to put all the beautiful theory into practice with you. You and I will learn about current theory on well-being, we will practice new ways of thinking and new habits, we will reflect on your current well-being and you will be invited to reflect on techniques you will try. You will have the opportunity to relate to some personal experiences from academia that I will share with you and we will plan specific steps on how to make you enjoy your life while feeling well. Thank you for doing this for yourself. I am excited to join you!

Your PERMA+4 Assessment

To know what to focus on and what activities to use to strengthen your well-being, it is important to know where you stand at the moment.

We are usually able to assess quite easily how satisfied we are with our life as a whole, marking our current situation on a scale of 0–10, where 0 stands for "I am not satisfied at all" and 10 stands for "I am rocking it!" But the simple scale does not assess our satisfaction within specific life domains, such as physical health, our relationships, meaning, and many more.

Completing your well-being wheel can provide you with a bigger picture of your health and well-being. Your personal assessment of how you see it right now. It gives you an opportunity to think about your current state and whether you might like to change anything or not. To contemplate what can be done to improve your well-being and what you would like it to be in the future. The well-being wheel lets you think of each key building block of your well-being and figure out where your well-being might be off-balance.

In this exercise, you will be asked to fill out your own **flower diagram**. You will be provided with a wheel that represents the **nine different building blocks** of your well-being, previously introduced as PERMA+4. These are positive emotions, engagement, relationships, meaning, achievement, physical health, mindset, environment, and economic security.

Here is a **set of statements** you might want to look at that can help you assess how well you feel about each well-being building block. You might find it helpful to reflect on those by reading the descriptions of the ideal states of all nine building blocks and assessing where you stand right now.

Positive Emotions

(Experiencing happiness, joy, love, gratitude, etc. in the here and now.)

I generally **experience positive emotions** (happiness, joy, love, gratitude, interest, etc.) either alone or with others often. I feel overall satisfied with my life, I devote a satisfying time to my hobbies and interests, and I enjoy what I do at work and at school.

Engagement

(Being highly absorbed or experiencing flow while engaged in activities of one's life.)

I generally **experience** flow and engagement in my everyday life activities, at work, and at school often. I feel engaged while doing my hobbies, while spending time with other people, or even while being alone.

Relationships

(Having the ability to establish and maintain positive and caring high-quality relationships with others, characterized by experiences of love and appreciation.)

I generally **experience** high-quality relationships with my boss or supervisor, classmates, co-workers, friends, family members, and significant other(s), and I have a great relationship with myself.

Meaning

(The experience of being connected to something larger than the self or serving a higher purpose.)

I generally **experience** meaning in everyday life activities, purpose in life, meaning in school activities, and purpose in school studies. I build meaningful relationships and I participate in meaningful activities in my community. I have faith and I cultivate my spirit.

Achievement

(Experiencing a sense of mastery over a particular domain of interest or achieving important or challenging life/work goals, as well as completing simple tasks of everyday life.)

I generally **recognize** and **celebrate** both my smaller and bigger achievements, and I accept my failures. I am generally satisfied with my personal life achievements, education achievements, relationship achievements, self-improvement achievements, and financial achievements.

Physical Health

(Operationalized as a combination of high levels of biological, functional, and psychological health assets.)

I generally feel **physically healthy** considering my body movement, body posture, nutrition, and sleep while being able to relax and breathe properly, and I successfully avoid risky behaviors, such as smoking, alcohol consumption, or social media overuse.

Mindset

(Adopting a growth mindset characterized by an optimistic, future-oriented view of life, where challenges or setbacks are seen as opportunities to grow. This may also be a function of positive psychological capital).

I generally **feel** resilient, confident in myself, responsible, hopeful, optimistic, future-oriented, persistent, and passionate about my long-term goals, and I have a growth mindset in important domains of my life.

Environment

(The quality of one's physical environment (including spatiotemporal elements such as access to natural light, fresh air, physical safety, and a positive psychological climate) is aligned to the preferences of the individual.)

I generally **experience** a positive, healthy, and supportive environment at home, in my family, at work or school, in my community, and online, and I spend a satisfying amount of time outdoors in nature.

Economic Security

(Perceptions of financial security and stability required to satisfy individual needs.)

I generally **feel financially secure** considering my income, savings, investments, and access to quality health care, and I am managing my financial expenses well.

So how do you assess your strengths? **Please imagine a ladder with steps numbered from 0 at the bottom to 10 at the top.**

The top of the ladder represents the best result (I feel very confident in this particular strength), while the bottom of the ladder represents the worst (I would like to build this particular strength better).

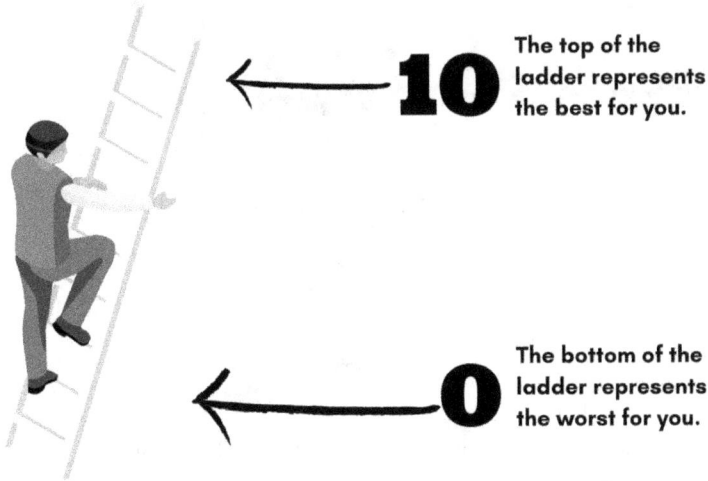

The top of the ladder represents the best for you.

The bottom of the ladder represents the worst for you.

Figure 1.8 Your well-being assessment ladder.

On which step of the ladder on a scale of 0–10 would you say you personally feel you stand at this time in terms of:

- positive emotions
- engagement
- relationships
- meaning
- achievement
- physical health
- mindset
- environment
- economic security

After you assess all your well-being building blocks, draw your very own well-being flower! Circle the resulting numbers of your building blocks on your well-being wheel ladders. Then, draw the petal shape from the center of the wheel through all the numbers on each ladder to create your own flower!

Let me show you an example of a filled-out flower diagram. This *fictive person* ranked their positive emotions as 7, engagement as 8, relationships as 6, meaning as 6, achievement as 8, physical health as 6, mindset as 7, environment as 7, and economic security as 9. Then, they drew a flower to understand their well-being better. So what do you think? Can you do the same?

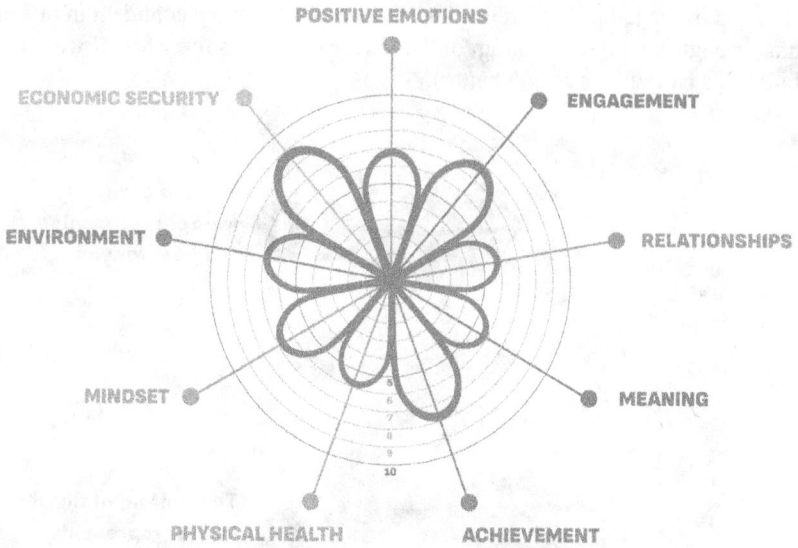

Figure 1.9 Example of your building blocks of well-being flower diagram.

Let's assess your **well-being** now! Figure 1.10 is a wheel created just for you to rate your individual building blocks of well-being. You will have a chance to reflect on them right away and the whole book is dedicated to learning about individual building blocks and practicing activities that will help you build the particular areas of your life. Enjoy drawing your own flowers and may your well-being garden grow and flourish!

Figure 1.10 Your well-being flower assessment.

YOUR WELL-BEING FLOWER REFLECTION

Great job! How do you feel?

Let's have a look at your personal **well-being flower together**.

Remember, there is no judgment here; this is just an awareness exercise.

The goal of this exercise is to become **aware of your situation and decide what your next goal should be**. Then, you will have a chance to think about what you can do to achieve the said goal. The nine upcoming chapters will present you with some **evidence-based recommendations and activities** you can try right away to see if those fit your personality and life style. You will also be asked to assess each particular well-being building block and to draw your very own well-being flowers throughout the whole book. It is fun to reflect on your flowers with your friends, but remember, the only one you can compare your flowers to is yourself. Enjoy checking on your flowers over time to track your progress or changes reflecting certain stages of your life. The goal shouldn't be to have perfect, long petals in all your flowers – you should come to terms with imperfection. Invite the possibility of gradual improvement rather than unhealthy, overnight perfection.

This flower reflects your **subjective perception** rather than your objective state. You might rate your *Physical Health Flower* lower while you objectively take good care of your physical well-being and actually eat pretty healthy. Why do we do that? Our perception of ourselves is rarely objective. Sometimes, this can be caused by having a certain idea, a vision of what our ideal *Physical Health* petal should look like. Sometimes, the *Physical Health* petal is disturbed by holidays that make you not follow your sleep regimen or by enjoying foods and a sedentary lifestyle on a vacation. Hence, it can be reasonable to believe we still have space for growth. Rating your petals gives you **the opportunity to reflect on** your current state in certain areas of your life that build up your well-being. It will also make you think about what areas you are satisfied with for now and what building blocks you might like to focus on.:-)

Let's see how you can **grow your well-being petals** throughout the course of reading and using this book!

> **Do It**   **Ten Empowering Questions to Support My Well-Being Flower Growth**
>
> 1 What actually is well-being to me?
> 2 What do I enjoy doing the most?
> 3 Who do I usually lose track of time with?
> 4 Who makes me feel accepted the way I truly am?
> 5 For whom or what do I get up from my bed in the morning?
> 6 What have I accomplished that makes me really proud of myself?
> 7 What is the smallest thing I can do for my body today?
> 8 What would a kind inner talk sound like?
> 9 Where and when can I get in touch with nature today?
> 10 What activity supports my well-being and is free of cost?

> **Do It**   **Ten Tips to Build My Well-Being Flower**
>
> 1 Laugh at yourself when messing things up!
> 2 Find time for your hobbies.
> 3 Text someone you care for and tell them you love them.
> 4 Remind yourself why you chose the major you are in.
> 5 Start your day by making your bed.
> 6 Drink plenty of water today.
> 7 When making any mistake, either small or big, ask yourself, "what have I learned?" next time.
> 8 Clean your desktop on your computer and enjoy the good feeling!
> 9 Do some activity you love doing in your free time that does not cost you anything at the same time.
> 10 Remind yourself why you want good health and well-being for yourself.

Care for Your Well-Being

Congratulations. By getting here and holding this book in your hands, you have already demonstrated that you care for your well-being. I would like to invite you to explore the upcoming chapters on the building blocks of well-being and to use this book as much as you can to improve your positive functioning. Come back to the readings, assessments, and exercises anytime you feel like you could benefit from them again. Caring for your well-being is a lifelong process.

In this book, each chapter lies on a foundation of three pillars. The first pillar and the opening of each chapter are a bit of up-to-date theory, presenting the thoughts and perspectives of the world's leaders in the science of well-being. The second pillar and the middle part of each chapter is your well-being self-assessment, helping you to become more conscious of how you are doing in a particular area of your life. And lastly, the third is a pillar of practice. This pillar at the end of each chapter represents my desire to provide you with ideas, tips, and evidence-based activities you can pick and choose from. You will be seeing bulb stamps that represent suggestions on where to learn more. You will also run into stamps saying "Do it!" inviting you to try an activity or a new strategy. And each chapter closes with ten empowering questions to support your well-being flower growth and ten tips to build your well-being flower. But only you can decide what is a good fit for you and what is not. Because remember, please. One size doesn't fit all and it is ok to choose to follow only advice or practices that you feel are the right ones for you at the moment. Or feel free to read the pages without the intention to change anything. Just to get some inspiration to generate your own thoughts and to build your own unique lifestyle, because let me kindly add one important thing for me. Even though this book is packed with tips on how to grow, change, and improve, the last thing I want is to make you feel like you have to change. Or even worse, that you are not good enough. The opposite is true. Not only are you good enough the way you are, you are exactly what the world needs right now. We hear from almost every direction that we should be more productive, do more, achieve more, and be better. But I personally believe that all our flourishing starts with meeting ourselves where we are at this moment and knowing that we are enough. Only from here can we work on ourselves in a healthy way. I would like to kindly invite you to read this book not for so-called self-improvement but as an act of self-care or simply just for fun. Not necessarily knowing what will happen next :-).

Also, it does not matter whether you choose to start with the chapter you are most interested in or read the chapters one by one chronologically. The chapters are designed so you can freely jump in between them based on what topic draws your attention at the moment. Any way you choose to read this book will work as soon as you have fun and enjoy the process. Knowing that you enjoyed reading this book as much as I enjoyed writing it would be the greatest reward I could ever ask for. I truly wish you to be well no matter what that means for you, and you can always let me know how you feel about your journey or about the book at jana@uniwellsity.com.

May this book help you to have fun and to enjoy the journey of caring for yourself. May this book help you to build the well-being you desire, and may your well-being help you generate any success you wish to achieve. May your life *be-well.*

I appreciate you.

Jana

References

Albert, D., & Steinberg, L. (2011). Judgment and decision making in adolescence. *Journal of Research on Adolescence, 21*(1), 211–224. doi:10.1111/j.1532-7795.2010.00724.x

Bryant, B. K. (1982). An index of empathy for children and adolescents. *Child Development, 53*(2), 413–425. doi: 10.2307/1128984

Cabrera, V., & Donaldson, S. I. (2023). PERMA to PERMA+4 building blocks of well-being: a systematic review of the empirical literature. *Journal of Positive Psychology,* DOI: 10.1080/17439760.2023.2208099

Centers for Disease Control (2018). Well-being concepts: https://www.cdc.gov/hrqol/wellbeing.htm

Cooke, R. (2006). Measuring, monitoring and managing the psychological well-being of first year university students. *British Journal of Guidance & Counselling.* Routledge, *34*(4), s. 505–517. ISSN: 0306-9885. https://doi.org/10.1080/03069880600942624.

Davidson, R. J., Kabat-Zinn, J., Schumacher, J., Rosenkranz, M., Muller, D., Santorelli, S. F., Urbanowski, F., Harrington, A., Bonus, K., & Sheridan, J. F. (2003). Alterations in brain and immune function produced by mindfulness meditation. *Psychosomatic Medicine, 65*(4), 564–570.

Deci, E. L., & Ryan, R. M. (2010). *Self-Determination.* New York, NY: John Wiley & Sons, Inc. http;//dx.doi.org/10.1002/9780470479216.corpsy0834

Donaldson, S. I. (2019). Evaluating employee positive functioning and performance: A positive work and organizations approach. Doctoral Dissertation, Claremont Graduate University.

Donaldson, S. I., Cabrera, V., & Gaffaney, J. (2021a). Following the science to generate well-being: Using the highest quality experimental evidence to design interventions. *Frontiers in Psychology.* https://doi.org/10.3389/fpsyg.2021.739352.

Donaldson, S. I., Gaffaney, J., & Caberra, V. (2023). The science and practice of positive psychology: From a bold vision to PERMA+4. In H. S. Friedman (Eds.), *The 3rd edition of the encyclopedia of mental health.* Cambridge, MA: Academic Press.

Donaldson, S. I., Heshmati, S., Young, J. Y., & Donaldson, S. I. (2021b). Examining building blocks of well-being beyond PERMA and self-report bias. *Journal of Positive Psychology,* https://doi.org/10.1080/17439760.2020.1818813.

Donaldson, S. I., Van Zyl, L. E., & Donaldson, S. I. (2022). PERMA+4: A framework for work-related well-being, performance and positive organizational psychology 2.0. *Frontiers in Psychology,* 12, 817244. https:/doi.org/10.3389/fpsyg.2021.817244.

Emmons, R. A. (2007). *Thanks!: How the New Science of Gratitude Can Make You Happier.* New York, NY: Houghton Mifflin Harcourt.

Gable, S. L., Reis, H. T., Impett, E. A., & Asher, E. R. (2004). What do you do when things go right? The intrapersonal and interpersonal benefits of sharing positive events. *Journal of Personality and Social Psychology, 87*(2), 228–45. doi:10.1037/0022-3514.87.2.228

Gallup Global Emotions (2022). Positive Experience Index in 2021. Available at: https://img.lalr.co/cms/2022/06/29185719/2022-Gallup-Global-Emotions-Report-2022_compressed.pdf

Geelong Grammar School (2011). What is positive education. Available at: https://www.ggs.vic.edu.au/learning/wellbeing/what-is-positive-education/

Hendriks, T., Schotanus-Dijkstra, M., Hassankhan, A., Jong, J., and Bohlmeijer, E. (2020). *The efficacy of multi-component positive psychology interventions: A systematic review and meta-analysis of randomized controlled trials.* J. Happiness Stud. Interdisciplin. Forum Subject. Well-Being 21, 357–390. doi: 10.1007/s10902-019-00082-1

Koci, J. (2022). Health and well-being tips for distance learning university students. Volume 6, Number 3, University Counseling – Current Challenges and Trends.

Koci, J. (2023). *How to build well-being in university and college students – Methodology of academic well-being promotion.* Prague: Charles University. ISBN: 978-80-87489-38-3

Koci, J., & Donaldson, S. I. (2022). *Zdraví a mentální well-being studentů distančního vzdělávání.* Prague: Charles University. ISBN: 978-80-7603-357-3

Koci, J., & Koptikova, D. (2022a). *Podpora mentálního well-beingu žáků středních škol v době digitalizace – teoretická východiska*. Praha: UK PedF. ISBN: 978-80-7603-360-3.

Koci, J., & Koptikova, D. (2022b). *Budování mentálního well-beingu žáků středních škol v době digitalizace – jak aplikovat praktická doporučení v praxi*. Praha: UK PedF. ISBN: 978-80-7603-361-0.

Marin, L. M., & Halpern, D. F. (2011). Pedagogy for developing critical thinking in adolescents: Explicit instruction produces greatest gains. *Thinking Skills and Creativity, 6*(1), 1–13. doi:10.1016/j.tsc.2010.08.002

Peterson, C. (2008). What is positive psychology, and what is it not? *Psychology Today*. Retrieved from https://www.psychologytoday.com/us/blog/the-good-life/200805/what-is-positive-psychology-and-what-is-it-not

Peterson, C., & Seligman, M. E. (2004). *Character strengths and virtues: A handbook and classification* (Vol. 1). New York, NY, Washington, DC: Oxford University Press, American Psychological Association.

Roberts, L. M., Dutton, J. E., Spreitzer, G. M., Heaphy, E. D., & Quinn, R. E. (2005). Composing the reflected best-self portrait: Building pathways for becoming extraordinary in work organizations. *Academy of Management Review, 30*(4), 712–736.

Seligman, M. E. P. (2002). *Authentic happiness: Using the new positive psychology to realize your potential for lasting fulfillment*. Free Press.

Seligman, M. E., Rashid, T., & Parks, A. C. (2006). Positive psychotherapy. *American psychologist, 61*(8), 774 -788. doi:10.1037/0003-066X.61.8.774.

Seligman, M. E. P. (2011). *Flourish: A visionary new understanding of happiness and well-being*. Free Press.

Seligman, M. E. P., & Adler, A. (2018). Positive education. In J. F. Helliwell, R. Layard, & J. Sachs (Eds.), *Global happiness policy report: 2018*. (pp. 52–73).

Steinberg, L. (2014). *Age of Opportunity: Lessons from the New Science of Adolescence*. New York, NY: Houghton Mifflin Harcourt.

Tejada-Gallardo, C., Blasco-Belled, A., Torrelles-Nadal, C., and Alsinet, C. (2020). *Effects of school-based multicomponent positive psychology interventions on well-being and distress in adolescents: A systematic review and meta- analysis*. J. Youth Adolesc. 49, 1943–1960. doi: 10.1007/s10964-020- 01289-9

Van Agteren, J., Iasiello, M., Lo, L., Bartholomaeus, J., Kopsaftis, Z., Carey, M., et al. (2021). *A systematic review and meta-analysis of psychological interventions to improve mental wellbeing*. Nat. Hum. Behav. 5, 631–652. doi: 10.1038/s41562-021-01093-w

World Economic Forum (2020). This is what makes people around the world happy right now: https://www.weforum.org/agenda/2020/11/global-happiness-survey-2020-coronavirus/

World Health Organization (2022). Constitution. [online]. Available at: https://www.who.int/about/governance/constitution

World Health Organization (2022). Mental Health. [online]. Available at: https://www.who.int/news-room/fact-sheets/detail/mental-health-strengthening-our-response

York, T., & Gibson III, C., & Rankin, S. (2015). Defining and measuring academic success. *Practice Assessment, Research & Evaluation*, 20.

2 Building Your Positive Emotions

Positivity opens us. The first core truth about positive emotions is that they open our hearts and our minds, making us more receptive and more creative.

– Barbara Fredrickson

It is Monday morning and your alarm starts to ring. It takes only seconds to wake up and to realize how desperately you want to stay in your bed. The room feels cold and the sun is not even up yet. You quickly scan your upcoming day in your head and you immediately feel the resistance to go to school and do the presentation you are not even sure you are prepared enough for. "I wish I did not play the volleyball tournament yesterday." You think to yourself. "I should have memorized the lines I wrote for my presentation," you beat yourself up. Today is going to be hard. Sigh.

All right. Let's try this one more time.

It is Monday morning and your alarm starts to ring. It takes only seconds to wake up and to realize how great it feels to start a brand new week. The cool sheets feel good on your skin and you will have a chance to see the sunrise in a few moments. You quickly scan your upcoming day in your head and you immediately feel the excitement to join Mrs. Erickson's class this morning. There is also the presentation you need to do later today. "I've got this. I am glad I took a day off from school yesterday. The volleyball tournament was so much fun," you think. "Today is going to go well."

Which one sounds more like you? Well, let me say that both scenarios are inside of us. We all have been there. We know what it feels like to get out of bed with the left foot. But we all also know the feeling of a great start of the day! Who do you prefer to be? And can we actually choose our Mondays?

Let's explore what can be done to bring more joy in your everyday life. This chapter will provide you not only with the theory behind emotions and the importance of positivity, but it will also invite you to try some evidence-based activities to see what might work for you to experience more positive emotions as you go through your days. Ready? Let's do this.

DOI: 10.4324/9781003378365-3

Introduction to Positive Emotions

Naturally, rather than focusing on the good aspects of life, our attention is mostly focused on unplesant emotions, such as sadness, boredom, fear, anger, shame, and guilt. Compared to these uncomfortable experiences, we tend to take pleasant emotions for granted. Still, we all want to experience **joy, interest, contentment, happiness,** and **love**. Positive emotions are as natural as negative emotions, and there can be no well-being without cultivating these positive emotions.

But why do we tend to focus on the negative **more than the positive**? And do unpleasant emotions even serve us?

Absolutely! Negative emotions have been helping humanity to evolve and to survive for many years. Noticing danger and responding appropriately in risky or even life-threatening situations is crucial for safety – even in the modern world. Positive emotions, as Professor Fredrickson discusses in her article (1998), *are in comparison more subtle, fewer in number, and we respond to positive emotions in others less intensively than to negative emotions.*

The Berkeley Well-Being Institute (2022) concludes that **emotions** are functional biological states that come about as a result of our **thoughts, feelings,** and **behaviors** existing in a continuum from pleasure to displeasure. They prepare us to respond to a **stimulus** and our **translation** (perception) of it. Such a stimulus can be sleepiness after a long study night, mid-afternoon hunger after skipping your lunch, pain in your body after you hit your ankle while parking your bike, a waving friend in a car driving by, or your successfully passed exam. Our translations (perception) of diverse situations stimulating us can vary from student to student and even from situation to situation. They can result from feeling discomfort, fear, or anxiety to experiencing excitement, relief, joy, or much more. We can list emotions from as elementary as six basic emotions (fear, anger, joy, sadness, disgust, and surprise) by Ekman (1992b) to hundreds! (Search for Berkeley's List of Emotions: 271 Emotion Words.)

According to psychologist Professor Fredrickson (1998), positive emotions **broaden** the scope of **attention, cognition,** and **action**. That results in **widening the array of precepts, thoughts, and actions presently in mind**. A corollary of the narrow hypothesis states that **negative emotions shrink** these same arrays. This leads us slowly to an explanation of why, according to strong evidence, the functioning of students who experience higher levels of positive emotions differs from that of students who experience lower levels of positivity.

Research shows that being positive is **essential** for our well-being. But let me emphasize that positivity is not about ignoring negative emotions. Negative emotions are as necessary for a healthy life as the positive ones. Positivity means that we consciously pay attention to the positive events and expectations in our lives while we acknowledge and engage with the whole **portfolio of all our emotions**. Emotions carry important messages and are valuable sources of impulses that help us overcome obstacles. Fear helps us avoid danger. Disgust helps us avoid unhealthy food, objects, and/or situations. Anger helps us fight or defend ourselves, while joy helps us to pay attention to what is important and valuable to us. And what about trust? Trust helps us connect with the right people when we need help, just like sadness makes us reach out to loved ones.

Rather than arguing that positive emotions should replace negative emotions, the premise of the broaden-and-build theory (Fredrickson, 1998) is that both types of emotions must coexist. Positive emotions build resources to cope with negative emotions. Pushing ourselves into positivity can have negative effects. Instead, we can find effective ways to **slowly change our mindset**. Focus on being **authentic, curious,** and **open to trying new things**. Quieting down your expectations that could limit your sensitivity and ability to perceive the good things in life that are already here might help too. Strive to be **thankful, track** your positive emotions daily, and **find time for** what makes you feel good.

Building positivity can be supported by processing frustrations and negative emotions. For example, imagine you did not cover everything you wanted to share with your class while presenting your project and you feel upset. It can be very helpful for you to sit with what is here and now for a while and don't push your rage anywhere. Honor all your emotions. Welcome everything you are experiencing. By acknowledging your discomfort you let it slowly dissolve and you make room for the positive part of your experience to arise. But please, even though negative emotions help us not only to survive but also to connect to what is important to us, it is also important to take care of yourself if it is too much. If you feel like negative emotions are getting too overwhelming for you and it is hard to manage them, ask for help at students' health services please. Asking for help can be the highest act of self-care and it is such an important part of your well-being to ask for professional help if you need it.

Generally, looking at the good side of an event helps us to be more objective. Ask yourself what actually went well? What part of your presentation was your favorite? What did your classmates seem to like? Train yourself to be more sensitive and perceive the good around you too. **Pay attention, become aware, and celebrate the good things** happening in your life and in the lives of others. You can also contribute to the good by being **compassionate, kind, and loving** towards your family, friends, community, and nature around us. Take to heart your core values and try to **act on them** through everything you do.

Learn More About Emotions on Coursera Positive Psychology Course Instructed by Dr. Barbara L. Fredrickson (The University of North Carolina at Chapel Hill)

Enroll for free! This course discusses research findings in the field of Positive Psychology, conducted by Barbara Fredrickson and her colleagues. It also features practical applications of this science that you can put to use immediately to help you live a full and meaningful life.

https://www.coursera.org/learn/positive-psychology

Benefits of Positive Emotions for Students' Well-Being

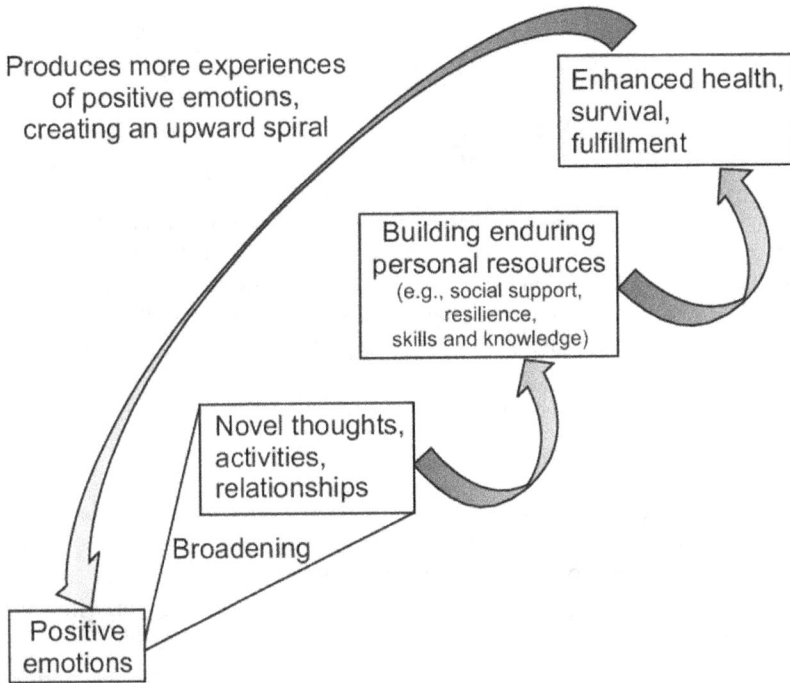

Figure 2.1 What good are positive emotions? (Fredrickson, 1998).

The **broaden-and-build theory** (Fredrickson, 1998) as a well-being model states that positive emotions are the stepping stones for all of us, including university students, broadening our ways of **thinking** and **behaving**. This helps you build **resources** for quality of life and positive functioning, which enhance your health as a result. But positive emotions themselves are not the sole goal. They are the beginning of a **great process of positive changes** that generate **students' well-being, health,** and a **prosperous life**.

Feeling joyful, excited, interested, peaceful, and loved broadens your momentary thinking and acting, which has a positive effect on building your **physical, intellectual,** and **social resources**. When you experience positive emotions, it naturally broadens your ability to

• think in new ways
• try new things
• try new behaviors

By nature, you become **open** to new ideas, think in new ways, adopt new mindsets, and learn in general. Over time, this broadened behavioral repertoire lets you build **useful skills** with no extra effort. By being willing to try something new, you gain

- new skills
- new friends and relationships
- new knowledge

All the above lead to **enhanced health and fulfillment**. You feel better physically, socially, and emotionally. That itself generates more positive emotions which then continue the cycle. Once you experience positive emotions, you naturally tend to think in new ways and try new things. You spontaneously build more resources that enhance your health and this, again, brings about more positive emotions into your life as a result.

Your Positive Emotions Flower Assessment

We have learned in Chapter 1 that positive emotions are one of the **nine essential building blocks** generating well-being. One of the things that can be very useful is to reflect and to think about your potential **positive emotions strengths**. By understanding the importance of positive emotions for your well-being, you will have an opportunity to assess your strengths and areas for future development!

In this exercise you will be asked to fill out your own **flower diagram**. You will be provided with a wheel that represents **seven different** possibilities for building your positive emotions. These go from positive emotions experiences (happiness, joy, love, gratitude, etc.), life satisfaction, time devoted to your hobbies and interests, positive emotions experienced with other people, enjoyment of what you do at school, enjoyment of what you do at work or your part-time job, and shared positivity, and there is also room for your own choice of another positive emotion strength you might feel needs to be reflected in your life as well.

Here is a **set of statements** that will help you to assess how well you feel about each positive emotions strength area. You might find it helpful to reflect by reading the descriptions of all seven strengths and assessing where you stand.

Experiencing Positive Emotions (Happiness, Joy, Love, Gratitude, etc.)

I **experience** positive emotions such as happiness, pride, contentment, and joy **often in my life**.

Life Satisfaction

I am **highly satisfied** with my life.

Time Devoted to Your Hobbies and Interests

I know the importance of **making time** for my **hobbies, relaxation,** and **regeneration** and to **energize** myself. I make sure that I prioritize my leisure and free time to enjoy my hobbies **regularly.**

Positive Emotions Experienced with Other People

I enjoy **spending time** with **other people.** I **laugh often** in others' company. I feel good about myself while being with others; I feel **included** and **safe** to **fully express** myself.

Enjoyment of What You Do at School

I enjoy **every activity** I do as a part of my **studies.** Even though it might be hard sometimes, I generally enjoy **going to school, learning** in classes, **studying** at home, **completing assessments,** and **preparing** for another school day.

Enjoyment of What You Do at Work or Part-time Job

I **enjoy** my work. I look **forward to** going to work every time it is scheduled. I enjoy my **work role** and all the work-related **tasks** I get to do during my shifts.

Shared Positivity

I genuinely enjoy seeing other people **experience positive emotions.**

Other Positive Emotions Strengths

Are there any other positive emotions strengths on your mind you would like to assess? If yes, scale them please as you did with the previous strengths.

So how do you actually assess your strengths? **Please imagine a ladder with steps numbered from 0 at the bottom to 10 at the top.**

The top of the ladder represents the best result (I feel very confident in this particular strength), while the bottom of the ladder represents the worst (I would like to build this particular strength better).

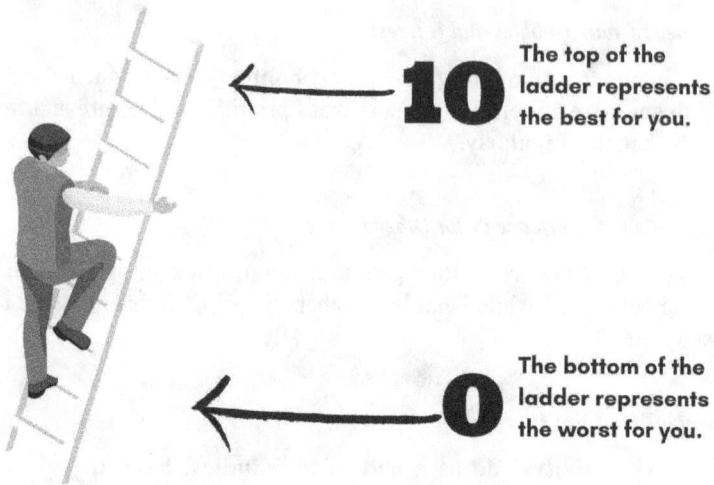

The top of the ladder represents the best for you.

The bottom of the ladder represents the worst for you.

Figure 2.2 Your well-being assessment ladder.

On which step of the ladder on a scale of 0–10 would you say you personally feel you stand at this time in terms of:

- positive emotions (happiness, joy, love, gratitude, etc.)
- life satisfaction
- time devoted to your hobbies and interests
- positive emotions experienced with other people
- enjoyment of what you do at school
- enjoyment of what you do at work or a part-time job
- shared positivity
- other positive emotions strengths

After you assess all your positive emotions strengths, draw your very own positive emotions flower! Circle the resulting numbers of your strength on the positive emotions wheel ladders. Then draw the petal shape from the center of the wheel through all the numbers on each ladder to create your own flower (see Figure 2.3 for an example of the flower diagram).

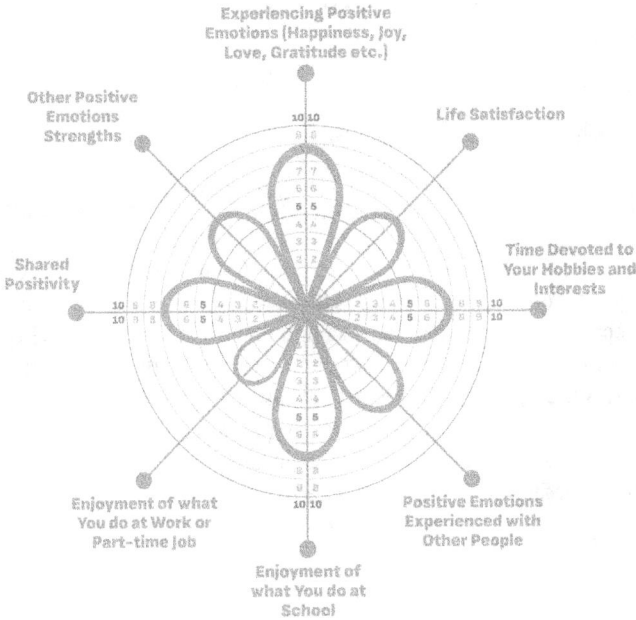

Figure 2.3 Example of your positive emotions flower diagram.

Let's assess your **positive emotions strengths,** and later you can reflect on them and learn how to build particular strengths (if needed) in the upcoming chapter.

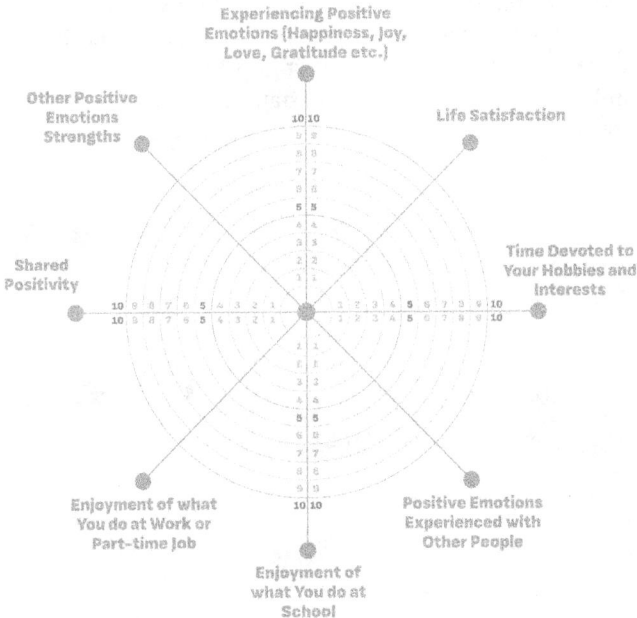

Figure 2.4 Your positive emotions flower assessment.

YOUR POSITIVE EMOTIONS FLOWER REFLECTION

Great job! How do you feel?

Let's have a look at your personal **positive emotions flower**.

Remember, there is no judgment here; this is just an awareness exercise.

The goal of this exercise is to become **aware of your situation and decide what your next goal should be**. Then you will have a chance to think about what you can do to achieve the said goal. This chapter will present some **evidence-based recommendations and activities** you can try right away to see if those fit your personality and lifestyle. It is fun to reflect on your flowers with your friends, but remember, the only one you can compare your flowers to is yourself. Enjoy checking on your flowers over time to track your progress or changes reflecting certain events in different stages of your life. The goal shouldn't be to have perfect, long petals in all your flowers – you should come to terms with imperfection. Invite the possibility of gradual growth of your flower petals, rather than unhealthy overnight perfection.

Each flower reflects your **subjective perception** rather than your objective state. You might rate your *Shared Positivity* petal lower while being content when seeing others experience positive emotions. Why do people do that? Our perception of ourselves is rarely objective. Sometimes, this can be caused by having a certain idea, a vision of what our ideal *Shared Positivity* petal should look like. Sometimes, the *Shared Positivity* petal is disturbed by, for example, not feeling fit and in the mood to socialize with friends and people around you. Hence, it can be reasonable to believe we still have space for growth. Rating your petals gives you **the opportunity to reflect on** your current state in certain areas of your life. It will also make you think about what strengths you are satisfied with for now and what strengths you might like to focus on. :-)

Let's see how you can **grow your positive emotions petals**.

Growing Your Positive Emotions Flower Petals

We experience positive emotions when we are experiencing pleasant feelings and deep connections. Psychologist Professor Fredrickson (2013) listed the ten most important positive emotions, namely joy, gratitude, serenity, interest, hope, pride, amusement, inspiration, awe, and love.

The University of Pennsylvania (2020) reminds us that the route to well-being is also hedonic – by increasing our experiences of positive emotions. Within limits, we can increase **our positive emotion about the past** (e.g., by cultivating gratitude and forgiveness), our **positive emotion about the present** (e.g., by savoring physical pleasures and mindfulness), and our **positive emotion about the future** (e.g., by building hope and optimism). To grow your positive emotions, this essential building block of well-being, pick and try some of the evidence-based interventions (that are proven to boost positivity) listed below!

Experiencing Positive Emotions (Happiness, Joy, Love, and Gratitude)

We have already learned about negativity bias; thus, when compared to subtle positive experiences, we are more inclined to notice negative emotions. West and Fredrickson (2020) summarize a body of scientific research that demonstrates cultivating positive emotions leads to higher levels **of well-being and flourishing**. People who experience numerous positive events, experiences, or emotions related to each negative one tend to flourish in their lives.

So, what causes positive emotions? What causes happiness? What causes experiencing the feelings of relaxation or excitement? Positive emotions are **the result of experiencing something subjectively meaningful**. For example, if spending time with family and friends is something you enjoy and find meaning in, spending time with loved ones **will result in positive emotions**. The same could be said about walking in nature, reading, or playing with a pet. **It is important to identify and prioritize what is meaningful to you and what brings you joy!**

Studying in general can be very stressful and demanding on one's mental well-being. So, what else can you possibly do to minimize the impact of study-related stress to balance your mental well-being? Research shows (Summer, 2018) that simple acts of **gratitude can significantly increase the levels of positivity** in people's everyday life.

But why does gratitude work with anxiety and stress relief? Greater Good Science Center (GGSC, 2021b) points out that when we deliberately focus on feeling and expressing gratitude, we build our **muscle for noticing the positive people and events in our lives** that we might otherwise take for granted.

Robert Emmons (2010), a leading scientific expert on gratitude, explains that gratitude carries powerful benefits to our mental, physical, and social health because it's **an affirmation of goodness**. We affirm that there are good things in the world, gifts, and benefits we've received.

When we express gratitude, our brain releases **serotonin and dopamine** – two hormones that help us feel peaceful and joyful inside. The simple act of practicing gratitude can help us to balance stress hormones such as cortisol with serotonin and dopamine by switching our negative mindset into the positive. Create your thankful mind; it creates you afterwards.

So how do we **practice gratitude**?

It is very simple. Ask yourself one or two of these questions from the list of ten below (originally designed by Christopher Littlefield in *Harvard Business Review* (2020) – redesigned to suit university students), write your answers down ideally, and see how you feel! When you find yourself stuck in a constant state of worry or hyper-focused on what is not working around you, try to pause for a second and ask yourself one or two of the following questions:

1   What have I gotten to learn at school recently that has helped me grow?
2   What opportunities do I currently have thanks to my studies that I am grateful for?
3   What physical abilities do I have but take for granted?
4   What did I see today or over the last month that was beautiful?
5   Who at school am I happy to see and why?
6   Who is a person that I don't speak to often but, if I lost them tomorrow, it would be devastating? (Take this as a cue to reach out today!)
7   What am I better at today than I was a year ago thanks to my college experience?
8   What material object do I use every day to be able to study that I am thankful for having?
9   What has someone at school done for me recently that I am grateful for?
10   What are the three things related to my college experience that I am grateful for right now?

Do It   **Thnx!**

By taking time to **write down** your answers, you will consciously redirect your attention to that which you are grateful for. And there is usually a lot to be grateful for in our lives. We just have to train ourselves to notice the good. This is not so hard, because thankfully, **being grateful feels great** :-)

You can also register at **Thnx4.org** to start your mobile-friendly online gratitude journal that makes it easier to give thanks, enjoy the benefits of thankfulness, and see what happens when you strengthen your own "**attitude of gratitude**." Thnx4 was created by the GGSC (2021b) at the University of California, Berkeley. It draws on two decades of research suggesting that people who regularly feel grateful:

- report better health, reduce their risk of heart disease, and get better sleep
- strengthen feelings of connection and satisfaction in their relationships
- feel more satisfied with their lives, more joy and optimism, and less anxiety

Register here: https://nurseschallenge.thnx4.org/about

Do it   What Went Well

Research suggests practicing *What Went Well* (Seligman et al., 2006) to generate positive emotions leading to mental well-being. How can such activities be implemented in university students' lifestyles? The *What Went Well* suggests you to record **three events that went well today and spend some time describing why they went well**. Acknowledge what went well and generate positive emotions to support your mental well-being today.

Here's how to get started. Scan your previous day (24 hours) and identify three things that went well and made you feel positive. Look for something that was related to your student life and even beyond (things that went well at school or in your personal life that made you experience positive emotions such as joy, gratitude, serenity, interest, hope, pride, amusement, inspiration, awe, and love). For example, you felt pride after successfully writing your essay and your statement might sound like: "I got finally done with my assignment today!"; or you felt joy while studying an interesting chapter on your favorite topic that was so easy to read and your statement might sound like: "I read a chapter of a book I like."; or you felt inspired by your classmate after a great discussion talking about a topic of your mutual interest and your statement might sound like: "I had a good discussion with Natalie today!"; or you felt completely engaged in the interesting lecture that went by so fast thanks to how engaged you were and your statement might sound like: "I had a really good class today!".

Should you assess your life beyond school life? Absolutely! Search and reflect on what went well in your friendships and in your dating life as well. Reflect on your hobbies, going on new adventures in the area, or how well attending cultural events went. Write all your thoughts down. And if you find it hard to recall some good things within the last 24 hours, try to come up with some things you simply find to be good generally with no set time frame. **Monitor the things that went well in your life and start a diary if this exercise sounds interesting to you.**

Do It   **Let's Cope with Our Emotions!**

Research shows (Deci & Ryan, 2010 in Roth et al., 2019) that **emotional regulation can be crucial for your well-being and has benefits for your volitional functioning, your personal well-being, and high-quality relationships**. But it is also important to choose the right strategy!

The study above compared different emotional regulation styles such as:

- focusing on diminishing emotions through avoidance
- suppression
- enforced expression in controlled emotion regulation and reappraisal
- amotivated emotion regulation, in which emotions are uncontrolled or dysregulated
- integrative emotion regulation

Integrative emotion regulation was found to be the most effective among all the above. This strategy focuses on **emotions as a means of carrying information that is brought to awareness**. Integrative emotion regulation represents a beneficial style of processing your emotions, which develops most effectively in a **non-judgmental** and **autonomy-supportive environment**. In other words, allowing your emotions to be as they are at the moment, sitting with them, and exploring what this emotion is trying to tell you can be a very healthy way to process your emotions.

Try to look at your emotions as messengers carrying some important information for you. Develop a healthy relationship with your emotions and ask yourself: *What are you trying to tell me?*

Practice identifying, understanding, and managing your emotions, particularly positive emotions by asking yourself **what** am I feeling? **Why** do I feel this? **How** is this related to my core values and what is important in my life? Give yourself a few moments to feel and process the emotions before you react.

Do It   **Your Emotions Are Your Friends!**

Would you like to get better at processing your emotions? Please try to learn how to become friends with all of your emotions. Get to know yourself through both pleasant and unpleasant emotions, reveal your life values by being curious about the messages your emotions are trying to deliver to you, and become emotionally agile! Learn

from fascinating expert on emotional agility and resilience Susan David, PhD and read her book *Emotional Agility: Get Unstuck, Embrace Change, and Thrive in Work and Life*. Or watch her amazing TED Talk here:

https://www.ted.com/talks/susan_david_the_gift_and_power_of_emotional_courage

Life Satisfaction

What makes you well in terms of how close your life is to ideal, your living conditions, satisfaction with your life, achieving the important things in your life, and believing that if you had a chance to live your life over again, you would change almost nothing? Life satisfaction is an **appreciative attitude towards our life**. It is when we evaluate our life positively as a whole. The good news is we can increase our life satisfaction. Make a list of people, things, and activities that are important to you and prioritize them. What makes you happy? What do you love to do? What brings meaning to our life? Who do you always love to see?

To get inspired, let me remind you of the list of what makes people around the world happy that we already saw in Chapter 1 (World Economic Forum, 2020):

- our health and physical well-being
- our relationship with our partner or spouse
- our children
- feeling that our life has meaning
- our living conditions
- our personal safety and security
- feeling in control of our life
- having a meaningful job and employment
- satisfaction with the direction our life is going
- having more money
- our personal financial situation
- our friends
- our hobbies and interests
- finding someone to be with
- the amount of free time we have
- well-being of our country

Time Devoted to Your Hobbies and Interests

Let me ask you a question. Of all the things you love to do and that bring you joy, how many are on your calendar for the next week? Constant progress in learning is important. But finding time to relax, regenerate, and enjoy what you love doing in your life the most is just as important. We all have that something we sometimes wish we had more time for. But it is your human right to enjoy your life, and it is your responsibility to make sure you always find time for yourself. There is a lot of evidence that when we **invest time into activities we enjoy doing and choose to do them for their own sake,** we feel energized, relaxed, and more prosocial; we learn faster; we are more creative; we feel more alive; and we are overall happier.

Research shows (Princeton's study on Leisure Time in Hygge, 2017) that when we assess our activities from the previous 24 hours (time spent at school, at work, at home, with friends, family, or alone, etc.), we enjoy our leisure time activities the most. Such activities we decided to do ourselves when we are free from work or school, and there is no obligation to do what we do. We do it simply because we want to. And as a kind reminder: please don't forget that finding time for doing nothing is also a necessary leisure activity!

Do it **What Do I Enjoy Doing?**

You can benefit a lot from sitting down and making **a random list of activities you generally enjoy doing**. Be creative. Put no limitations to your imagination. Think about the good times. Don't think about how feasible it would be to do this activity now. Just dream, reflect, and write it all down.

Now look at the list and try to rate your top five activities. Don't think, just feel. Circle what makes you excited and like your true self. And now look at the list and think of how you can incorporate any of these listed activities into your schedule. Pay extra attention to the circled activities. **Look for any opportunities to do those things**. Be creative. Remember – if you won't do it, no one else will do it for you. You can make time for what you love!

Positive Emotions Experienced with Other People

Do you feel like emotions are contagious sometimes? We all have experienced a friend's sadness making us feel down or a family member's happiness transferring to us, making us feel energized and excited. Studies suggest that other people's moods may be as easy to catch as germs. This phenomenon is called **"emotional contagion,"** and it happens when we mimic, usually without conscious effort, the emotions and expressions of people around us.

Research shows that we are all affected by feelings, while negative emotional states and bad moods affect us stronger than the good ones. It is a natural part of our lives to have good and challenging relationships. We cannot always escape interaction with someone we don't feel very comfortable around, and running away from them would not solve much. Life is not about avoiding the uncomfortable. But what we can certainly do to maintain your health and build your well-being is **to be conscious of who makes you feel good**. People who make you feel safe are authentic with no judgment. Someone who makes you feel heard, seen, and loved. Prioritize spending time with them. Share with them how good they make you feel and tell them you appreciate having them in your life.

Also, think of how you show up for others and how you can create positivity for people around you. Be kind; help if the situation and your energy level allow it. Listen actively, be curious about others' lives, and ask open questions to show others that you want to know more. Don't interrupt them when they're sharing something with you. Let them talk. Be fair. Be a team player. Be funny and less serious if the situation lets you do that. Make people laugh! **Be here for people**. People will like you better and will want to spend more time with you. This, in return, can bring even more positivity into your life. :-)

Enjoyment of What You Do at School

Imagine this. It's mid-December of your freshman year. You spent an all-nighter studying for your economics final. You're tired and shaky and questioning whether you should have another coffee or a nap. You have two more finals to go this week before heading home for the holidays. As you wipe the sleep from your eyes, you question whether this will all be worth it one day. Were you unprepared this semester, or is this just what to expect? It sure would be nice to have a guide to what it all means and how best to get there.

Your time spent at school is significant. But what is even more important is whether you see the invested time as a bad investment or a good investment. We all experience boredom (and it could be a good thing!) and resentment to do things we don't feel like doing. But **there is no well-being without love and enjoyment of what you do.** It is understandable that you might not love every school activity you, as a student, encounter. However, you should at least **see the meaning in what you do** and enjoy the majority of school activities. Assess what it is that you love to do at school and do it more often. Schedule such activities and make time for what you enjoy the most.

Do it   60 Seconds Investment

Everything feels different if we enjoy what we do or if we at least see meaning and purpose in it. Keep reminding yourself why you started doing the things you do, what you like about doing them, and why they are important to you. Before diving into a school activity, ask yourself upcoming questions. **What do I enjoy about this? What is exciting here? How will this help me reach my goals in life? How can this contribute to my growth? What am I learning? How will I use this in the future? Who else can benefit from me doing this?** Learn to invest 60 seconds into thinking to answer such questions before you do any school activity and benefit from stronger inner motivation, sharper focus, and better productivity!

Enjoyment of What You Do at Work or Part-Time Job

Have you ever thought of this? **We spend a third of our lives at work or by preparing for our occupation – for example like you, right now, by studying.** You might have a part-time or full-time job as you take college classes like approximately 60%

of students. Whether you work or are preparing for your career as a student, it is important for all of us to do what we enjoy and to work in a positive work environment, surrounded by good people. Not all jobs or positions we try must fit our life vision perfectly – and that is ok. Any type of work experience is a great starting point! But always keep in mind – it is worth having a vision for an occupation that will make you excited to rise from your bed in the morning. If you still hesitate about what kind of occupation it is that could be the right one for you, look at **the Japanese concept of Ikigai**, a concept which generates your life's worth, meaning, and purpose. Your Ikigai can be an expression of your passion, dream, a mission, or anything else that gives you the reason to live. Finding your Ikigai means finding your ideal job or even a dream career, provided that the ideal career includes these four qualities:

- what you love
- what you're good at
- what you can be paid for
- what the world needs

Ask yourself these four simple questions: **What do I really love and enjoy doing? What am I noticeably good at and where can I use my strengths? What does the world need that I may offer at the same time and what can I be paid for?** Get inspired by your own thoughts! Be creative. Think big. Think out of the box. And believe that sooner or later you **will** find your Ikigai.

Shared Positivity

Did you know that witnessing good and savoring positivity that happens around you can also have a positive **impact on you**? Observing people who experience pride, love, joy, happiness, and all the good emotions can also make **you** feel good! This happens thanks to **the mirror mechanism of your brain**. The mirror mechanism is a basic brain mechanism that transforms sensory representations of observed behavior into your motor or visceromotor representations concerning that behavior. Translated to common English, it is rather usual that we suddenly experience sadness when seeing someone crying, amusement when hearing someone laughing, or insecurity when seeing someone scared. **Knowing that you have this superpower, why don't you tune in to the good that happens around you?** Just open your eyes and savor the positivity whenever you can!

(Do it)   **Savor It!**

In this activity, we're going to focus on **savoring**. First off, what is savoring? Well, Professor Laurie Santos in her Happiness Course (Coursera, 2019) teaches that savoring is just the simple act of stepping out of your experience to review it and **really appreciate it while it's happening**. Why should we take time to savor? Well, it turns out savoring can boost our mood in at least three ways. First, savoring can thwart hedonic adaptation, thus a natural tendency to return to our default happiness level after major events or life changes. It can make us remember the good stuff in life. Second, savoring can help thwart mind wandering. It keeps us in the moment. And finally, savoring can help increase gratitude. It can make us thankful for the experiences we're having as we're having them.

How do we make the most of the savoring activity? Well, first off, you just have to take part in a positive experience, and then you have to savor it during that experience. Take a second to **realize why it makes you happy**. You can use your phone to help you by taking a picture, which will help you remember it later. Then track what you savored that day. As we've seen, tracking can help turn savoring a moment into a habit. So, get out there and savor something good. Go out and really enjoy the good things in life.

Ten Empowering Questions to Support My Positive Emotions Flower Growth

1 What am I looking forward to doing today?
2 What and who makes me laugh?
3 What do I appreciate about today?
4 What went well yesterday?
5 Who do I really enjoy spending time with?
6 What hobbies do I miss doing and I will make time for this week?
7 What is the smallest thing I can do to make my mood positive today?
8 Where can I eat today to savor my food better?
9 What can I do for others today to feel better about myself?
10 What else can I do to support my positive emotions today?

Ten Tips to Build My Positive Emotions Flower

1 Give thanks. Whatever your day brings you, don't take anything for granted and express your gratitude.
2 Laugh out loud! Let your whole body feel the excitement in moments that make you laugh and let it all out!
3 Savor. Whether it is your morning coffee, a walk through a park, a phone call with your loved one, or lunch on the bench in front of your dorms. Savor the little things and make the most out of your everyday life.
4 Process your emotions when feeling uncomfortable. Ask yourself what is here now? What sensations do I feel in my body? What kinds of emotions

are present? Why do I feel this way? What could be the message behind this feeling? How is this feeling related to my core values in life?

5 Share the good with others! Whether it is good news, an anecdote, or a cup of ice-cream. Good things are meant to be shared.

6 Enjoy the positivity around you! Look around for moments when people laugh, are kind to each other, and savor witnessing the good in the world.

7 Find time for what you love. Whether it is art, music, sports, relaxation, socializing, or spending time alone. Doing what you enjoy has the same priority as doing homework at school.

8 Look for meaning in both the big and small activities you do in your everyday life.

9 Take care of your body. Sleep, relax, move, eat real food, and dress up comfortably, rather than nicely. Put on your tennis shoes, your baggy hoody, and provide your body with the comfort it deserves.

10 Start a what-went-well diary. Journal about what good your previous day gave you and stick to this habit for a few weeks to enjoy great changes in your life!

Tips to Positive Emotions Snacking

Building your positive emotions does not have to be complicated nor time demanding. Look at Figure 2.5 and try some of the tips right now.

TIPS TO YOUR POSITIVE EMOTIONS SNACKING

Make it quick, easy and fun!

Time	Tip	Time	Tip
1 min	SEND A LOVED ONE A TEXT TO SAY HI AND TO REMIND THEM YOU CARE	5 mins	CALL SOMEONE YOU LOVE
10 mins	TREAT YOURSELF WITH YOUR FAVORITE COFFEE	4 mins	LISTEN TO YOUR FAVORITE SONG
1 min	SMILE AT SOMEONE	1 min	PET A DOG IN A PARK
15 mins	STRETCH YOUR BODY WITH SOME MOVEMENT	15 mins	TAKE A WARM SHOWER
3 mins	EXPOSE YOURSELF TO THE SUN AND GET SOME SUNBATH	3 mins	WRITE DOWN THREE THINGS YOU ARE THANKFUL FOR

Figure 2.5 Tips to positive emotions snacking.

A joyful life is an inseparable part of our well-being. If there is one thing you can do for your well-being with immediate effect, **do something that brings you joy**. Choose any activity that makes you excited and is doable for you today. Go to your favorite coffee shop and read a book. Dance. Bake yourself a cake. Call a friend you love spending time with and hang out tonight. Whatever it is that brings you joy, always make time for your hobbies. Leisure time activities allow us to disconnect from the world and connect us to ourselves. To the present moment. Being fully engaged not only feels good, it also generates your well-being. How? Let me invite you to another chapter, fully devoted to a good, engaged life. Is there anything you can do to increase your engagement? Absolutely. Pick and choose any of the presented activities onward, generate engagement, and invite more flow into your life!

References

Davis, T. (2022). *Emotion: Definition, theories, & examples*. Berkeley Well-being Institute. Available at: https://www.berkeleywellbeing.com/list-of-emotions.html

Deci, E. L., & Ryan, R. M. (2010). *Self-determination*. New York: John Wiley & Sons, Inc. https//dx.doi.org/10.1002/9780470479216.corpsy0834Ekman, P. (1992b). Are there basic emotions? Psychol. Rev. 99, 550–553. doi: 10.1037/0033-295X.99.3.550

Emmons, R. (2010). Why Gratitude is Good? Greater Good Science Center. Available at: https://greatergood.berkeley.edu/article/item/why_gratitude_is_good

Fredrickson, B. L. (2013). "Positive emotions broaden and build," in Advances in Experimental Social Psychology. Vol. 47. eds. P. Devine and A. Plant (Academic Press), 1–53.

Fredrickson, B. L. (1998, September). What good are positive emotions? *Review of General Psychology*, 2(3), 300–319. https://doi.org/10.1037/1089-2680.2.3.300. PMID: 21850154; PMCID: PMC3156001.

Greater Good Science Center (2021a). Online gratitude journal. [online]. Available at: https://thnx4.org/?_ga=2.4097204.542645702.1625729744-336604110.1625559203

Greater Good Science Center (2021b). Thnx4 gratitude journal. [online]. Available at: https://ggsc.berkeley.edu/what_we_do/online_courses_tools/thnx4_gratitude_journal

Littlefield, Ch. (2020). Use gratitude to counter stress and uncertainty. *Harvard Business Review*. [online]. Available at: https://hbr.org/2020/10/use-gratitude-to-counter-stress-and-uncertainty

Positive Psychology Center (2020). PERMA Theory of well-being and PERMA workshops. University of Pennsylvania. [Cited July 10, 2022] Available at: https://ppc.sas.upenn.edu/learn-more/perma-theory-well-being-and-perma-workshops

Roth, G., Vansteenkiste, M., & Ryan, R. (2019). Integrative emotion regulation: Process and development from a self-determination theory perspective. *Development and Psychopathology*, 31, 1–12. https://doi.org/10.1017/S0954579419000403

Santos, L. (2019). Coursera happiness course. Available at: https://www.coursera.org/learn/the-science-of-well-being

Seligman, M., Rashid, T., & Parks, A. (2006). Positive psychotherapy. *American Psychologist*, 61, 774. https://doi.org/10.1037/0003-066X.61.8.774.

Summer, A. (2018). The science of gratitude. Greater Good Science Center. Available at: https://ggsc.berkeley.edu/images/uploads/GGSC-JTF_White_Paper-Gratitude-FINAL.pdf

West, T. N., & Fredrickson, B. L. (2020). Cultivating positive emotions to enhance human flourishing. In S. I. Donaldson, M. Csikszentmihalyi, & J. Nakamura (Eds.), *Positive psychological science: Improving everyday life, well-being, work, education, and socie-ties across the globe* (pp. 38–51). New York: Routledge.

Wiking, M. (2017). *The little book of hygge: Danish secrets to happy living.* New York: William Morrow.

World Economic Forum: This is what makes people around the world happy right now (2020). Mental Health. [online]. Available at: https://www.weforum.org/agenda/2020/11/global-happiness-survey-2020-coronavirus/

3   Building Your Engagement

It is by being fully involved with every detail of our lives, whether good or bad, that we find happiness, not by trying to look for it directly.

— Mihaly Csikszentmihalyi

Introduction to Engagement

There is no doubt that the level of our engagement in our everyday life generates a great amount of our well-being. You might remember from Chapter 1 that Martin Seligman, in his very popular book *Authentic Happiness* (2002), discusses that authentic happiness is derived from three major sets of experiences in life:

- experiencing **pleasantness** regularly (the pleasant life)
- experiencing a high level of **engagement** in satisfying activities (the engaged life)
- experiencing a sense of **connectedness** to a greater whole (the meaningful life)

Just to kindly remind you, Professor Seligman added two more sets of experiences generating well-being (life shared with others and life filled with achievement) in his book *Flourishing* (2011) and introduced us to PERMA, an acronym that stands for the five elements that account for what makes up the "good life" – an authentic and sustained happiness and well-being. The PERMA+4 model was introduced in 2019 (Donaldson, 2019; Donaldson & Donaldson, 2021; Donaldson et al., 2021, 2023) and presents the nine building blocks of well-being as we know them today:

1 positive emotions
2 engagement
3 relationships
4 meaning
5 achievement
6 physical health
7 mindset

DOI: 10.4324/9781003378365-4

8   environment
9   economic security

Below is an example of the second building block – engagement – the focus of this chapter.

Try to recall the last time you were surprised that the class was suddenly over. *You were sitting in the middle of the room, fully sunk into the discussion that was happening between you, your classmates, and the professor. You almost felt like everyone in the class became a part of one living organism that is fully here and now, chewing on the provocative ideas that had been thrown at you by the professor with a fox smile on her face. You found the counterarguments being returned straight back to her by one of your classmates brilliant. The rhythm of the talk started to feel like they were playing tennis, waiting for someone to hit a perfect forehand with a final argument. You all got so caught up in the topic that you forgot to track the time. The professor suddenly ended the class with the words "All right everyone, let's quit it here today and we can come back to this next week. What a discussion!" You were excited about the tools you just learned and you almost felt like you did not want the class to end. You wanted more now. "Next week is so far away!" You thought about the class discussion while you packed your backpack, leaving the room still processing all the good ideas that were just born there.*

Do you recall a similar feeling? Whether it's generated by flow in class or flow you got into while reading a chapter of your favorite book, writing an essay, or simply talking to your friend about a topic that caught your interest so much.

Student engagement can refer to the degree of **attention, curiosity, interest, optimism, and passion** that you all show when you are learning or being taught. How engaged you are in school-related activities often reflects the level of motivation you have to study, to learn, and to make progress in your education.

So we understand that engagement co-creates our well-being. But what if you want more full involvement in your everyday life? You can build more engagement and flow, thus *relaxed peak performance and optimal experience in* your life with two different approaches (see Csikszentmihalyi, 1990, 1997; Yan & Donaldson, 2022):

1   creating time and space to engage in more activities that bring you to flow
2   crafting activities that you are already doing in order to engage more and to bring more flow into them

So let's dive deeper into this chapter together looking at how you can create more space for **flow** in your life through seeking **meaningful goals**, **deeper presence**, **stronger focus**, and through **reflection** on your flow experiences. Ready, set, flow!

Benefits of Engagement for Students' Well-Being

Research shows that for university students, boredom is experienced at school around one-third of the time. So what is boredom, what amount of it is "normal" and what does it generate as a result? While some amount of boredom is to be expected in our lives, or even desired to let our brain recharge and to stimulate creativity, boredom is an unpleasant state when we experience a lack of interest or enthusiasm, leaving us feeling weary and impatient. We often experience lower motivation, poorer focus, weaker ability to remember, and, mainly, zero joy while being bored. We can experience situational boredom such as not knowing how to "kill the time" when missing the bus to school or existential boredom that feels more like a permanent lack of meaning in our everyday lives turning into low motivation to finish or even start different activities. Luckily, both scenarios can be solved by building up engagement in your day-to-day lives.

The opposite of boredom is **engagement**. Students who are more engaged in classes or at home while studying report higher levels of motivation, ability to focus, better memory, joy, and satisfaction and experience academic success.

University students are usually emotionally engaged:

- when they feel safe at school
- when they like spending time at school
- when they are interested in classes and topics they learn about
- when they identify with the whole school culture

You as students are usually very cognitively engaged. You attend a great amount of classes where you pay attention to what is **being taught and discussed**. Many students put in a lot of effort to **do well in school**, naturally oftentimes as a result of our fear of failure (Koci et al., 2023) which can lead to high academic engagement as well. But emotional engagement at the school level also reflects **our relationships with classmates** and **our professors**. We naturally pay more attention and feel more engaged **with teachers we connect with** or with those who are **easier to bond with**.

How can you tell you are frequently engaged as a student?

- You feel alert and you are listening to what teachers or classmates are saying
- You often take notes, create mind maps, or draw pictures as part of your notes
- You don't hesitate to ask questions and to offer your comments
- You gladly offer your own input when invited
- You respond to questions, often with a level of enthusiasm
- You even look and feel interested. Your face, eyes, body posture, and gestures show that you are involved in the lesson
- You react, according to the lesson, with expressions of happiness, surprise, and concern, and you don't hesitate much about expressing your opinion when being asked
- You are curious and ask questions on your own
- It is not difficult for you to make connections to other ideas and offer insights accordingly

But how about in your life outside of your academic experiences?

- You often find yourself caught in the moment while spending time in nature
- You are listening closely to what your friends are saying when meeting them
- You like to stop for a small talk with your neighbors when you see them
- You enjoy the presence of your loved one and even forget to check your phone for a longer period of time
- You are generally interested about what is going on in the world around you
- You find time for your hobbies
- You lose track of time even while doing small, simple things in your daily life
- You rarely feel bored

But please, keep in mind, our engagement goes hand in hand with your energy levels. It is very usual and normal to feel less engaged when your energy levels are low. If you find yourself feeling rather disengaged, tired, or even avoiding interactions, listen to your body and provide it with what it needs the most right now. Do you feel like you are the half empty glass that has nothing left to be poured from for others? Do you feel like even small things to do evoke feelings of resistance? It might be worthwhile to stop and to observe your mind – does it ruminate on negative thoughts and generate negative feelings that need to be processed? If yes, try to process your emotions in an activity from the previous chapter on emotions. Or do you rather feel like you lack sleep, relaxation, and proper nutrition? If yes, go to the chapter on physical health and remind yourself how to eat, sleep, and relax better. Prioritize yourself now and do what you can to recharge. Add some "me time" to your calendar. Find space for leisure time activities, or maybe now is the moment for doing nothing and using the advantage of being bored. :-)

Your Engagement Flower Assessment

We have learned in Chapter 1 that engagement is one of the **nine essential building blocks** for generating well-being. One of the things that can be very useful is to reflect and to think about your personal **engagement strengths**. By understanding the importance of engagement for your well-being, you will have the opportunity to assess your engagement strengths!

In this exercise, you will be asked to fill out your own **flower diagram**. You will be provided a wheel that represents **nine different strengths** for building your engagement. These go from your ability to focus to your engagement in everyday life activities, engagement in school, engagement in work or a part-time job, engagement in your hobbies, engagement with other people, engagement in your alone time, your creativity, and experiencing flow. There is also room for your own choice of another engagement strength you might feel that needs to be reflected in your life as well.

Here is a **set of statements** that will help you to assess how well you feel about each engagement strength. You might find it helpful to reflect by reading the descriptions of ideal states of all nine strengths of yours and assessing where you stand.

Ability to Focus

I am **able to focus** and **shift my focus** in the direction I desire using my willpower. I avoid multitasking and I strengthen my ability to focus with different strategies, such as breathing exercises or meditation.

Engagement in Everyday Life Activities

I experience a great amount of engagement in everyday life activities such as **self-care, housekeeping,** or **spending time with my loved ones**. I am engaged when I **study** or when I have some **time for myself** no matter what activities I decide to choose.

Engagement in School

While understanding that boredom is a natural part of our life, I experience a great amount of engagement at school. In my **classes**, in **seminars**, and in my interactions with **classmates and teachers**. I don't feel bored during breaks; I enjoy lunch breaks and purposefully motivate myself to engage at school as much as possible.

Engagement in Work or Part-time Job

While understanding that boredom is a natural part of our life, I experience a great amount of engagement at work. I feel engaged while performing my **regular work duties** and also while working on **new projects** or **activities**. I engage with my **colleagues** and my **boss** in our **meetings** or **discussions**.

Engagement in Your Hobbies

I experience a great amount of engagement while doing what I enjoy in my free time. I do my best to find time for **my hobbies** and I **prioritize my hobbies** to learn, grow, and relax.

Engagement with Other People

I experience a great amount of social flow and engagement while interacting with other people. I experienced engaged **conversations** and **high quality time**. I like to **talk to people** and I enjoy **listening to them**.

Engagement in Your Alone Time

I experience a great amount of engagement in my alone time. I manage my time well to do **activities I enjoy, to learn, or to practice**. I know well what activities make me feel engaged and I participate in those when I'm alone. While understanding that boredom is a natural part of our life, I **don't usually get bored** when spending time on my own.

Creativity

I am happy with the time in my life I invest in my creativity. I let myself be creative while **writing essays, working on projects,** and even when **I cook or decorate** my home! I make time for activities that make me creative (e.g. drawing, crafting, writing, and photographing).

Experiencing Flow

I often experience flow, the state of **relaxed peak performance**, where I feel like being one with the activity I am doing.

Other Engagement Strengths

Are there any other engagement strengths on your mind you would like to assess? If yes, please scale them as well as the previous strengths.

So how do you actually assess your strengths? **Please imagine a ladder with steps numbered from 0 at the bottom to 10 at the top.**

The top of the ladder represents the best result (I feel very confident in this particular strength), while the bottom of the ladder represents the worst (I would like to build this particular strength better).

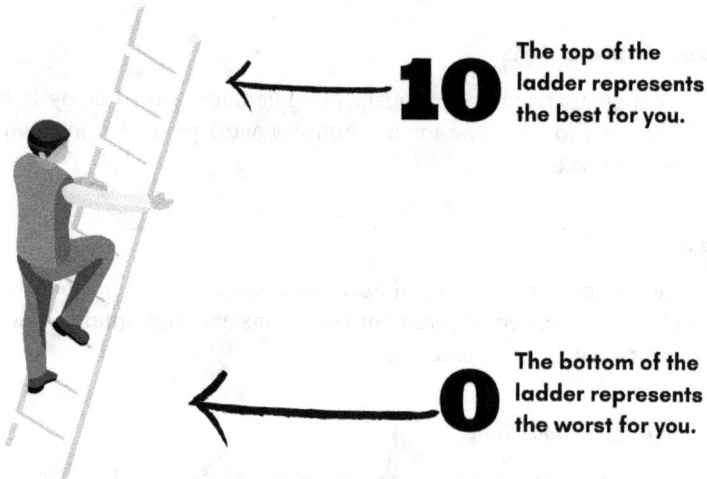

The top of the ladder represents the best for you.

The bottom of the ladder represents the worst for you.

Figure 3.1 Your well-being assessment ladder.

On which step of the ladder on a scale of 0–10 would you say you personally feel you stand at this time in terms of:

- ability to focus
- engagement in everyday life activities
- engagement in school
- engagement in work or a part-time job
- engagement in your hobbies
- engagement with other people
- engagement in your alone time
- creativity
- experiencing flow
- other positive emotions strengths

After you assess all your engagement strengths, draw your very own engagement flower! Circle the resulting numbers of your strength on the engagement wheel ladders. Then draw the petal shape from the center of the wheel through all the numbers on each ladder to create your own flower (see Figure 3.2 for an example of the flower diagram).

Figure 3.2 Example of your engagement flower diagram.

Let's assess your **engagement strengths** and later you can reflect on them and learn how to build particular strengths (if needed) in the upcoming chapter.

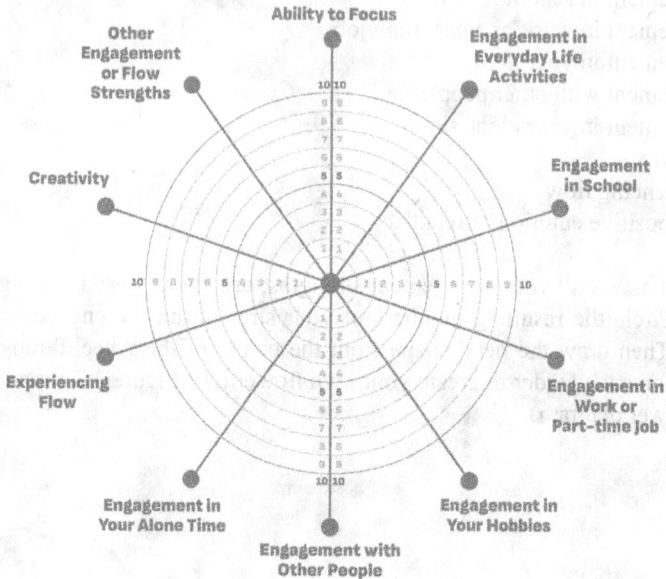

Figure 3.3 Your engagement flower assessment.

YOUR ENGAGEMENT FLOWER REFLECTION

Great job! How do you feel?

Let's look at your personal **engagement flower**.

Remember, there is no judgment here; this is just an awareness exercise.

The goal of this exercise is to become **aware of your situation and decide what your next goal should be**. Then you will have a chance to think about what you can do to achieve the said goal. This chapter will present some **evidence-based recommendations and activities** you can try right away to see if they fit your personality and style. It is fun to reflect on your flowers with your friends, but remember, the only one you can compare your flowers to is yourself. Enjoy checking on your flowers over time to track your progress or changes reflecting certain events in different stages of your life. The goal shouldn't be to have perfect, long petals in all your flowers – you should come to terms with imperfection. Invite the possibility of gradual growth of your flower petals rather than unhealthy overnight perfection.

The flower reflects your **subjective perception**, rather than your objective state. You might rate your *Creativity* petal lower while you are objectively creative and creating on a daily basis. Why do people do that? Our perception of ourselves is rarely objective. Sometimes, this can be caused by having a certain idea, a vision of what our ideal *Creativity* level looks like. Sometimes, the *Creativity* petal is disturbed by a specific time of the semester such as weeks of finals that don't allow you to devote time to your creative hobbies as much. Hence, it can be reasonable to believe we still have space for growth. Rating your petals gives you **the opportunity to reflect on** your current state in certain areas of your life. It will also make you think about what strengths you are satisfied with for now and what strengths you might like to focus on. :-)

Let's see how you can **grow your engagement petals**.

Growing Your Engagement Flower Petals

Being engaged means being highly focused on the activity you do, whether it is cooking your dinner, doing your morning yoga, reading a book, or discussing it with your classmate. Being in flow means being in a state of peak performance while being relaxed. But increasing your engagement or even getting to flow starts with your ability to focus, devoting your time to your interests and passions, and practicing. Does that sound like fun? Let's take a look at what you can do to grow your engagement flower!

Ability to Focus

In his book *Good Business* (2003), Professor Mihaly Csikszentmihalyi describes focus as the brain's capacity to process information and guide a person's actions. **Focus is mental energy**, and as with physical energy, if we don't devote at least some of it to a certain task, then we won't move forward with it one bit.

According to Professor Csikszentmihalyi, **the brain can process about 110 bits of information per second**. For example, to understand what the other person is saying to us, we use about 40 bits, which explains why we cannot understand more than two people who are talking to us at the same time. Here is Professor Csikszentmihalyi's math. If we are awake for 16 hours every day and live to be 75 years old, we can absorb a limited number of about 173 billion bits of information.

Every experience we have – every thought, feeling, wish, or memory, every action, or conversation – passes through the net of our attention and consumes some part of those 173 billion bits. What we refer to as our life is a summary of all these experiences that we have filtered through our attention during this time. From this point of view, it is easy to understand that the context and quality of **our life determines what and how we focus our attention.**

As you might think now, where you put your attention is crucial to your life goals, well-being, fulfillment, and happiness. But can we train our ability to focus on things that matter the most to us? Absolutely! There are actually a few things we can do.

Do it   **Single Task!**

Start feeling productive with **single tasking**. Switching tasks is not as effective as it is believed to be. Before we can focus our mind on a difficult problem and create the conditions for its meaningful solution, it takes us about 15 minutes to 1 hour. Professor Csikszentmihalyi says in his books that it is better to work on one task until we are exhausted. When we switch to another problem at this point, it will feel like a relief. When we get tired of the new task, we can return to the original problem feeling refreshed!

Loving-Kindness Meditation

You can do breathwork and practice focusing on your breath. But to feel good, you can also practice being mindful and try meditation! Have you ever tried mindfulness meditation? If interested, listen to a guided **loving-kindness meditation** created by scientist Barbara Fredrickson with current knowledge on how to regulate your emotions on her www.positivityresonance.com page!

Box Breathing

To train your focus, you can also try the box breathing exercise. Imagine a box with four sides. Make one slow breath out, releasing all the air from your lungs.

1 Breathe in through your nose as you slowly count to four in your head.
2 Hold your breath for a count of four.
3 Exhale for another count of four.
4 Hold your breath again for a count of four.

Repeat for three to four rounds, but stop if you start feeling dizzy or uncomfortable.

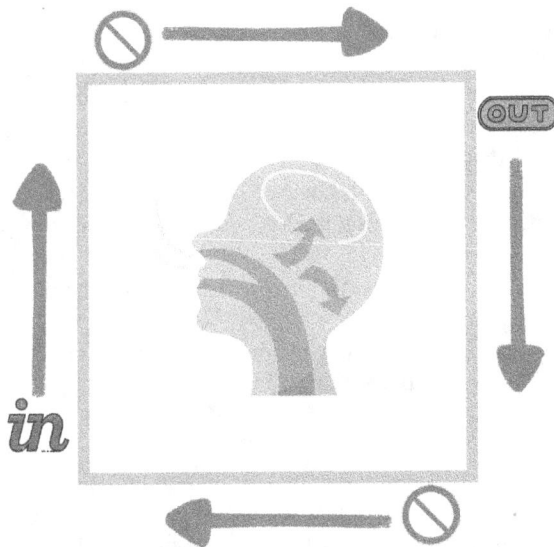

Figure 3.4 How to box breathe to stay focused.

Engagement in Everyday Life Activities

What can **block your engagement** or ability to get in flow? What to avoid? Let's take a look. If possible, try to stay off:

- dilemmas
- ineffective habits
- worries
- negative stress
- too strong excitement
- not having enough time
- weak inner motivation

But what can you, in contrast, do to increase the potential to **feel engaged or even experience flow**? Try to:

- focus intentionally (e.g. set an intention to limit distractions and to focus on reading your favorite book for a certain amount of time)
- have previous experience (getting engaged in activities we are already familiar with is easier. Don't despair if new activities feel distractive)
- have clear goals (e.g. writing one page of an essay, cooking pasta with tuna, running around the neighborhood for 25 minutes)
- vision of success (e.g. imagine the feeling of being done with your exam and walking proudly through your campus)
- get in a good mood (e.g. getting excited when thinking about doing this activity)
- create peace and quiet (e.g. close your window, shut your door, or even use ear plugs if helpful)
- take initiative (e.g. buy yourself new workout clothes, check out the library hours, watch some Ted Talks that will get you inspired before diving into your project)
- receive positive feedback or feedback in general (set your milestones, e.g. a number of pages you want to read so you can track your progress)
- adopt a mindset that it is not important what others think about the process or your results (e.g. I am doing this because I love doing this)
- create mind maps (e.g. throwing the key words on the sheet of paper and connecting those that are related)
- brainstorm before doing something (e.g. write down your ideas, discuss your plan with your roommate)
- have fun! (e.g. get excited, laugh when making mistakes, and let your body feel the enjoyment of what you are doing).

Engagement in School

Students often experience engagement related to school while studying, being in class, or while talking or socializing with classmates who are like-minded. But how can you work with activities that you are already doing in order to bring more flow into them? **Use your superpowers**! You say you don't have any? What if I tell you that character traits like being kind, fair, grateful, funny, curious, or being a good team player are the true superpowers that change lives?

Students who use their **character strengths** during their studies or in daily life report greater study and life **satisfaction** and **engagement**, and are more likely to see what they are studying as **meaningful** or as a **calling**, than those not using their strengths. This means:

- Identify your strengths.
- Use them and get creative!
- Try to apply them also in a new way.
- How does this look in real life?

Andrew, a student of mine came to class one day with a smile from ear to ear. We were about to start the lecture while he stood in the main door waving to my students to get their attention. He asked loudly if we could all sing happy birthday to Tom once he arrives since it is his day. "Including you," and he gave me this funny look. He said, "Tom is running late because he forgot something in another building so it will be the perfect surprise to start singing when he enters the room." And so we did. We all started to sing loudly and inharmoniously Happy Birthday when Tom entered the room. Tom did not believe what was happening and he was obviously touched. We were all smiling and clapping our hands like little kids and Andrew was patting Tom's back as he was sitting down. This was a beautiful example of how Andrew used his character strength. He made thirty people laugh, celebrate life, and he completely changed the dynamics of our class. You don't have to sing nor joke to make people around you happier. Instead, think of what your superpower is, what feels good to you, and what comes naturally to you and share that with the world around you. Small gestures can have a tremendous impact on someone's day.

Do it   **What Are Your Character Strengths?**

Identify your personal character strengths at VIA Character Strengths Survey (https://www.viacharacter.org/) and think of how concretely your strengths can help you to study more effectively, joyfully, and with a sense of meaning.

To identify your character strengths you might also like to ask yourself:

- What gives you energy?
- When do you feel alive?
- When do you lose track of time?
- When do you feel challenged and engaged?

Generate three new ways to use your character strengths at school and in your everyday life! For example, if curiosity is your character strength, you can grow it and expand your knowledge about a topic you are currently curious about such as your physical health through books, journals, magazines, TV, radio, or the internet. Devote half an hour, three times a week paying attention to what new knowledge about your health promotion you have gained and are ready to apply to your everyday life! To tap into your curiosity, ask yourself what topic seems the most exciting to you at this stage of your life? It can be even something out of the range of what you study or usually care about. And that is perfectly ok! Any topic that makes you excited deserves your attention. You can apply your curiosity strength in your day-to-day life by awakening it before any project you are about to work on. Raise some provoking questions and dive into your creative thinking.

Also, don't hide your weaknesses please. We all have them. This might surprise you, but I would like to ask you to love them. Our weaknesses make us who we are. Celebrate your uniqueness from both sides – acknowledge and use your character strengths, respect them, and don't hide your weaknesses. Be you. Even if this book is full of tips on how to grow and change our behavior, I would like you to know that you are already perfect the way you are. Don't ever forget that. Your desire to grow and evolve is just a bonus.:-)

Engagement in Work or Part-time Job

While for all of university students studying can actually be seen as a "full-time job," more than half of you are also working while in college. You might have a job in retail or in a restaurant, or on campus sorting library books. Let's look closer at how you can approach those types of work assignments for maximum engagement, while we can also think ahead to your professional lives after college.

We discussed two approaches to generate more engagement in your life at the very beginning in the introduction to this chapter: Creating time and space or crafting activities.

So **craft the activities that you are doing already** in order to bring more flow into them!

Professor Csikszentmihalyi introduced core characteristics and elements of flow that were generated based on 10 000 interviews. Let's learn how you can use those to increase your engagement at your work through job crafting! We experience flow when:

1   Our goals are clear.
    Specify your goals as much as possible. Define for yourself what is your main goal and what are the steps that will lead you there. Try to understand the goals that have been set for you. If your goals are not clear to you, ask your boss or coworkers what exactly is expected from you.

2 We get immediate feedback.

It is not always true that we get immediate feedback at work. We often get a task that is expected from us to do but not always are we fortunate to have immediate feedback about how we are doing. But what if you set the milestones yourself, and what if you tracked your progress with no external help? **Create a specific plan and vision, and track your steps to stay motivated!**

3 We balance between challenges and our abilities.

We get in flow when our abilities meet the needs of the challenge. If our abilities are too progressive for the activity, we get bored soon. If our abilities are stretched too much, we might get anxious. So how do we balance challenges and our abilities at work? If you feel like getting bored at work, challenge yourself to stay engaged. And vice versa. **When the task is too challenging for you, balance the expectations!** Discuss with your boss if you can get more time to get things done. Ask your colleagues for help. There is nothing wrong with asking for assistance. You only show that you are responsible and look for ways to get your work done right!

4 Our concentration deepens.

When we experience flow, our concentration deepens with time. **Protect it!** Make enough time for certain projects on your calendar. Limit distractions. Use this increasing focus to flow with the activity you are participating in and enjoy it!

5 Only the presence matters.

We forget about what went wrong this week, we forget about what we still need to do today, and we forget even about ourselves when we get in flow. Only your presence matters. When working on a project, try not to worry about the outcome. Try not to think about what your colleagues or boss will think about our results and don't even compare yourself to others. **Focus only on now and enjoy here and now.**

6 We have no problems controlling the situation.

We feel like we control the situation while in flow. We set the speed, we set the rhythm, and we decide where we go next from where we are. To get in flow, visualize the activity already successfully done and **trust your abilities**. Believe in yourself, and believe you can. Because, as Henry Ford once said, whether you think you can, or you think you can't – you're right.

7 The perception of time is altered.

When in flow, we feel like time slows down, our senses get more reactive, and the experience gets richer. But when we get out of flow and look back at how much time we actually invested in the activity, we often cannot believe how fast the time flew by. You can get a lot done in this particular state. Care for it! Place boundaries at the time you book for your deep work. Don't let anyone make you sacrifice your time for focused work because they need your assistance. **Your deep work time on the calendar is as important as any other activity.**

8 Loss of ego.

When we get in flow, we become one with the activity we do. We do not think of ourselves separately from the activity and our ego fades away. But there is a paradox in the loss of ego due to flow. On the contrary, after we "wake up" from a flow state, we feel more complete than before. Our sense of self deepens and we know ourselves a bit better than before the activity. **Check for the activities that make you feel like you lose yourself in them at work and prioritize them!**

Engagement in Your Hobbies

Working with my students for thirteen years, I noticed one thing. Students who have a hobby, something that is "their thing" and who regularly find time for what they love and enjoy **seem much more relaxed**. They smile more; they seem more energized and grounded. I would almost say laid back. The mindset of "school is important, but so is my life" brought some light into their faces.

Another thing I noticed is that students can get really creative in their leisure time. Asking how my students love spending their free time is one of my favorite questions to ask. You immediately see their eyes light up. We use anonymous word clouds to answer this question so students can open up and some of the most frequent answers I get are:

- Sleeping
- Painting
- Reading
- Cooking and baking
- Doing some sports
- Crafting
- Spending time with my pet
- Spending time with friends and family
- Watching Netflix

But also:

- Crocheting
- Geocaching
- Shopping and window-shopping
- Coffee hopping
- Traveling
- Working
- Cuddling
- Eating
- Doing NOTHING (and being good at it!)

No matter what is "your thing," you deserve to find time for what makes you feel alive. The study-life balance (like work-life balance) that college students often struggle with is a very real thing. Students aren't always sure how best to manage their time and what is the "right" way to go about it. There is one thing you cannot go wrong with. Find time for your hobbies. Studying is important, but so is what brings you joy.

(Do It)   **Make Time For Yourself**

What do you like to do? What brings you joy? What do you love? Create time and space to engage in more activities that **might bring you flow.** Whether in or out of your student life. Prioritize your hobbies and make them as important as studying or making time for others. **Making time for yourself to recharge and to do what you love is an essential building block for your life satisfaction and well-being.** Make a list of activities you know you should do more often and try to squeeze them into your calendar. This might be the best investment you've made in a while!

Engagement with Other People

Our **relationships and how happy we are in our relationships have a powerful influence on our health.** Growing our positive relationships is a form of **care for our well-being** too. Close relationships, more than money or fame, are what keep us happy throughout our lives. Harvard (2022) concludes that positive relationship ties protect us from life's discontents, help to delay mental and physical decline, and are better predictors of long and happy lives than social class, IQ, or even genes.

If engagement in your hobbies is about answering what you like to do, engagement with others is about even easier questions. Ready? **Who do you like to spend time with? Who makes you smile and laugh? Who do you love to listen to when they talk? Who makes you forget about the struggles of everyday life when you are with them?** Those are your people! Make sure you make room in your calendar for them. Prioritize spending time with them. Such a high-quality relationship boosts your well-being and is healthy for you. The world's oldest and happiest people often say that the key ingredient to their happiness and longevity is to make time for what they love and for who they love. Go ahead! Grab your phone and reach out to someone you want to see to make a walk and coffee date to increase your social flow.

Engagement in Your Alone Time

Spending time alone can be comfortable for each of us to different degrees. The fact is, those of us who report high levels of engagement in our alone time also enjoy being on our own more.

Do It   **Mind Mapping Your Engagement in Your Alone Time**

When in your alone time do you **experience joy? What do you enjoy doing? When do you experience a high level of engagement or even flow?** Let's mind map this so you get to know yourself better!

1 Prepare for **mind mapping**: bring a paper (the bigger the better), colors, and your painting skills :-)
2 Follow the rules: the faster the better. Do not think, do not judge (no one has to see it), and just WRITE or DRAW what comes to your mind.
3 Write the topic "My engaged self in my alone time!" in the middle of your paper.
4 Create 3–5 branches and describe them a bit with words.
5 Extend each with another three branches and continue expressing what's on your mind with words.
6 After you get done, go through your mind map. Link what feels like needs to be linked. Draw. Have fun.
7 Now look at your masterpiece. Circle 3 ideally different things that caught your attention. You will know what they are when you see them. Listen to your gut.
8 Think how you can incorporate those three into new ideas, new inspiration, new realizations, and how can you experience more engagement in your alone time!
9 Share what have you learned about yourself with a family member; discuss this with a classmate. :-)

Experiencing Flow

As a peak form of engagement, flow state is an optimal experience. It is a holistic sensation that people feel when they act with total involvement, as Professor Mihaly Csikszentmihalyi, the pioneering co-founder of the field of positive psychology and author of the theory of flow, described it. Flow state is a particularly important part of engagement and it can be very rewarding. Flow can be seen as an engagement on steroids or one might say like the nirvana state of engagement. Being in flow not only feels good, we also get very productive and we tend to learn fast in flow. Are you wondering how often, if at all, you experience flow and if there is anything you can do to increase such an experience in your day-to-day life? There is actually a lot you can start practicing to experience peak performance more often. First, let's have a look at how to use flow to create engagement and your intrinsic motivation. It is as simple as:

1 Identifying your personal flow activities
2 Planning a flow activity
3 Carrying out a flow activity

How to build flow?

We all know that feeling of losing ourselves in an activity and performing the best while being relaxed. But we all experience flow while doing different activities. Have a look back at your life and think of moments when you felt relaxed, but also productive and consumed by what you were doing.

Ask yourself a question:

"What activities make me not only lose myself in what I am doing but also feel like I flow effortlessly with the activity as one? Write your thoughts and ideas down and be specific!"

Example:

Flow activities supporting my high engagement and almost effortless performance: running, drawing, reading, writing essays, long walks with my dogs in nature, talking to my friends, spending time with my parents, bike trips with family and friends, walks with my classmates, healthy cooking with friends, supportive calls and texts with friends making us feel relaxed, relaxing walks by the river in the sun, walking instead of driving everywhere, brisk walking to school instead of using the tram, walks on the beach, and Yoga! **Create your own unique and authentic list.**

Look at the list and think of what activity you could actually **plan on doing next week**. Try to fit it into your schedule and put it on your calendar.
Example:
Healthy cooking with my friends and family! (over the weekend)
Long walk by the river. (on Friday night?)
Last step: Carry out a flow activity and have fun!

Do it   **My Recent Flow**

Have you experienced flow lately? How much flow did you experience the preceding week? When? With who? What were you doing? Get curious and identify when and how you experienced flow in the current days using the **AEIOU technique**.

The AEIOU acronym stands for areas to be explored: activity, environment, interaction, objects, and users.

ACTIVITY:
What activity was I doing?
Example:
I was meeting with Alice, my new coach. We had coffee at the University cafeteria. It was a planned activity. It was an unstructured activity. My role was: a visitor, a client.

ENVIRONMENT:
What environment was I in?
Example:
University environment.
New environment.
New school (I study at a different college).
Feelings: excitement, curiosity, and admiration.

INTERACTION:
Who/what was I interacting with?
Example:
Interaction with University employees and a specialist in the field of public health.
Informal interaction. New type of interaction. Self-initiated interaction. High level of importance.

OBJECTS:
What were the objects that took a part in the interaction?
Example:
Discussion with a coach about how to plan my future coaching. University building while receiving the tour. University garden I took a walk in. A bike I used to get to school.

USERS:
Who were you with and what was their role in your experience?
Example:
Coach Alice who was kind and caring.
University employees.
Barista at the coffee shop who smiled.
Students.

So what can this activity give you? The answer is simple. **Awareness of what helps you to get in flow.**

See the possible conclusion:

I was in flow thanks to **being in a new, exciting environment** and **planning my future coaching** I am looking forward to. Also because the activity **involved positive people** and **great coffee**. I also **stretched my body** and **biked** there and back.

Now is your turn. Think of the last time you were in flow and analyze what activities, environments, interactions, objects, and people helped you to get there!.

Activities	**E**nvironments	**I**nteractions	**O**bjects	**U**sers

Figure 3.5 Your flow activity assessment using AEIOU technique.

Ten Empowering Questions to Support My Engagement Flower Growth

Do It

1 What can I do to make my engagement a priority?
2 What activities do I enjoy doing?
3 What work activities make me forget about the world?
4 What school activity makes me feel fully absorbed in the moment?
5 What activities make me connected to myself?
6 Who do I lose track of time with?
7 What can I do to hang out with them more often?
8 What is the smallest thing I can do today to increase my engagement?
9 What was I doing last time I found myself in flow?
10 What can I do to incorporate engaging activities into my life more often?

Ten Evidence-based Tips to Build My Engagement Flower

Do It

1 Make your autotelic activities list. A list of things you do for your own sake. For the activity itself, not for the result.
2 Get clear about what activities, situations, or people make you more engaged using the AEIOU technique.

3   Find ways to make time for such activities and for people who help you feel engaged.
4   Book enough time for your flow activities in your calendar. Getting fully engaged and absorbed in the activity takes some time and once you get there, you don't want to interrupt your flow because you have other responsibilities to deal with.
5   Make intention. Before you start your creative process, think of what you want it to be like and even visualize your successful achievement.
6   Set your environment to support your engagement (e.g. find a place where you can focus the best, eliminate distractions, and set realistic goals).
7   Balance your skills and challenges that certain activities demand. Either lower the pressure you put on yourself or raise the bar to challenge yourself.
8   Try to stay relaxed throughout your creative process. Whether you write an essay, paint, or dance.
9   Try to stay away from thoughts about whether people will like what you are doing/working on or not. Do it for yourself and for the feeling it generates for you.
10   Recover from the flow. Longer periods of deep concentration can be physically and mentally demanding. Hydrate, eat, and rest.

Tips to Engagement Snacking

Building your engagement does not have to be complicated nor time demanding. Look at Figure 3.6 and try some of the tips right now!

Figure 3.6 Tips to engagement snacking.

Feeling "lost" in an activity feels great. Having a great conversation, reading a fascinating book, playing with your dog in the park, or just having yourself fully focused on the project you are working on for your favorite class. While many of us build our well-being on activities that generate engagement, I would like to invite you to dive into another strong and interesting topic of positive relationships. The upcoming chapter will reveal how high-quality relationships impact our well-being, shape our days, and improve our overall health. Being engaged can be extremely rewarding but caring for our relationships can do the work as well!

References

Csikszentmihalyi, M. (1990). *Flow: The psychology of optimal experience*. New York: HarperCollins.

Csikszentmihalyi, M. (1997). *Finding flow: The psychology of engagement with everyday life*. New York: HarperCollins.

Csikszentmihalyi, M. (2003). *Good business: leadership, flow, and the making of meaning*. New York, Viking.

Donaldson, S. I. (2019). Evaluating employee positive functioning and performance: A positive work and organizations approach. Doctoral Dissertation, Claremont Graduate University.

Donaldson, S. I., Gaffaney, J., & Caberra, V. (2023). The science and practice of positive psychology: From a bold vision to PERMA+4. In H. S. Friedman (Eds.), *The 3rd edition of the encyclopedia of mental health*. Cambridge, MA: Academic Press.

Donaldson, S. I., Heshmati, S., Young, J. Y., & Donaldson, S. I. (2021). Examining building blocks of well-being beyond PERMA and self-report bias. *Journal of Positive Psychology*, https://doi.org/10.1080/17439760.2020.1818813.

Koci, J. (2023). How to Build Well-being in University and College Students – Methodology of Academic Well-being Promotion. Prague: Charles University, 2023, ISBN: 978-80-87489-38-3

Seligman, M. E. P. (2002). *Authentic happiness: Using the new positive psychology to realize your potential for lasting fulfillment*. New York, NY: Free Press.

Seligman, M. E. P. (2011). *Flourish: A visionary new understanding of happiness and well-being*. New York, NY: Free Press.

Valliant, G. E., McArthur, C. C., Bock, A., & Waldinger, R. J. (2022). Grant study of adult development, 1938–2000, February 20, 2022. 1938/2000. V4_Academic achievement, College students. Longitudinal, field study. Harvard Dataverse. Available at: https://doi.org/10.7910/DVN/48WRX9

4   Building Your Relationships

Other people matter. Period.

– Christopher Peterson

Introduction to Positive Relationships

Research shows that the good quality of our relationships can positively influence **every aspect of our well-being**. In fact, the longest scientific study on happiness (more than 80 years) conducted by Harvard University researchers **clearly shows that positive relationships keep us healthier and happier** (Waldinger & Schulz, 2023). Science has come to a realization that caring, loving, and respectful relationships are as important for our health and well-being as our diet, exercise, or environment we live in. And it is rather the quality of our relationship that matters more than the quantity of friends and family members we hold good relationships with. Thus, whether we can say **we feel** supported, loved, and cared for and that we are capable of loving back regardless of the number of relationships that provide us with such experience. Relationships and all those brief everyday life connections. The micro-moments of connection are when you smile at the cashier at the local coffee shop and they smile back at you. When you share your funny weekend story with a classmate and you laugh together. When you call your parents to say quick hi and you tell them you miss them. When you tell your partner you did not pass the exam and they just sit there silently with you in your disappointment. All these moments matter and count.

This chapter will cover the **"what, why, and how" of every flourishing relationship** as a fundamental building block of a good life. We will learn social skills that will help you to build high-quality relationships at home, at school, at work, and in your community. You will be invited to explore your own feelings and needs, and to create positivity through gratitude, honest appreciation, complementing, and acknowledging others' actions. To acknowledge others by being kind, empathetic, and a good, active listener. To prioritize the relationships you want to flourish and to be hopeful, trusting, and laugh as much as you can.

DOI: 10.4324/9781003378365-5

YOUR RELATIONSHIPS

GREAT SOCIAL SKILLS

RELATIONSHIPS WITH CLASSMATES

RELATIONSHIPS WITH PEOPLE IN YOUR COMMUNITY

RELATIONSHIPS WITH TEACHERS

RELATIONSHIP WITH YOURSELF

RELATIONSHIP WITH BOSS OR SUPERVISOR

RELATIONSHIPS WITH SIGNIFICANT OTHER

RELATIONSHIPS WITH CO-WORKERS

RELATIONSHIPS WITH FAMILY MEMBERS

RELATIONSHIPS WITH FRIENDS

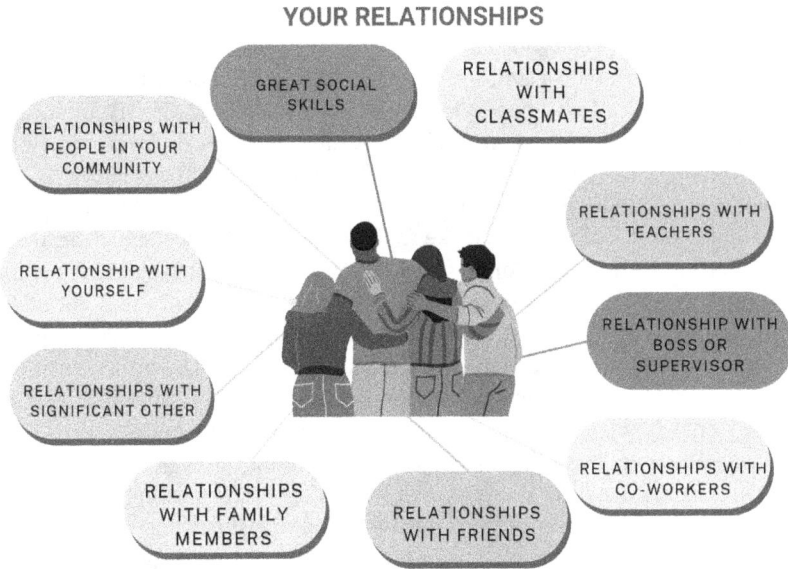

Figure 4.1 The portfolio of our relationships.

Seligman states that while spending time with other people, we get to experience more positive emotions, leading to greater happiness and well-being. That also works vice versa; when we're happier, our relationships are better. This, in turn, leads to more positive emotions and being on an **"upward spiral" of well-being and happiness**. Seligman concludes that connecting with others is the single most important thing we can do for happiness.

As mentioned above, the Harvard Study of Adult Development is one of the world's longest studies of adult life assessing data on human physical and mental health. The single most surprising finding over many decades of Harvard's research is that our **relationships and how happy we are in our relationships have a powerful influence on our health**. Taking care of our body is important, but growing positive relationships is, according to the Harvard Study of Adult Development, a form of **self-care** too. Close relationships, more than money or fame, are what keep us happy throughout our lives, the study revealed. The Harvard study concludes that positive relationship ties protect us from life's discontents, help to delay mental and physical decline, and are better predictors of long and happy lives than social class, IQ, or even genes (Waldinger & Schulz, 2023).

Let me share with you my regular day at the university and how much all the micro-moments of connections with the school community boost my well-being. I usually start my day with a walk through the old city of Prague. I jump on a bus in the morning and I get off a few stops early so I can stretch my legs first thing in the morning. I like to use the front bus door so I can greet the driver and thank him for the ride. Once I get closer to the university, I stop for a coffee at a local coffee shop. The barista always makes me smile when she knows my weird order (iced decaf coffee with soy milk and regular whipped cream) without me reminding her. Once I get to the university entry hall, I wave to greet the lady in the gatehouse who always greets me back with a smile on her face "Have a good day Ms. Koci." I climb two sets of stairs and I give back a few smiles to the students who are sitting in the halls. Once I open my office door, due to our different schedules, I never know who is there. Whether I'll see my colleagues Ivo, Magda, or Jiri. But whoever is there, we usually get loud by greeting each other and we hug. We briefly catch up with what is going on in our lives, we make fun and we laugh but we also share worries and ask for advice when any of us struggles. We create a safe space for anything. And even though not all days are bright, my colleagues usually pull out of their sleeves some funny stories they collected within the last couple of days and make me laugh. I go to see our secretary who greets me informally by my first name and she immediately makes me feel at home. Once I get to the classroom, I appreciate every student who made time for the class and who came here to learn (and chat :-). I start every meeting by asking my students how are they doing. We share our past week experiences, we discuss actual topics, we discuss some fresh theory and how we understand it, and we try to find answers to all questions that arise together. I don't have a better view of my day than seeing all the young students facing my direction. Watching you being curious, smiling, yawning, complaining about all the stuff you needed to do but still managed to come, teasing your classmates, and giggling together. Leading classes has always been very energy-demanding for me, but I always get rewarded with many micro-moments of positivity resonance my students help to create. I usually go home from school quite exhausted, but there is always a smile on my face and I feel so connected to all of you. Starting with the bus driver, coffee house barista, lady in the entry hall, my colleagues, and you, my dear students. Can my day really be only this positive? No. My feelings and moods fluctuate as much as yours. I get stressed every time I am running late for my meetings, I get nervous easily, I slip into the worst possible scenario in my mind often when facing challenges, and I tend to be oversensitive sometimes. I used to try to control my thoughts by focusing on the positive and I used to run away from negative feelings. I know today that doing that feels worse than actually embracing those experiences. I am doing my best to be fully present, in my own skin, in the moments, feelings, and thoughts that are uncomfortable and not always fun as well. But even though we are not always in a good mood and we all feel stressed or tired sometimes, I truly believe that this is what a good life is about. About truly seeing each other, sharing thoughts, sharing our concerns and supporting each other, making each other feel understood, laughing with each other, or just sitting in the room together silently, working on our computers. My life would not be even close to what it is without you all.

Benefits of Positive Relationships for Students' Well-Being

We all experience feelings of **connectedness** throughout the course of our days. Unique moments that are much more than just shared positivity. This shared positivity that generates a beautiful interpersonal connection is called **positivity resonance**. The moment when you smile and wave at your neighbor who just passed by in a car waving at you too. The moment when a friend brings you a soup after you missed a class today because you feel sick and they come by to ask how you are feeling. Or the moment when a cashier jokes about some item you are buying and they make you laugh.

There is strong evidence of the relationship between such moments of **positivity resonance** and our well-being (West & Fredrickson, 2020). According to Professor Fredrickson, the author of the book *Love 2.0* (2014), "Love is that micro-moment of warmth and connection that you share with another living being." While we usually think of love predominantly as built over time and enduring, research shows that our well-being correlates with our perceived everyday life positivity resonance. Thus, also with the number of momentary positive social connections **we believe we experience**.

Moments of positive resonance are **unique moments** that can be shared between two or more people. Such moments occur when we vibrate at the same frequency and make deep connections.

Positivity resonance as an interpersonal connection is **characterized by three elements**.

- **shared positivity** and positive emotions
- mutual **care** and concern
- and biological and behavioral **synchrony**

Shared positivity means being on the same emotional wavelength. We experience positive emotions with others, such as feeling hopeful together, feeling grateful together, or simply laughing together.

Mutual care and concern are experienced when we and others show that we are invested in each other's well-being.

Bio-behavioral synchrony is our alignment with another person(s) on a behavioral, emotional, and neuronal level. We experience such synchronicity through non-verbal behavior, such as body language (we tend to mirror the same gestures as the other person unintentionally, we lean towards each other, etc.), or through verbal behavior and vocal sounds, such as both laughing and using the same words more often. We can also experience synchronicity marked by autonomic nervous systems, such as increased or even decreased heart rate, decreased muscle tension, or slowed breathing. Other common examples can be mutually increased levels of "the love hormone" oxytocin. Another category of synchronicity is neuro-synchronicity. When two or more people are connecting, they show similar patterns in their brain activity.

The good thing is that positivity resonance is **buildable**. We all can build deep connections and thus build well-being in those around us. But not only that. We can also be **more conscious and aware of moments of already-existing positivity resonance** to savor them and enjoy the benefits of those beautiful connections.

How do we build positivity resonance in our relationships?

It is important to not only ask for good relationships but **to build and nurture them** as well. Listen and be curious. Be more empathetic. Avoid judging people. Care for people and wish them well. Help someone if you have a chance and you feel like you have the capacity to do that. Create positivity by sharing with people what you appreciate about them. Acknowledge it when they do something right. Complement them sincerely. Trust people. Be hopeful. Positive. Try to be more relaxed and less serious. Joke around :-)

In this chapter, you will be presented with the social skills needed to build, nurture, and care for healthy, prosperous relationships.

Your Positive Relationships Flower Assessment

We have learned in Chapter 1 that relationships are one of the **nine essential building blocks** for generating well-being. One of the things that can be very useful is to reflect and to think about your personal **relationship strengths**. By understanding the importance of relationships for your well-being, you will have the opportunity to assess your relationship strengths!

In this exercise, you will be asked to fill out your own **flower diagram**. You will be provided with a wheel that represents **ten different strengths** for building your relationships. These go from high-quality relationships with classmates, high-quality relationships with teachers, high-quality relationships with boss or supervisor, your high-quality relationships with co-workers, high-quality relationships with friends, high-quality relationships with family members, high-quality relationships with significant other(s), high-quality relationships with yourself, high-quality relationships with people in your community, great social skills, and there is also room for your own choice of another relationship strength you might feel that needs to be reflected in your life as well.

Here is a **set of statements** that will help you to assess how well you feel about each relationship strengths. You might find it helpful to reflect by reading the descriptions of ideal states of all ten of your strengths and assessing where you stand.

High-Quality Relationships with Classmates

I **enjoy seeing** my classmates and **spending time** with them. I feel like **a part of the group** and I was even able to develop some friendships within our class. We try to be friendly to each other and we help each other out with school tasks if needed.

High-Quality Relationships with Teachers

Even though my relationships with teachers are formal, I have a **good feeling** about our interactions. I found my teachers to be friendly, respectful, and helpful if needed. I can **openly express** my opinions in our classes and I can **talk to them** about any issues I am facing with my studies if necessary.

High-Quality Relationship with Boss or Supervisor (feel free to skip if you don't have any)

My relationship with my boss or supervisor feels safe, empowering, and full of trust and respect. I can discuss my ideas **openly** and ask for **advice** or **their mentorship** anytime. I feel comfortable coming to my boss or supervisor **for support** in times of work overload.

High-Quality Relationships with Co-workers (feel free to skip if you don't have any)

I feel good about my relationships with my coworkers. I **enjoy** working with them and I feel like **a part of the team**. We trust each other and respect each other's work. We help each other out with some tasks when feeling overloaded with work.

High-Quality Relationships with Friends

I have developed **loving** and **close relationships** with friends throughout my life. I know that the number of friends does not matter. What matters is the good quality of friendships I have. I care for my relationships with my friends by initiating contact and making sure my friends know I am here for them. I know they are here for me if needed too.

High-Quality Relationships with Family Members

My relationships with my family are **empowering and respectful: they provide me with a sense of trust, they allow me to be my authentic self,** and they help me feel great in my **family**.

High-Quality Relationships with Significant Other(s) (feel free to skip if you don't have any)

I **feel loved** in my relationship with my significant other(s), and I am capable **of sharing** my love. It is based on mutual **care, trust, support,** and a **desire to grow** together. We respect each other's boundaries and we are able to openly communicate about our feelings. We care for and help to build each other's well-being.

High-Quality Relationship with Yourself

I **deeply care** for myself. I am aware of my strengths and I support myself to use them. I also have compassion for my flaws. I **know** what I need and I **prioritize** my needs over pleasing others. I work daily with a respectful and loving attitude towards myself and I care for my own well-being.

High-Quality Relationship with People in Your Community

I enjoy positively interacting with people in my community (e.g., with my **neighbors, cashiers in stores, teachers, and classmates**) and I care for their well-being.

Great Social Skills

I actively **listen** to others; I am **empathetic, authentic, forgiving, respectful, positive**, and a **team player;** I express **gratitude** to others; and I **help others** while expecting nothing back.

Other Relationships Strengths

Are there any other positive relationship strengths on your mind you would like to assess? If yes, please scale them as well as the previous strengths.

So how do you actually assess your strengths? **Please imagine a ladder with steps numbered from 0 at the bottom to 10 at the top.**

The top of the ladder represents the best result (I feel very confident in this particular strength), while the bottom of the ladder represents the worst (I would like to build this particular strength better).

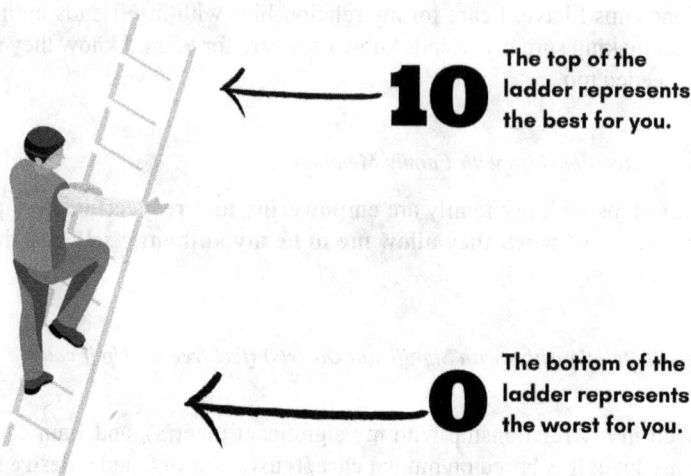

The top of the ladder represents the best for you.

The bottom of the ladder represents the worst for you.

Figure 4.2 Your well-being assessment ladder.

On which step of the ladder on a scale of 0–10 would you say you personally feel you stand at this time in terms of:

- high-quality relationships with classmates
- high-quality relationships with teachers
- high-quality relationship with the boss or supervisor
- your high-quality relationships with co-workers
- high-quality relationships with friends
- high-quality relationships with family members
- high-quality relationships with significant other(s)
- high-quality relationship with yourself
- high-quality relationships with people in your community
- great social skills
- other relationships strengths

After you assess all your relationships strengths, draw your very own relationships flower! Circle the resulting numbers of your strength on the relationships wheel ladders. Then draw the petal shape from the center of the wheel through all the numbers on each ladder to create your own flower (see Figure 4.3 for an example of the flower diagram).

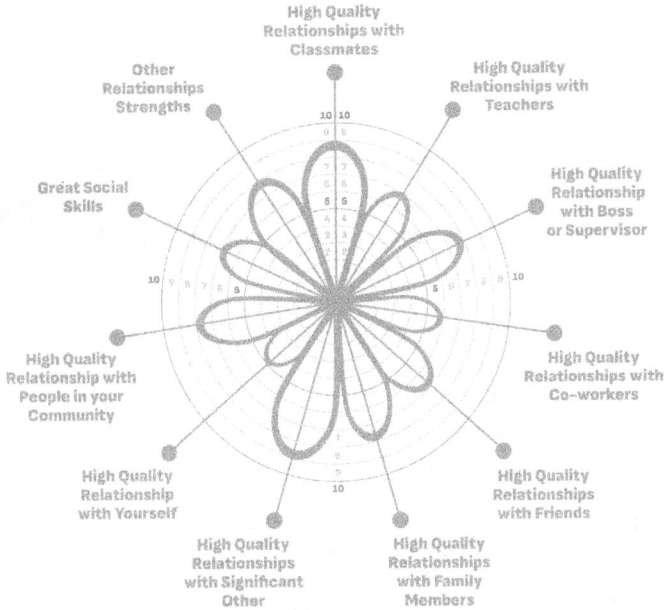

Figure 4.3 Example of your relationships flower diagram.

Let's assess your **relationship strengths,** and later you can reflect on them and learn how to build particular strengths (if needed) in the upcoming chapter.

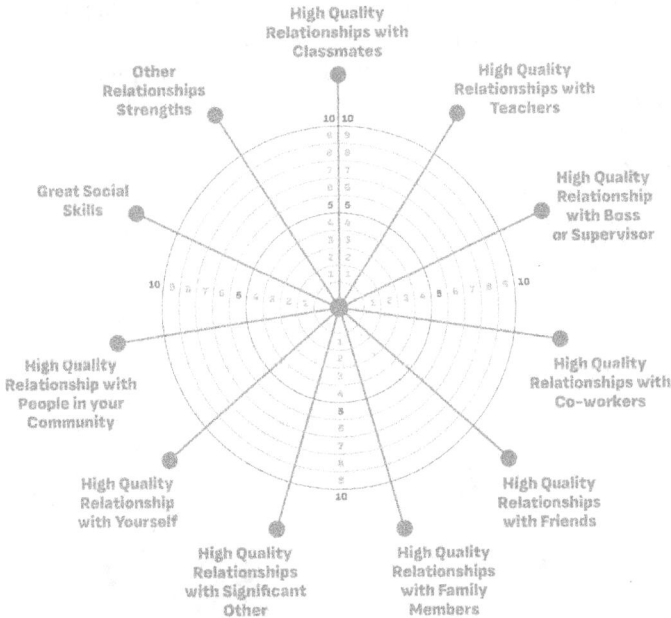

Figure 4.4 Your relationships flower assessment.

YOUR RELATIONSHIPS FLOWER REFLECTION

Great job! How do you feel?

Let's have a look at your personal **relationships flower**.

Remember, there is no judgment here; this is just an awareness exercise.

The goal of this exercise is to become **aware of your situation and decide what your next goal should be**. Then you will have a chance to think about what you can do to achieve the goal. This chapter will present some **evidence-based recommendations and activities** you can try right away to see if they fit your personality and lifestyle. It is fun to reflect on your flowers with your friends, but remember, the only one you can compare your flowers to is yourself. Enjoy checking on your flowers over time to track your progress or changes reflecting certain events in different stages of your life. The goal shouldn't be to have perfect, long petals in all your flowers – you should come to terms with imperfection. Invite the possibility of gradual growth of your flower petals rather than unhealthy overnight perfection.

Each flower reflects your **subjective perception** rather than your objective state. You might rate your High-Quality Relationships with Family Members petal flower low, even while objectively maintaining high-quality relationships with your family. Why do people do that? Our perception of ourselves is rarely objective. Sometimes, this can be caused by having a certain idea, a vision of what our ideal High-Quality Relationships with Family Members petal should look like. Sometimes, the petal is disturbed by a negative family event; those usually pass as time progresses. Hence, it can be reasonable to believe we still have space for growth. Rating your petals gives you **the opportunity to reflect on** your current state in certain areas of your life. It will also make you think about what strengths you are satisfied with for now and what strengths you might like to focus on. :-)

Let's see how you can **grow your relationship petals**.

Growing Your Relationships Flower Petals

High-quality relationships are crucial for our well-being, overall health, and good life. And what's more – **good relationships are buildable**. It is important to not only look for good relationships; we also need to **create** them and care for them. The relationship with ourselves is included. Research shows that even though we spend a lot of time with our friends while younger, we spend most of our overall life **alone**, with our **partner** and our **co-workers**. This chapter will discuss the importance of different relationships for your well-being, and you will be provided with tools and practices known to increase high-quality relationship support and positive relationship skills.

In this chapter, I would like to invite you to try some activities that can support your traits, characteristics, or skills you can use to maintain great social health:

- gratitude visit
- positivity
- fostering authenticity
- collaborating and cooperating
- respecting and setting boundaries
- empathy training
- forgiveness
- active-constructive responding
- self-compassion
- altruism

Trying on or even practicing the activities above will help you build, nurture, and care for healthy and prosperous relationships in your everyday life. But please, remember, one size doesn't fit all. Play with different activities, try them on, and keep only those in your life that you feel like keeping. Don't push yourself too much but at the same time, if you feel like, try to expand your comfort zone one step at a time :-).

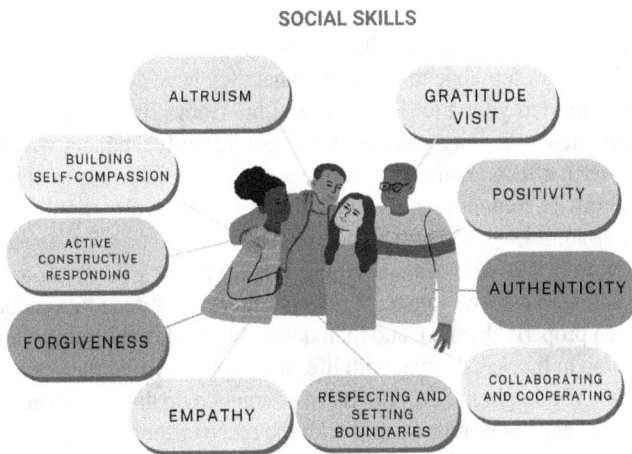

Figure 4.5 The portfolio of social skills to learn, strengthen, and perform to maintain healthy relationships.

Your High-Quality Relationships with Classmates

Some of the most important people in our lives were once our classmates. **We often build our fun group, safety net, and lifelong friendships at school.** And there is something especially extraordinary about friendships we make during university studies. You build relationships with people who chose the same major, who have similar interests, and, in many ways, live a similar lifestyle. Some classmates can become our friends, but it is also very natural to maintain a less personal relationship with many of our peers. But there are always ways to maintain healthy relationships with those we study with. For example, by making time for social interactions, being empathetic, and taking healthy advantage of social media.

Creating positive relationships with classmates can be done through **appreciating** your schoolmates and their strengths, appreciating their actions, and giving them your thanks when they do something nice for you. VIA Institute on Character (2023) points out that gratitude involves feeling and expressing a deep sense of thankfulness in life, and more specifically, **taking the time to genuinely express thankfulness to others.** This thankfulness is not only for gifts or thoughtful acts. It could also reflect the recognition of what **that person contributes to your life**. We can be grateful for deliberate acts of others, such as help with the essay structure from a peer, or for spontaneous, treasured moments, such as feeling a cool breeze on your face while walking around the campus on a hot day. Grateful people are **happier** and **more resilient**. Gratitude positively impacts our health as well. We experience a variety of positive emotions, and those emotions inspire us to act in more virtuous ways – to be humbler, more persistent, or kinder to each other. Gratitude tends to foster the character strengths of kindness and love and is therefore closely associated with **empathy** and **connection to others**.

Do it　　**Thanks!**

How can the new science of gratitude make you happier?

There is always someone to thank for what they have done for you and how they have impacted your life. Emmons and his team (2007) have shown that there is a particular activity you can do to feel instantly amazing with surprisingly long-term effects. Something called a **gratitude visit**. It is as simple as it sounds. **Think of someone you would like to express your thanks to.** It can be your classmates, your teacher, your family member, or even someone you don't know well but who did something important for you. Write a letter of gratitude and read it to the source. Writing a letter of gratitude to someone who has not been properly thanked, and then delivering the letter in person increases your meaning in life, satisfaction with life, and happiness after the gratitude visit intervention. You might need a little bit of courage to do this in person, but such activity can change your relationship with the receiver forever. If you don't feel comfortable in reading the letter out loud to them, you can always hand them the letter to read it themselves. Or we can go even further. If you feel like you need to express all those thanks but you don't want anyone to read it, don't provide the letter to anyone. Just write all your feelings and thanks down and keep the letter for yourself. Ask yourself **who do I want to thank from my heart? Why is this person important to me? What exactly do I want to thank them for? What do I want to tell them?** And give it a try! Write it all down and go see them in person. Read the letter and watch the beautiful miracle you yourself have created.

Your High-Quality Relationships with Teachers

Teachers play **a big role in our lives**. Apart from conveying information, they teach us how to act, think, and even how to live. Besides our parents, whether we realize it or not, they are oftentimes **the second strongest adult influence** we face in our lives.

But so are you to us teachers, dear students. **You play a big role in our lives.** You are the ones who teachers spend the most of their work time with. For example, I personally have a deep belief that you students are the best thing that has ever happened to me. You share your unique ways of thinking with me, you stretch my thinking, you share your personal stories that inspire me, and you are my daily source of positivity resonance. Your curiosity, kindness, and humor influence my days tremendously.

I enjoyed watching students laughing while climbing chairs and playing the game "floor is lava" as a part of their school assignment. I had students sing happy birthday to each other, or I witnessed students bringing each other coffee without being asked, just as an act of kindness. One student played an instrument in the worst possible way for us in our wellness class just to make us laugh, or we even met with a group of students over the holidays because my students did not want to skip the opportunity to meet with each other. Some of the best memories I have created are thanks to my students and I know I can speak for many of my colleagues too by saying I am not the only one. Whether your positive personal traits are humor, trust, courage, enthusiasm, being easy-going, realistic, or responsible, share your gifts with us.

Expressing **positive personality traits** can help strengthen all your relationships, including those with your teachers. But what does it actually mean to be "more positive"? "Being positive" is a large umbrella term. The Berkeley Well-being Institute (2023) posted 100+ positive character traits to express, learn, and practice.

Below are a few of the aforementioned traits. Choose those that are **natural** and **characteristic** to you and express them anytime you can, beyond your interactions with teachers!

> **Do It**   **Choose Those That are Natural and Characteristic to You and Express Them Anytime You Can, Beyond Your Interactions with Teachers!**
>
> Warm, friendly, clean, honest, loyal, trustworthy, dependable, open-minded, thoughtful, wise, mature, ethical, courageous, constructive, productive, progressive, individualistic, observant, neat, punctual, logical, prompt, accurate, self-reliant, independent, inventive, wholesome, attentive, frank, purposeful, realistic, adventurous, relaxed, curious, modern, charming, modest, enthusiastic, polite,

patient, talented, perceptive, forgiving, ambitious, respectful, grateful, resourceful, courteous, helpful, appreciative, imaginative, self-disciplined, decisive, humble, self-confident, easy-going, consistent, positive, artistic, fashionable, convincing, thrifty, bold, suave, methodical, interesting, unselfish, responsible, reasonable, likable, clever, cooperative, romantic, and proficient.

To learn more, go to: https://www.berkeleywellbeing.com/positive-qualities-activity.html

High-Quality Relationship with Boss or Supervisor

Professor Mihaly Csikszentmihalyi once said, "People feel really most alive when they are able to express who they are and how they feel."

One of the **healthiest things** we can do for ourselves and for others is to **be ourselves.** To be authentic. To be honest with ourselves and with others. To be true to our personality and to act (think, talk, do) in alignment with our values, regardless of the pressure to act otherwise. It might take some self-awareness and practice to correct yourself to be able to be more and more authentic in our everyday lives, especially in relationships with authorities. A relationship with our boss or teacher is probably the most challenging of all for expressing authenticity, but it is so worth the effort. Oftentimes, we rather think, "What should I say?" "What would be the most appropriate answer?" or "What do they want to hear?" is better than thinking, "What do I think about this?" "What is important to me about this and why?" or "What is my current opinion I can share now to honor my truth?" Try to slow down your thinking process. Pay attention to what you truly believe or think of the raised question, and express your true opinion.

You can practice authenticity in any area of your life. Learn to be conscious of what you think, what you say, and what you do by asking yourself:

Is this really me?
Do I really believe this?
Does this align with my values?
May I be saying this just to please others?
What can I say to honor my truth?

Be kind to yourself if you **"catch"** yourself saying or doing something different compared to what you truly think or believe in. Whether it is at work, at school, or in your personal life. Reflect on what happened and think about what you would say or do next time in the same situation. You can try to be more **you** next time. Be patient and **acknowledge yourself** for becoming more and more authentic in every little situation like this. You got this. :-)

High-Quality Relationships with Co-workers

Not many of us work alone. **We are usually part of large groups and big organizations.** At work, we spend a lot of time with people. Learning how to collaborate and cooperate with our co-workers can be beneficial for our everyday well-being, as well as for the well-being of others. How do we achieve that?

- Be optimistic and spread positivity if you are in a good mood. But if you feel down, don't ever push yourself. Respect and feel all your emotions, whether they are pleasant or not, please. Suppressing your emotions can harm your body as much as bad food or toxins in your cleaning supplies.
- Trying to use your strengths more can help too. Perhaps you're fair, courageous, creative, or incredibly organized! Use it to be an even more valuable part of the team.
- Understand the team's goals and share the team vision. Don't be afraid to ask if you don't understand something or see the meaning in certain activities.
- Be an innovator. Think out of the box.
- Be reliable. Before saying yes to things, assess whether what you are about to promise is realistic or not.
- Try to be a good communicator. Ask questions, listen carefully, and reflect on what others have to say.
- Support other people on your team. Genuinely appreciate the good in people around and help without expecting to receive anything back.
- Share information and resources with your team. Trust your teammates and, in return, they will trust you too.

But what if things don't go as planned or as you wanted? Situations like this are also part of our day-to-day lives. Reflect on what happened and what could be done differently next time. But try not to slip into negative self-talk. Acknowledge your effort and remind yourself, we all have room to grow as well as we all have a full right to have a bad day. If you caused some discomfort to someone else, it is never too late for an honest apology.

High-Quality Relationships with Friends

Life is simply better with friends. We often like to say that "our friends are the family we can choose." It is very important to nurture our friendships and to care for the well-being of our friends as well. That can be done by showing love, care, and respect. By respecting the boundaries of others and setting boundaries of our own. Setting personal boundaries can be difficult for many of us. But we could hardly find someone better to start practicing with than our friends.

So what is a boundary? **A boundary is a clear line**. It tells us and others where to stop. In any relationship, boundaries can be set in physical contact (it can be expressed, for example, when not feeling comfortable hugging a person you've just met, thus not doing it), verbal interactions (not wanting a friend to speak in a certain tone to you and expressing that you don't feel comfortable about it), or in your own personal space (choosing to not have others using your personal stuff you have in your dorm room when you aren't there).

Communicate openly about what is comfortable, safe, and acceptable in your relationships, and also learn to talk about what makes you feel unsafe or uncomfortable and what you won't tolerate even though it might not be easy to express out loud. You can even be open about your desire to change and to learn how to set boundaries.

Share with your friends that you learn to respect the boundaries of people around you and you also try to learn to set boundaries for yourself in any relationship you have and ask them if you can practice your authenticity with them. It is a **healthy way to build, care for, and nurture relationships** with the people around us.

High-Quality Relationships with Family Members

Someone once said that families are like branches on a tree. We grow in different directions, yet our roots remain as one. We are born into our nuclear family, which often consists of our parents or any other caregivers and siblings. But we are also being born into an extended family that includes our grandparents, aunts, uncles, and cousins. We do not choose our family members, but we can certainly choose how to behave toward them.

There are many character traits that help us build good relationships in our lives and foster high-quality relationships with our family members. We all appreciate when people show us empathy and forgiveness. Being **empathetic and forgiving are crucial skills that increase our emotional intelligence**, which can be described as being aware of and understanding our feelings and thoughts, as well as the feelings of those around us (VIA Institute on Character, 2023). **Learning about and using empathy techniques** can be beneficial for everyone (Bryant, 1982). **Showing our interest in our family members by expressing curiosity and genuine attentiveness in others can help us understand our family members better.** When having discussions with your family members, express interest by using simple phrases such as "tell me more about it" or by asking open-ended questions and actively listening to what our family members have to say. What are open-ended questions? Questions that won't let us respond with a simple yes or no. We ask the Wh-questions, beginning with **what, when, where, who, whom, which, whose, why,** and **how,** or we also ask **how much, can you describe,** or **could you tell me about it**?

Open-ended questions require a person to pause, think, and reflect. Answers often include personal feelings, opinions, or ideas about the subject of the discussion. This tends to lead us to **deeper** and **more personal** conversations, letting us get to know each other better and connect with greater intensity. The listener then **feels heard**. Both you and the other person enjoy mutual conversations better. Your relationship grows deeper, becomes more personal, and becomes much healthier.

Another social skill that can help us with our family relationships and beyond is forgiveness. While forgiving someone can sometimes seem impossible, I would like to kindly invite you to consider learning **how to forgive those who have harmed us**. The Greater Good Magazine (2022) defines forgiveness as a **conscious, deliberate decision to release feelings of resentment or vengeance toward a person or group who has harmed you, regardless of whether they actually deserve your forgiveness**. Whether it is a single person, a group of people, or even yourself who you decide to forgive, that Greater Good Magazine points out that it is important to also realize that forgiveness does not mean forgetting, nor does it mean condoning or excusing the offenses. Though forgiveness can help repair a damaged relationship, it doesn't obligate you to reconcile with the person who harmed you or release them from legal and moral accountability.

How do we forgive? We do acknowledge that someone did, indeed harm us. We let the emotions come to the **surface**, but we also decide to renounce our anger and resentment. We don't deny what happened; we don't even have to try to fix the relationship, especially if we don't feel like doing so. Forgiveness can sometimes be done for **our sake** rather than for the sake of others. We decide not to feel the anger anymore, and to carry it on with our lives.

But also, please don't feel bad if you feel like you cannot or don't want to forgive someone right now. It might just mean that you are not ready yet, and that is ok as well. Don't push yourself into something that does not feel right to you. All your emotions, even if they are not pleasant, are very valid. If you are still angry or feel disappointed, acknowledge your emotions and take your time to process what you feel.

High-Quality Relationships with Significant Other

Our significant other is our spouse or the person we **care for** and are **in an intimate relationship with**. Someone who is important to our **well-being**.

And it is natural for us to wish to build a joyful, trustworthy, and stable relationship with our significant other. Evidence shows (Gable et al., 2004) that a valuable skill that can be learned in strengthening our relationships, especially the intimate ones, is something called **active constructive listening**. It is an effective way of responding when someone shares **good experiences or information** with us. Research describes (Lambert et al., 2013) that when the receiver of the good news responds actively and constructively, it can often provide a boost in well-being to both people involved in the conversation!

Shelly Gable has described four main ways people respond to good news:

- active-constructive
- passive-constructive
- active-destructive
- passive-destructive

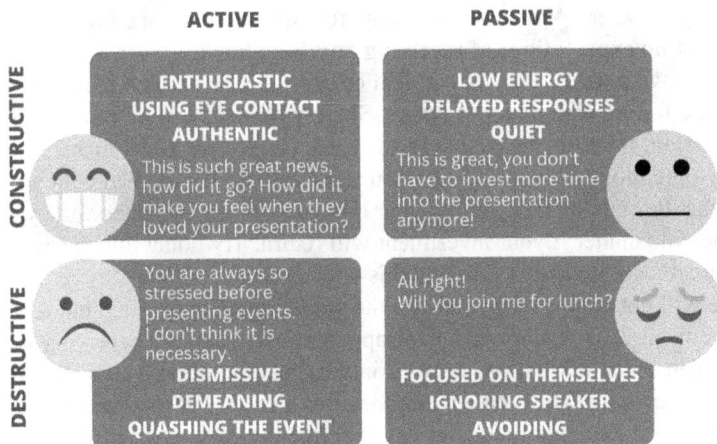

Figure 4.6 Examples of ways to respond to a positive event.

Shelly Gable (2004) and her team found that only active constructive responses led to an increase in daily positivity, satisfaction with life, and overall well-being, and this might be a great contributor to building relationship quality between you and your significant other. It is important for us to learn to **respond constructively** to another person's victories. But how exactly does it look? When someone shares a great event with you, such as a successful presentation in class, rather than responding passively-destructively (All right! Will you join me for lunch?) or active-destructively (you are always so stressed before presenting events. I don't think it is necessary), or passive-constructively (This is great, you don't have to invest more time into the presentation anymore!), respond actively-constructively (**This is such great news, how did it go? How did it make you feel when they loved your presentation?**). Put some effort into your responses. Look into your partners' eyes. Be present. Listen to what they say. If you feel like at, you can even reflect and repeat what you hear. This might look like:

> Your loved one: "I shared the numbers and they were surprised!"
> You: "They looked surprised?"

This might feel odd, but it works. Repeating some parts of what you hear makes the other person feel seen and heard. Just give it a try and see for yourself. Try to be active-constructive in your reactions and enjoy the benefits of being consciously supportive towards your partner.

High-Quality Relationship with People in Your Community

One of the biggest contributors to our health and well-being are the **micro-moments of positive interactions** with people in our **everyday lives and our community**. Do you remember my story with the bus driver, the barista from a coffee shop, and members of my university community? If there is anything that will certainly help you boost them, it is altruism.

Oxford Languages define **altruism** as disinterested and selfless concern for the well-being of others. **We help, do things for others, and care for others' well-being with no expectations of receiving anything back**.

How do we practice this? If you feel comfortable and if you feel like you can share, care for the well-being of others. Share with people your **resources**, **ideas**, and **attention**. Invest in the people around you. Invest your **time**, **focus**, **attention**, or even some **money** if you feel like you can afford it. Try to unlearn doing things with "what this could bring me" on your mind. Try doing things because you want to do them no matter if your investment will return. Try doing things because it is who you are. Ask yourself "Can I do this with no expectation of any return?" This exercise will not only reward you with the good feeling of sharing, but it will also lower your negative experience or disappointment when not receiving anything back. Because that is what you decided in the first place. To give for its own sake. Not to gain anything. But please remember, this also applies to yourself. If you feel like you are stressed and tired, and you feel like the half empty glass that has not much to pour from, save your acts of kindness for yourself. Guard your free time so you can relax. Pay extra attention to your needs and try to meet them for yourself. Be kind to yourself, and don't feel guilty for saying no to others. You can think of them once you recharge.

High-Quality Relationship with Yourself

And this gets us to the most important relationship we will ever experience, which is the one with ourselves. This relationship is as important as any other relationship in our life, and it deserves as much of our attention, love, and care as other relationships – if not more.

Researchers (Schotanus-Dijkstra et al., 2017) suggest **self-compassion training** to develop a positive mindset that generates our mental well-being. How can such an activity be implemented in university students' lifestyles? When not performing at school as planned, please show yourself some self-compassion. Self-compassion can seem difficult at the beginning because many of us are hard on ourselves and find it difficult to try an opposite approach. But please, don't give up. Give yourself time. Keep applying kindness toward yourself, and your self-compassion muscle will become stronger and stronger as you practice.

Psychologist and Stanford University researcher Carol Dweck has shared that students who have adopted a growth-mindset believe that hard work, perseverance, and learning from mistakes give them the ability to learn and continually develop their knowledge and skills. Practice self-compassion every time you perform not as well as planned, and remember that you can learn from this. **Use your inner voice to repeat your compassionate wish and learn how to learn from your own mistakes.**

Here are four ways to give your self-compassion skills a quick boost (originally published by Harvard, 2021):

- **Comfort your body.** Eat something healthy. Lie down and rest. Massage your own neck, feet, or hands. Take a walk. Anything you can do to improve how you feel physically gives you a dose of self-compassion, especially after a long day at school.
- **Write a letter to yourself.** Think of a situation that caused you to feel pain (a breakup with a lover, a job loss, poorly received homework at school). Write a letter to yourself describing the situation, but without blaming anyone – including yourself. Use this exercise to nurture your feelings.
- **Give yourself encouragement.** Think of what you would say to a good friend if he or she were facing a difficult or stressful situation, such as getting ready for an exam. Then, when you find yourself in this kind of situation, direct these compassionate responses toward yourself.
- **Practice mindfulness.** Even a quick exercise, such as meditating for a few minutes, can be a great way to nurture and accept ourselves while we're in discomfort experienced at school, at home, or in our personal lives.

Do It　**With Self-compassion to a Better Sleep**

Several studies found that there was a significant association between self-compassion and self-reported sleep quality. As a student, you can always benefit from practices like writing yourself a self-compassion letter. You can try this technique developed by the University of California, Berkeley right now here:

https://ggia.berkeley.edu/practice/self_compassionate_letter?_ga=2.163801023.1489895161.1628069520-336604110.1625559203

Do It　**Ten Empowering Questions to Support My Relationships Flower Growth**

1　What is the smallest thing I can do today to foster my relationships?
2　Who are the most important people in my life?
3　How can I show love to people I care about today?
4　What are my character superpowers and how can I contribute to the well-being of others today?
5　What is the smallest thing I can do today to show myself love?
6　What do I need and how can I provide it to myself?
7　What can I do to be a better team player today?
8　What do other people love about me?
9　How can I serve my community today?
10　Who can I call to show my love today?

Do It　**Ten Tips to Build My Relationships Flower**

1　Prioritize your social health.
2　Reflect on your relationships. What relationships are healthy for you and what are not so much?
3　Make the relationships that make you feel safe, seen, heard, and loved unconditionally for who you are a priority.

4 Use your character strengths as your natural ways to foster your relationships, whether it is kindness, humor, teamwork, leadership, fairness, or vitality.

5 Check the community website and search for ways to volunteer to see how you could contribute to supporting your neighborhood.

6 Practice social skills (e.g. active constructive listening, teamwork, or foster your authenticity) to be able to grow your relationship well-being.

7 Ask your loved ones how you can contribute to their well-being.

8 Care for yourself as much as you would care for someone very dear to you.

9 Practice setting healthy boundaries and respect boundaries of people around you.

10 Initiate positive interactions first. Smile at people, open doors for them, or start a small talk. Majority of the people will respond back to you very positively!

Tips to Relationships Snacking

Building your relationships does not have to be complicated or time-consuming. Look at Figure 4.7 and try some of the tips right now.

TIPS TO YOUR RELATIONHIPS
SNACKING
Make it quick, easy and fun!

1min	SMILE AT SOMEONE
10mins	CALL SOMEONE YOU LOVE
1min	SEND A LOVED ONE A TEXT TO SAY HI AND TO REMIND THEM YOU CARE
15mins	SHARE YOUR SNACK WITH A FRIEND
1min	HOLD THE DOOR FOR SOMENONE
5mins	BUY YOURSELF AN ICECREAM
4mins	WRITE DOWN 3 THINGS YOU LOVE ABOUT YOURSELF
1min	WRITE SOMEONE A NOTE TO REMIND THEM THEY ARE AWESOME
15mins	ASK YOUR FRIEND HOW ARE THEY DONIG AND ACTIVELY LISTEN
3mins	MAKE A SMALL TALK WITH SOMEONE AT WORK

Figure 4.7 Tips to relationships snacking.

High-quality relationships bring laughter, love, care, trust, and sense of safety and belonging to our day-to-day lives. But they can also be a great source of meaning in our existence. In the upcoming chapter, we will reveal the science behind meaning and we will look closer at the importance of meaning for our well-being. Let me invite you to try some hands-on activities and to reflect on what gives meaning to your life. Are you ready to look closer at one of the most important questions you can ever be asked? What makes your life worth living? See you in the upcoming chapter!

References

Berkeley Greater Good Magazine: What is Forgiveness (2023). Available at: https://greater-good. berkeley.edu/topic/forgiveness/definition

Berkeley Well-being Institute (2023). Positive qualities: Discover 100+ positive character traits. Available at: https://www.berkeleywellbeing.com/positive-qualities-activity.html

Bryant, B. (1982). An index of empathy for children and adolescents. *Child Development*, 53, 413–425.

Emmons, R. A. (2007). *Thanks!: How the new science of gratitude can make you happier*. New York: Houghton Mifflin Company.

Fredrickson, B. (2014). *Love 2.0: Creating happiness and health in moments of connection*. New York: Plume.

Gable, S., Reis, H., Impett, E., & Asher, E. (2004). What do you do when things go right? The intrapersonal and interpersonal benefits of sharing positive events. *Journal of Personality and Social Psychology*, 87, 228–245.

Harvard Medical School, Harvard Health Publishing (2021). 4 ways to boost your self-compassion. https://www.health.harvard.edu/mental-health/4-ways-to-boost-your-self-compassion

Lambert, N. M., Gwinn, A. M., Baumeister, R. F., Strachman, A., Washburn, I. J., Gable, S. L., & Fincham, F. D. (2013). A boost of positive affect: The perks of sharing positive experiences. *Journal of Social and Personal Relationships*, 30(1), 24–43. https://doi.org/10.1177/0265407512449400

Schotanus-Dijkstra, M., Drossaert, C. H., Pieterse, M. E., Boon, B., Walburg, J. A., & Bohlmeijer, E. T. (2017). An early intervention to promote well-being and flourishing and reduce anxiety and depression: A randomized controlled trial. *Internet Interventions*, 9, 15–24. https://doi.org/10.1016/j.invent.2017.04.002

VIA Institute on Character (2023). The 24 character strengths. Available at: https://www.viacharacter.org/

Waldinger, R. W., & Schulz, M. S. (2023). *The good life: Lessons from the world's longest scientific study on happiness*. New York: Simon & Schuster.

West T. N., & Fredrickson, B. L. (2020). Cultivating positive emotions to enhance human flourishing. In S. I. Donaldson, M. Csikszentmihalyi, & J. Nakamura (2nd ed.), *Positive psychological science: Improving everyday life, well-being, work, education, and society*. New York, NY: Routledge Academic.

5 Building Your Meaning

Those who have a WHY to live can bear almost any HOW.

— Viktor E. Frankl

Introduction to Meaning

Professor Frankl gave us a profound understanding of the importance of meaning and purpose in our lives in his classic best-selling book *Man's Search for Meaning* (1946). **In your studies**, a strong sense of **meaning and purpose** can motivate you and help you generate the determination to **fulfill your school-related goals**. However, modern life has a way of distracting us from our true, authentic goals. Not many of us have invested much time in **deep thinking** about who we truly are, what we believe in, and what we find important in our lives. Some students can even find it hard to define their purpose and why they selected to study their major. And I want you to know that it is perfectly normal. As young adults, living on your own often for the first time, it might be common to experience the social pressure to build a **"perfect" life**. We feel the weight on our shoulders to show our families, friends, and community that we are doing "great". This oftentimes causes us to focus on "what we think we need to do" rather than following up on our deep-felt **values and passions**. "What actually are my values and passions?" you might be asking now. "Do I have some?" "And do I honor them in my life at all?"

Questions like this can make you interested in a structured way of finding meaning in your studies through interventions. Luckily, research (Schippers & Ziegler, 2019) offers **evidence-based ways of finding purpose** in studies through a tested process called "life crafting".

There has been evidence (Bruch & Ghoshal, 2004; Bundick, 2011) that **personal goal-setting and goal attainment plans help students gain direction or a sense of purpose in their life**. Studies on purpose and meaning in life (Fredrickson, 2001) also link meaning in life to better mental and physical health. Going back to positive emotions as the building block of well-being for a minute, one way to experience pleasant emotions in everyday life is by finding positive meaning in ordinary events (Fredrickson, 2000). A simple act of **personal goal-setting** can also help you to **focus on what is valuable to you** and it can help you to

DOI: 10.4324/9781003378365-6

sustain your school plans with better **clarity**, **confidence**, **engagement**, **enthusiasm**, and **accomplishment**. The goal-setting technique is the main tool in the life-crafting exercise that researcher Michaéla Schippers from Rotterdam School of Management (University of Erasmus) developed for her students. She aimed to motivate them to learn and to succeed at school and to make them persevere in their studies. And you will have a chance to benefit from this beautiful exercise today as well.

This chapter will lead you through **the theory of meaning**; you will have a chance to **assess the current state of meaning in your life**, to reflect on how you are performing in individual areas of your life generating meaning, and you will be invited to **try some life crafting**, so you can reveal the meaning in your life.

Benefits of Meaning for Students' Well-Being

Dekker et al. (2020) suggest that students who write about their values, passions, goals, and goal-attainment plans have shown to improve their academic performance and limited the probability of dropping out of the school.

Life-crafting interventions like the one we will later try together can help you find a meaning and purpose in your life. This journaling exercise will, at the same time, lead you through the process of making concrete plans to work towards finding your meaning. Revealing and caring for your meaning will enable you to take control of your life and, as a result, optimize your performance, life satisfaction, and happiness.

Not only will you increase your probability to succeed at school. You will feel more whole; you will become aware of your values and you will feel in control due to creating specific plans for directing your life towards your meaning and purpose. There is a high probability that both your academic performance and your well-being will improve as a result of a life-crafting exercise.

This chapter will discuss the science of meaning and I will do my best to help you realize your purpose. Life crafting might help you to live more consciously and authentically and to flourish in your everyday life as a result. But before we dive into it, I would like to invite you to reflect about the meaning in your life with me.

Your Meaning Flower Assessment

We have learned in Chapter 1 that meaning is one of the **nine essential building blocks** of generating well-being. One of the things that can be very useful is to reflect and to think about your personal **meaning strengths**. Understanding the importance of meaning for your well-being, you will be provided with an opportunity to assess your meaning strengths!

In this exercise you will be asked to fill out your own **flower diagram**. You will be provided with a wheel that represents **eight different strengths**, building your meaning. These go from meaning in life, meaning in everyday life activities, meaning in school activities, meaning in work activities, building of meaningful relationships, serving others, purpose in life, and faith and spirituality, and there is also room for your own choice of another meaning strength that you feel like needs to be reflected in your life as well.

Here is a **set of statements** that will help you to assess how well you feel about each meaning strength. You might find it helpful to reflect by reading the descriptions of ideal states of all eight of your strengths and assessing where you stand.

Meaning in Life

I have a strong sense of **meaning** in my life. I am aware of my **values and passion,** and I live my life in accordance with both. I have a good sense of where I would like my life to be **headed**.

Meaning in Everyday Life Activities

I see meaning in my everyday life activities. I set my personal **goals** and strategies to pursue said goals. I speak about my **goals publicly** if I feel comfortable to do so. I monitor my progress and I acknowledge my achievements.

Meaning in School Activities

I can **see meaning** in the majority of the school activities I do. If I don't, I am able to stop and think of how this particular activity will **support me** on **my way to reach my personal goals** or how it will **benefit others**. This helps me to be **motivated, focused,** and **effective**.

Meaning in Work Activities (feel free to skip if you don't work at the moment)

I can **see meaning** in the majority of work activities I do. If I don't, I am able to change my perspective and reveal meaning for either me, my organization, my coworkers, or how people beyond my work environment will benefit from what am I working on.

Serving Others

I am aware that it is important for my well-being to **serve** others in the best way possible. I take action and I try my best to **be there for people around me when I feel energized and able to share.** I use my **character strengths** in service of people and my community.

Building Meaningful Relationships

I realize how **meaningful** high-quality relationships are for my life. I reflect on my relationships and prioritize those that support my social health. I proactively **build** high-quality relationships, and I **care** for the well-being of people around me.

Purpose in Life

I am aware of my life mission. I feel motivated to pursue my life goals and I know what the purpose of my life is. The accumulation of my **meaningful goals has generated a life purpose** for me. I reflect on my purpose and I give myself the freedom to change my goals if they no longer seem to be aligned with my values.

Faith and Spirituality

I sense that faith and spirituality contribute to my well-being and both faith and spirituality increase the sense of meaning in my life. Whether I am religious or not, I **have faith** and I **cultivate my spirit** in my everyday life.

Other Meaning Strengths

Are there any other meaning strengths in your mind that you would like to assess? If yes, scale them, please, as you did for the previous strengths.

So how do you actually assess your strengths? **Please imagine a ladder with steps numbered from 0 at the bottom to 10 at the top.**

The top of the ladder represents the best result (I feel very confident in this particular strength), while the bottom of the ladder represents the worst (I would like to build this particular strength better).

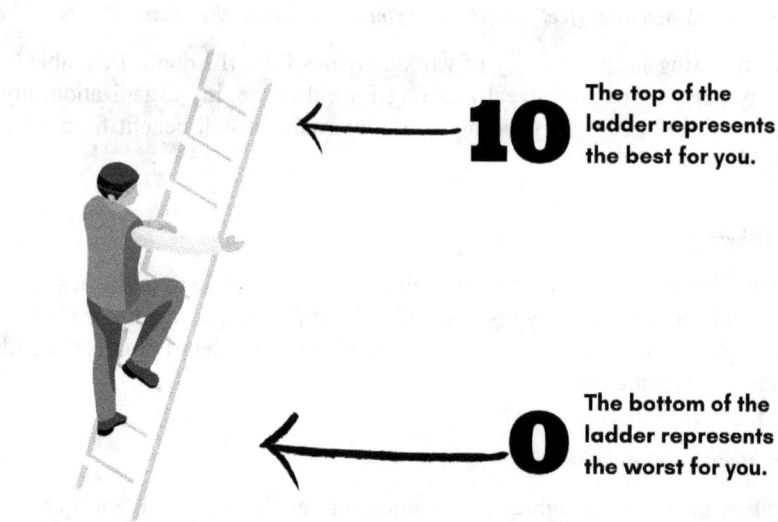

10 ← The top of the ladder represents the best for you.

0 ← The bottom of the ladder represents the worst for you.

Figure 5.1 Your well-being assessment ladder.

On which step of the ladder on a scale of 0–10 would you say you personally feel you stand at this time in terms of:

- meaning in life
- meaning in everyday life activities
- meaning in school activities
- meaning in work activities
- building of meaningful relationships
- serving others
- purpose in life
- faith and spirituality
- other meaning strengths

After you assess all your meaning strengths, draw your very own meaning flower! Circle the resulting numbers of your strength on the meaning wheel ladders. Then draw the petal shape from the center of the wheel through all the numbers on each ladder to create your own flower (see Figure 5.2 for an example of the flower diagram).

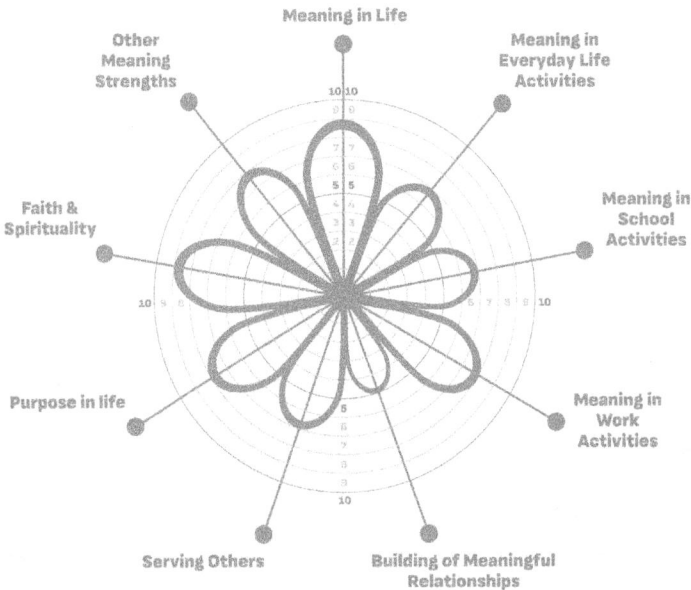

Figure 5.2 Example of your meaning flower diagram.

Let's assess your **meaning strengths,** and later you can reflect on them and learn how to build particular strengths (if needed) in the upcoming chapter.

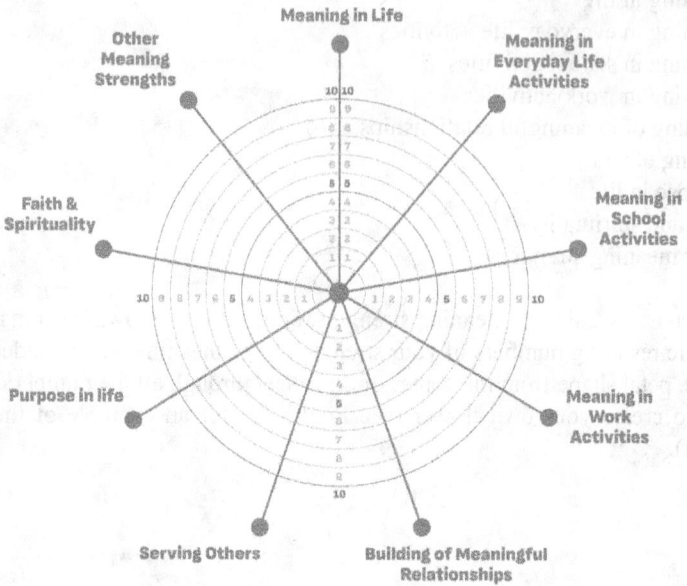

Figure 5.3 Your meaning flower assessment.

YOUR MEANING FLOWER REFLECTION

Great job! How do you feel?

Let's have a look at your personal **meaning flower**.

Remember, there is no judgment here; this is just an awareness exercise.

The goal of this exercise is to become **aware of your situation and decide what your next goal should be**. Then you will have a chance to think about what you can do to achieve said goal. This chapter will present some **evidence-based recommendations and activities** you can try right away to see if they fit your personality and lifestyle. It is fun to reflect on your flowers with your friends, but remember, the only one you can compare your flowers to is yourself. Enjoy checking on your flowers over time to track your progress or changes reflecting certain events in different stages of your life. The goal shouldn't be having perfect, long petals in all your flowers – you should come to terms with imperfection. Invite the possibility of gradual growth of your flower petals rather than unhealthy overnight perfection.

Each flower reflects your **subjective perception** rather than your objective state. You might rate your *Meaning in School Activities* petal low, even while enjoying being at school and seeing meaning in your studies. Our perception of ourselves is rarely objective. Sometimes, this can be caused by having a certain idea or vision of what our ideal *Meaning in School Activities* should look like. Sometimes, the *Meaning in School Activities* petal is disturbed by a short-term project that you cannot find any meaning in. Hence, it can be reasonable to believe we still have space for growth. Rating your petals gives you **the opportunity to reflect on** your current state in certain areas of your life. It will also make you think about what strengths you are satisfied with for now and what strengths you might like to focus on. :-)

Let's see how you can **grow your meaning petals**.

Growing Your Meaning Flower Petals

Life-crafting intervention is a method of improving both your **academic performance** and your **well-being** by helping you uncover your purpose in life. This chapter will help you define your purpose while also helping you make concrete plans to work towards its fulfillment. The life-crafting intervention (Schippers & Ziegler, 2019) consists of several integrated components. These components build on a range of empirically tested mechanisms that will aid you in reflecting on **your present and future lives, setting goals, making plans**, and **taking actions** in a way that is congruent with your values.

Grab a pen and a paper and let me lead you through the process of crafting your life! You will reflect on your values, passions, and goals, your best possible self, and your goal attainment plans. Important elements of this intervention are:

1 discovering values and passion
2 reflecting on current and desired competencies and habits
3 reflecting on present and future social life
4 reflecting on a possible future career
5 writing about the ideal future
6 writing down specific goal attainment and "if-then" plans
7 making public commitments to the goals set (only if you feel like it, of course!)

Elements	Tasks involved
1. Values and passion	Writing about:
	(1) What they like to do, (2) what kind of relationships they would like to have, both in their private life and their work life, (3) what kind of career they would like to have, and (4) lifestyle choices
2. Current and desired competencies and habits	(1) Qualities they admire in others, (2) competencies they have or would like to acquire, and (3) their own habits they like or dislike
3. Present and future social life	(1) Relationship that energize and de-energize them, (2) kinds of friends and acquaintances that are good for them, (3) kinds of friends and acquaintances they would like to have in the future, and (4) what their ideal family life and broader social life would look like

Figure 5.4 Elements and description of a life-crafting intervention (from Schippers & Ziegler, 2019).

4. Possible future career (path)	(1) What is important in a job, (2) what is it they like to do, (3) what kind of colleagues do they want, and (4) whom do they want to meet through their work?
5. Ideal versus less ideal future	Best possible self and future when there are no (self-imposed) constraints. Contrast this with "future if no changes are made"
6. Goal attainment and "if-then" plans	(1) Formulating, strategizing, and prioritizing goals, (2) identifying and describing ways to overcome obstacles, and (3) monitoring progress toward goals
7. Public commitment to goal	Photo with statement, which communicates their goals to the world; communicating goals to friends, co-workers

Figure 5.4 (Continued).

Meaning in Life

Professor Seligman once said that *"Just as the good life is something beyond the pleasant life, the meaningful life is beyond the good life."* Revealing meaning in your everyday life not only makes you feel **whole**, it is also very healthy for you. Meaning generally supports other building blocks of a student's life and a sense of meaning is known to impact their well-being. For example, positive relationships with other people are critical to students' positive functioning and well-being, and as reviewed in research, students with a strong sense of meaning report better **relationships** and experience **joy** and a deeper level of **engagement** in their lives.

Realizing your **core values** and **living your life in accordance with them** can generate meaning in your day-to-day life. A great value-realizing technique is simple reflection – writing about important areas of your life.

Are you ready? Now is the time to grab your pen and paper and write your thoughts down. Discover your **values** and **passion** (Schippers & Ziegler, 2019) by writing about:

1 what you like to do
2 what kind of relationships you would like to have, both in your private life and your work/school life
3 what kind of career you would like to have
4 lifestyle choices you would like to make for the elements of your values and passion

Write also about **your ideal future** (Schippers & Ziegler, 2019) by writing on this prompt:

1 describe your best possible self and future when there are no (self-imposed) constraints (contrast this with "future if no changes made")

Whether you choose a question that resonates with you the most or you try to think about all of the above, reflecting on these will help you to get clearer on the meaning of your life.

Meaning in Everyday Life Activities

Seligman suggested in 2002 **three paths to well-being**, and the pursuit of **pleasure**, the pursuit of **meaning**, and the pursuit of **engagement**. He added two more, positive relationships and accomplishment, in his 2011 PERMA theory of well-being and Donaldson added physical health, mindset, environment, and economic security in 2019. Despite meaning being highly discussed as an elementary part of our well-being in modern science, it has always been historically a foundation for religion and elementary topics in ancient philosophy and beyond.

There is no doubt that the overall meaning of life determines our well-being. But it is also healthy to **experience meaning in our everyday life**. As my dear colleague Ivo would say, not only existential meaning is important (whether we see meaning in our life overall) but also situational meaning (whether this situation or activity is meaningful to us). Situational meaning refers to seeing meaning in simple tasks we do repeatedly every day and to perceiving things we do as meaningful. So, what can you do to generate more meaning in your everyday life? I would like to gently invite you to be intentional in your everyday life. You already reflected on what is important to you in the activity above. Let's bring this to life now by setting intentions that reflect your values. **Set goals and try to pursue them**! Make a public commitment if it will help you to work toward your goals. And be SMART in setting them. Make your goals:

- **Specific** (clearly defined and focused on one target, knowing what you expect to achieve and what strategies will help you to reach the goal)
- **Measurable** (so you can clearly say you reached the expected quantity and quality, and you can track your progress at school and beyond)
- **Achievable** (knowing that you have the skills and capacity to reach the goal. Students usually have a lot on their plate. It is perfectly healthy to move toward your goals, one small step by another small step to make them achievable!)
- **Relevant** (the goal is aligned with your values and will help you reach your personal and academic growth)
- **Time-based** (you are able to set a deadline and milestones for your journey to reach the goal to make it easier to stick with your plan)

Write down specific goal attainment and "if-then" plans (Schippers & Ziegler, 2019):

1 formulate, strategize, and prioritize goals
2 identify and describe ways to overcome obstacles
3 monitor progress toward goals for the element of attainment and "if-then" plans

You can also make public commitments to the goals you have set (Schippers & Ziegler, 2019). Communicate goals to friends or family members. Or you can take and post/show someone a photo with a statement, which also communicates your goals to the world. If this does not scare you, as my dear student Francesco once shared in our class, just the idea of making a public commitment may feel scary for many of us. If you would rather keep your goals for yourself now, please, do that for you! Remember, one size does not fit all. Don't push yourself to do anything that makes you feel too unconformable. Pick and try only what sounds good to you.

Meaning in School Activities

You spend the **majority of your time at school**, working on school projects, being involved in many different school activities, or being at home doing what? Studying. That is a huge energy and time investment in school from you. Being able to see meaning in the activities above can help you **keep going** and **stay focused and engaged**. But to be true, looking at well-being assessments among our students (Koci et al, 2023), if there is something that our students are missing, it is seeing meaning in school activities. So is there any way to craft meaning in school activities? Luckily, there is one. Just because you feel like you don't see meaning in some of the everyday school activities sometimes does not mean that it is not there. Let me introduce you to an exercise my students and I like to call "60-second investment". Give yourself a minute every time you are about to work on something. Think about how a particular activity or skill you are about to learn is or can be meaningful to you or to others. Will you be able to use this in the future to help your clients as their lawyer? Will this help you to be a better teacher for your future elementary school students? Or will this skill help you be a more confident surgeon for your future patients? You will create **intrinsic motivation** that will give you energy to do what you want to do not only effectively but also with **greater joy**. So now, the upcoming activity might make much more sense to you. Take this opportunity to work on your skills portfolio to make reaching your goals easier in the future.

Reflect on your current and **desired competencies** and **habits** (Schippers & Ziegler, 2019) and write about:

1 qualities you admire in others
2 competencies you have or would like to acquire
3 your own habits you like or dislike the elements of current and desired competencies and habits

Meaning in Work Activities

If you work and study, like approximately 60% of students in Europe (Eurostudent, 2021), it is important to try to make sure that the work you do also **brings you energy**, not only consumes it. One way to do it is to teach yourself to see meaning in your work activities. Link the meaning to your values and life goals, and see your work as a practice to gain experiences and adopt skills that can never be taken from you. It is also important to know what your **career dream**, **vision**, and **plan** are. Just because your current job is not your dream job does not mean that it is not a great starting point for you!

Reflect on your possible future career or path (Schippers & Ziegler, 2019) by writing about:

1   what is important in a job
2   what is it you like to do
3   what kind of colleagues do you want
4   who do you want to meet through your work

Serving Others

Have you ever heard about the **hedonic** and **eudaimonic** views of well-being and happiness? The hedonic view of well-being equates our well-being and happiness with pleasure, comfort, and enjoyment (**activities we love to do for enjoyment and great feelings**). Whereas the eudaimonic view equates well-being and happiness with the human ability to pursue complex goals that are **meaningful** not only **to us,** but also **to our society**. And it does not necessarily have to be fun. It is important for your well-being to do what you enjoy, but ideally also to serve society and those around you in the best possible way. One way to determine where to focus our attention is to **define our Ikigai**. Ikigai is a Japanese concept that combines two terms. Iki, which means **"life"** and gai, meaning **"worth"**. Your Ikigai is what makes your life worth living. This beautiful concept is a combination of doing what you love, what you are good at, what you can make a living from, and doing what the world needs. I would like to kindly invite you to take some time to discover your Ikigai. Ask yourself the following questions and reflect on them through deeper thinking or even journaling:

• What do I love to do?
• What am I great at?
• What does the world need from what I love and am great at?
• What from all the above can I get paid for?

YOUR IKIGAI

Figure 5.5 Find your Ikigai.

Building of Meaningful Relationships

You already know how important your relationships are for your well-being and overall health. But did you know that high-quality relationships are also a **great source of meaning** in our lives? In order to manage your relational life and support meaningful relationships, it can be very beneficial for you to reflect on your present and future social life (Schippers & Ziegler, 2019). Write about:

1 relationships that energize and de-energize you
2 kinds of friends and acquaintances that are good for you
3 kinds of friends and acquaintances you would like to have in the future
4 what your ideal family life and broader social life would look like for the elements of present and future social life

Reflect on your writings and try to prioritize those relationships that support your ideal life vision!

Purpose in Life

When we create and feel meaning in our life, we also feel motivated and energized to pursue our life goals. Purpose can be seen as *the cumulative effect of meaningful goals we set for ourselves.*

There is rich evidence of the well-being and health benefits of living a purposeful life, both for our-selves and for others. But what can be a good strategy to pursue our meaningful goals and live our purpose? Martin Seligman defines meaningful life as knowing what your highest strengths are and "**using your signature strengths and virtues in the service of something much larger than you are.**" Ask yourself the upcoming questions, discover your character strengths, generate your purpose, and share with others your most natural self! This will bring pleasure not only to others but mainly to you. There are not many other things we love more than seeing our virtues in action, especially when they benefit others.

- What gives me energy?
- Where do I learn quickly?
- What makes me feel most alive?
- What makes me feel confident?
- Which activities make me lose track of the time?
- When do I feel challenged and, at the same time, fully engaged in what I'm doing?
- What positive things do others see in me?
- What do others love me for?
- How can I use my strengths more?

And remember, we all have weaknesses, and they are also what make us special. Don't be ashamed of having flaws. You can always work on them to become more familiar with them, accept them, and even learn to love them. Believe it or not, what might seem like weakness may be a big part of the holistic picture of your personality, making you so special to others.

Faith and Spirituality

Faith and spirituality have been found to be positive predictors of subjective well-being. Whether we discuss the role of having faith in combination with religious beliefs, spirituality, or simply believing in something larger than us, all those acts are usually positively related to life satisfaction, well-being, and our overall health. It seems that having faith and taking part in some practices, such as prayer, **positively contribute to inducing positive states such as gratitude, hope, and meaning**. Recent studies report the role played by self-transcendent emotions, such as awe, hope, love, and forgiveness, in mediating the relationship between spirituality and well-being. There are particular activities and practices that can help you deepen your sense of faith and spirituality, such as **meditation**, **mindfulness**, and **prayer**. No matter what you decide to believe in, find what helps you nurture your spirit and try to deepen your faith and spirituality in your everyday life.

Do it   **Mindfulness Meditation**

You can try a guided loving-kindness meditation created by scientist Barbara Fredrickson right now!

To listen to the meditation go to: https://www.positivityresonance.com/meditations.html.

You can practice this in the morning before you head to school, between your classes in a park to calm down or before bedtime to get relaxed and prepared for a good night's sleep.

Listen to Michaéla Schippers Ted Talk on Life Crafting through Personal Goal-Setting

As a Professor in Behavior and Performance Management, Michaéla Schippers talks about the importance of goal-setting and the impact this can have on your life and offers an innovative approach for effective goal-setting.

https://www.youtube.com/watch?v=Jhjw8bJy2tQ

Do it   **Ten Empowering Questions to Support My Meaning Flower Growth**

1   What are my core values?
2   What am I passionate about?
3   What are my life goals?
4   What would make me feel devastated if I lost it?
5   What relationships do I find most meaningful in my life?
6   How can I pursue my purpose today?
7   What am I looking forward to doing today that is meaningful to me?
8   How can I use my character strengths to make my day more meaningful?
9   How can I contribute to my community today?
10   What can I do for myself today to show myself some love? (Please take this also as a kind invitation to really do that!)

Do it   **Ten Tips to Build My Meaning Flower**

1   Buy a notebook you will enjoy looking at and create a habit of journaling. Journal about your ideal future, about your values, about people who inspire you, and about your life mission.

2   Discover your core values and use them as a compass for your life. Ask yourself what makes your life worth living and what is most important and dear to you.

3   Create a habit of dreaming big, make action plans, and set realistic goals that will help you move in the desired direction. Choose effective strategies and don't hesitate to change them if they no longer serve you. But you know what? You can also take a break from dreams, goals, and visions if you feel overwhelmed. Give yourself a grace, take a break, and plan absolutely nothing for a week. You will be surprised what life brings you when you have no agenda :-)

4   Visualize your ideal future. Try on the feelings of what it would be like to achieve what you wish to achieve right now!

5   Reflect on your life goals. Our life goals might change over time and it is worth it to check on your current dreams, plans, and strategies.

6   Use your character strengths to help you reach your goals naturally and more confidently.

7   Give thanks and express gratitude. Whatever your life gives you, don't take anything for granted and express your gratitude.

8   Collaborate. Look for mentors, colleagues, or friends who could help you to reach what you wish in your life. Learn from them. Don't hesitate to ask for help if needed.

9   Always find time for doing what you are passionate about and what you find interesting at this stage of your life. You can make room for your passion in your free time and who knows, maybe you will find a way to make a living at it one day.

10 Have faith. Practice believing and being hopeful, no matter what it means to you. Cultivate your unique spirituality.

Tips to Meaning Snacking

Building your meaning does not have to be complicated or time-consuming. Look at Figure 5.6 and try some of the tips right now.

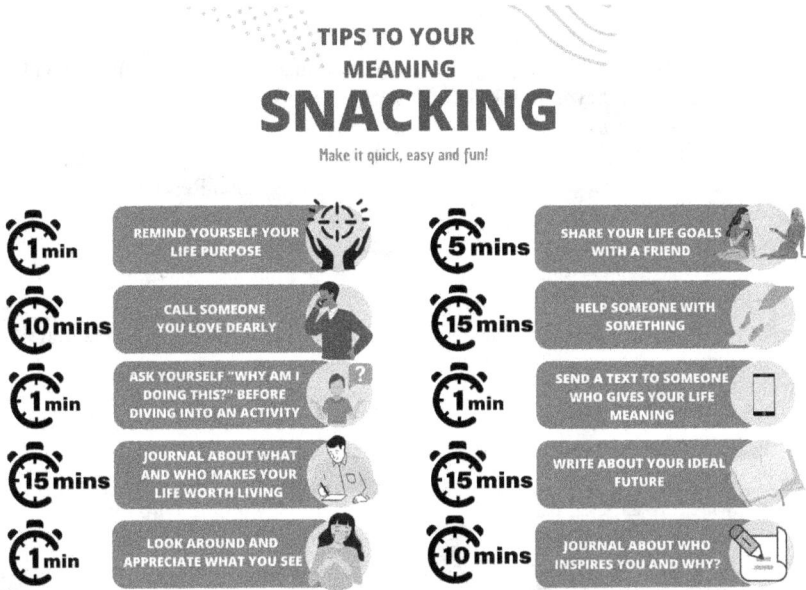

Figure 5.6 Tips to meaning snacking.

Meaning making is possible for each and every one of us. Having meaning in our lives not only motivates us to get up from our bed every morning, it also helps us to overcome tough times when they come. Seeing value in our lives is critical, and purpose is the center from which we can keep going forward. To live our lives fully and to pursue our dreams. But how do you turn your dreams into plans, and what strategies should you use to accomplish in life what you wish to achieve? Let me invite you to another chapter focused on building your achievements. You will be introduced to the science of GRIT, the magic behind success, and the use of your character strengths as your superpowers that can make everything easier for you. Try some of the presented activities in the upcoming chapter and build your achievements to support your well-being and success.

References

Bruch, H., & Ghoshal, S. (2004). *A bias for action: How effective managers harness their willpower, achieve results, and stop wasting time*. Boston, MA: Harvard Business School Press.

Bundick, M. J. (2011). The benefits of reflecting on and discussing purpose in life in emerging adulthood. *New Directions for Youth Development*, 89–103. https://doi.org/10.1002/id.430

Dekker, I., De Jong, E. M., Schippers, M. C., De Bruijn-Smolders, M., Alexiou, A., & Giesbers, B. (2020). Optimizing students' mental health and academic performance: AI-Enhanced life crafting. *Frontiers in Psychology*, 11, 1063. https://doi.org/10.3389/fpsyg.2020.01063. PMID: 32581935; PMCID: PMC7286028.

Donaldson, S. I., Heshmati, S., Young, J. Y., & Donaldson, S. I. (2021). Examining building blocks of well-being beyond PERMA and self-report bias. *Journal of Positive Psychology*, https://doi.org/10.1080/17439760.2020.1818813.

EUROSTUDENT VII Synopsis of Indicators 2018–2021. Social and Economic Conditions of Student Life in Europe. German Centre for Higher Education Research.

Frankl, V. E. (2006). *Man's search for meaning*. Boston, MA: Beacon Press.

Fredrickson, B. L. (2000). Extracting meaning from past affective experiences: The importance of peaks, ends, and specific emotions. *Cognition and Emotion*, 14, 577–606. [Google Scholar]

Fredrickson, B. L. (2001). The role of positive emotions in positive psychology: The broaden-and-build theory of positive emotions. *American Psychologist*, 56, 218–226. https://doi.org/10.1037/0003-066X.56.3.218

Koci, J. (2023). How to Build Well-being in University and College Students – Methodology of Academic Well-being Promotion. Prague: Charles University, 2023, ISBN: 978-80-87489-38-3

Schippers, M. C., & Ziegler, N. (2019). Life crafting as a way to find purpose and meaning in life. *Frontiers in Psychology*, 10, 2778. https://doi.org/10.3389/fpsyg.2019. 02778

Seligman, M. E. P. (2002). *Authentic happiness: Using the new positive psychology to realize your potential for lasting fulfillment*. Free Press.

Seligman, M. E. P. (2011). Flourish: A visionary new understanding of happiness and well-being. Free Press.

6   Building Your Achievement

When you multiply talent by effort, you gain skill. But when you multiply skill by effort, you gain achievement!

— Angela Duckworth

Introduction to Achievement

We all look at achievement with a different sense of importance and success means different things to different people. Planning and achieving goals might be a main source of meaning and joy for some of us, while many of us prefer to plan less and go with the flow of life. Both attitudes are right once you feel like they work for you. No matter what life approach we choose at this time, we all experience joy and a sense of accomplishment when things **"work out well"**. Whether we talk about our school achievements or achievements in our work, or personal and social life.

Our achievement **does not** necessarily have to be narrowed only to our **long-term goals** such as finishing the degree, writing the thesis, finding a job we enjoy doing, or moving to a place that is perfect for us. We can increase our achievement building blocks by accomplishing **small things** in our everyday life! We all get the boost of a good feeling when we finish what we started. When we prepared a good meal, cleaned up our room, fixed a dripping tap, or finished a chapter of a great book that we are reading. But what about our school life? There are **also many opportunities** to succeed and to feel accomplished. We only have to open our eyes to them. It feels good to close the book after the class we just managed to attend. It feels good to prepare for an essay by reading an article we found fascinating or by closing up our day by completing a few laps in the swimming pool at the university recreational center.

Becoming more aware of our daily accomplishments is one option. Another approach is to manage the process of setting up our goals, to think through the things we did to reach the goals, or to shape the beliefs we hold about our achievements. All our successes (not only the school ones) are related to **how realistically we can set our goals**, what **strategies** we use, or, believe it or not, what **importance** we assign to the desired outcomes. Students who fracture their long-term goals into smaller ones and turn them into more realistic "steppingstones" release pressure and anxiety. Students who use their **signature strengths** to achieve their

DOI: 10.4324/9781003378365-7

school-related plans **have more positive school experiences**, experience **success**, and report their studies as **satisfying** and **fulfilling**.

Benefits of Achievement for Students' Well-Being

Many scientific studies show that our well-being, achievement, and performance at school and work are strongly related to one another (Koci & Donaldson, 2022; Donaldson et al., 2022). That is, achievement feels good and contributes to our well-being, especially when we try to achieve something that is meaningful to us. Something we feel passionate about and are willing to stick to and work on. Those factors not only generate well-being and joy; they also increase our intrinsic motivation and our chance to succeed in our set goals. Research shows that **students who are passionate about what they study and persevere are more likely to graduate than their less passionate and less persevering peers**.

There is also evidence (Govindji & Linley, 2007) emphasizing that college and university students who become **aware of** what they are **good at** and use their **strengths in life** are more **satisfied** and **happier**, have **higher self-confidence** and **self-esteem**, and perceive their lives as **fulfilling**. Some evidence (Linley et al., 2010; Proctor et al., 2009) also confirmed a positive relationship between the **use of character strengths** and the achievement of **set goals**.

In my country, in order for students to graduate, they have to undergo an oral final state exam. During this final state exam, our students come in front of a committee, draw a question, have a moment to prepare their answer, and present their thoughts for 20 minutes in front of everyone. This can be very stressful for many of our students and even for us teachers, because we want our students succeed. But there is something I love about these exams. I love watching our students use their virtues in action and apply their strengths to help them to succeed. Some students have a great sense of humor and jokes to relieve the seriousness of the situation for all of us. Some love to be analytical and they draw mind maps to present their thoughts better. Some students are great at discussing; some tell stories; and some show their kindness, fairness, empathy, love of learning, curiosity, or honesty. Whatever your strengths are, know them, use them, and share them with the world around you. Our strengths are not only for us. They are meant to be shared.

This chapter will teach you about **the power of passion and perseverance** and you will learn how to be **"grittier"**. I will also invite you to shift your focus to your aforementioned character strengths. You will have a chance to think about how you can use your **personal superpowers** in your daily life to experience greater study and life **satisfaction**, more fulfilling **engagement**, and **more meaningful study experiences**. But first, let's have a look at your personal achievement and how exactly it might contribute to your well-being.

Your Achievement Flower Assessment

We have learned in Chapter 1 that achievement is one of the **nine essential building blocks** for generating well-being. One of the things that can be very useful is to reflect and to think about your personal **achievement strengths**. Understanding the importance of achievement for your well-being, you will be provided with an opportunity to assess your achievement strengths!

In this exercise you will be asked to fill out your own **flower diagram**. You will be provided with a wheel that represents **seven different strengths** that build your achievement. These go from satisfaction with your achievements, recognition and enjoyment of others' achievements, recognition and use of your character strengths, your responsibility, willpower, perseverance for long-term goals, and passion for long-term goals, and there is also room for your own choice of another achievement strength you might feel needs to be reflected in your life as well.

Here is a **set of statements** that will help you assess how well you feel about each achievement strength. You might find it helpful to reflect by reading the descriptions of ideal states of all seven of your strengths and assessing where you stand.

Satisfaction with Your Achievements

I am **aware** of my achievements. I **reflect** on my effort, and I **acknowledge** my successes. I **celebrate** when I accomplish something meaningful, as well as when I achieve small things in my day-to-day life. I am **satisfied** with what I have achieved in my life so far.

Recognition and Enjoyment of Others' Achievements

I **pay attention** to the achievements of **others**, and I **sincerely enjoy** when others are successful. I like to acknowledge others' successes by **telling them** that they have done great. I also feel **inspired** when I see others achieve something.

Recognition and Use of Your Character Strengths

I am well aware of my character strengths, and I use them in my everyday life. I reflect on my **top strengths** from time to time. I like to think about how I can **apply** my strengths in different situations to reach what I am aiming for **confidently** and with more **ease** and **joy**.

Responsibility

I have a great **sense of responsibility**. I consider myself an **accountable person**. I do my best to keep my promises, stick to my plans, and, if needed, develop extra effort to meet deadlines I agree to. Others would say that I am **easy to work with**.

Willpower

I feel like I have control over the actions I take in my life. I can **resist impulses** for the sake of my goals. I can **control** my own thoughts and behavior and I have **strong determination** to overcome obstacles when working toward my personal goals.

Perseverance for Long-Term Goals

I **persist** in my long-term goals despite obstacles, discouragements, or disappointments. When I fail, despite the fact that I might feel disappointment and demotivation in the moment, **I rarely give up** and I continue to work on my goals and dreams.

Passion for Long-Term Goals

My actions, plans, and behavior are **passion-driven**. I am aware of what I love and what is important to me, and I do my best to keep activities that are **filled with passion** in my everyday life.

Other Achievement Strengths

Are there any other achievement strengths on your mind that you would like to assess? If yes, please scale them as well as the previous strengths.

So how do you actually assess your strengths? **Please imagine a ladder with steps numbered from 0 at the bottom to 10 at the top.**

The top of the ladder represents the best result (I feel very confident in this particular strength), while the bottom of the ladder represents the worst (I would like to build this particular strength better).

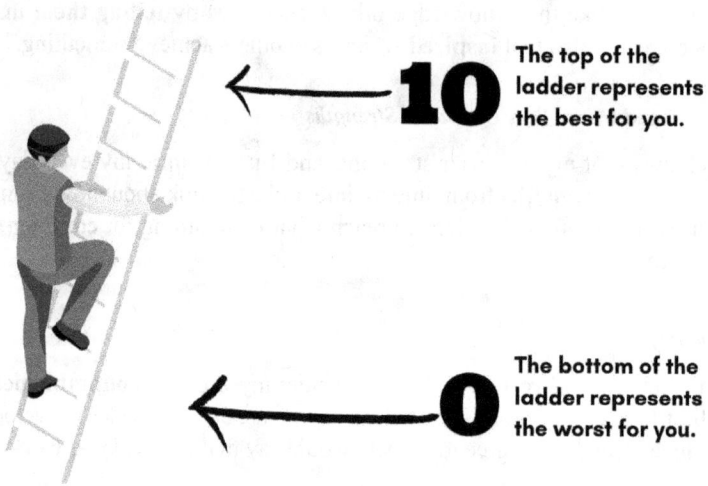

10 ← The top of the ladder represents the best for you.

0 ← The bottom of the ladder represents the worst for you.

Figure 6.1 Your well-being assessment ladder.

On which step of the ladder on a scale of 0–10 would you say you personally feel you stand at this time in terms of:

- satisfaction with your achievements
- recognition and enjoyment of others' achievements
- recognition and use of your character strengths
- responsibility
- willpower
- perseverance for long-term goals
- passion for long-term goals
- other achievement strengths

After you assess all your achievement strengths, draw your very own achievement flower! Circle the resulting numbers of your strength on the achievement wheel ladders. Then draw the petal shape from the center of the wheel through all the numbers on each ladder to create your own flower (see Figure 6.2 for an example of the flower diagram).

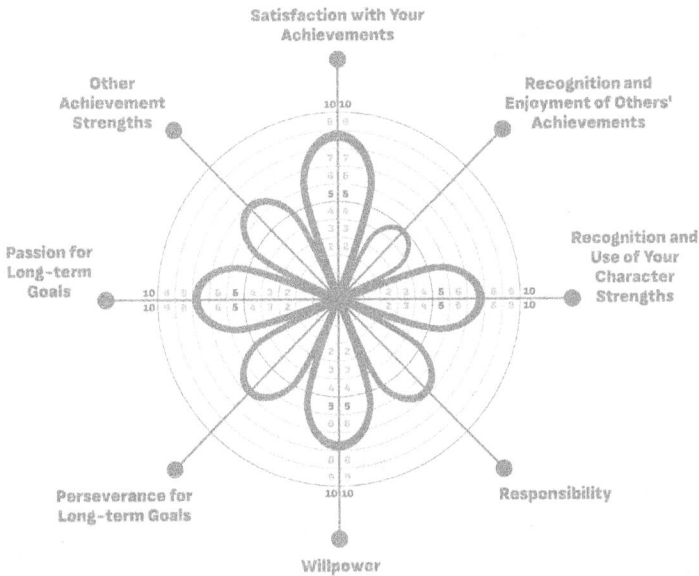

Figure 6.2 Example of your achievement flower diagram.

Let's assess your **achievement strengths** and later you can reflect on them and learn how to build particular strengths (if needed) in the upcoming chapter.

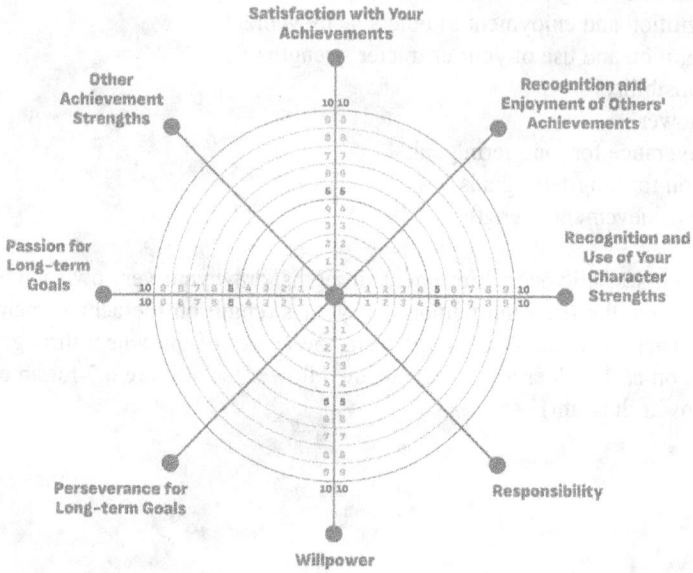

Figure 6.3 Your achievement flower assessment.

YOUR ACHIEVEMENT FLOWER REFLECTION

Great job! How do you feel?

Let's have a look at your personal **achievement flower**.

Remember, there is no judgment here; this is just an awareness exercise.

The goal of this exercise is to become **aware of your situation and decide what your next goal should be**. Then you will have a chance to think about what you can do to achieve said goal. This chapter will present some **evidence-based recommendations and activities** you can try right away to see if they fit your personality and lifestyle. It is fun to reflect on your flowers with your friends, but remember, the only one you can compare your flowers to is yourself. Enjoy checking on your flowers over time to track your progress or changes reflecting certain events in different stages of your life. The goal shouldn't be to have perfect, long petals in all your flowers – you should come to terms with imperfection. Invite the possibility of gradual growth of your flower petals rather than unhealthy overnight perfection.

Each flower reflects your **subjective perception** rather than your objective state. You might rate your *Responsibility* petal lower while being a responsible, accountable person. Why do people do that? Our perception of ourselves is rarely objective. Sometimes, this can be caused by having a certain idea or vision of what our ideal *Responsibility* petal should look like. Sometimes, the *Responsibility* petal is disturbed by a short-term project you feel unmotivated to do, resulting in feeling irresponsible as well as unmotivated, too. Hence, it can be reasonable to believe we still have room for growth. Rating your petals gives you **the opportunity to reflect on** your current state in certain areas of your life. It will also make you think about what strengths you are satisfied with for now and what strengths you might like to focus on. :-)

Let's see how you can **grow your achievement petals**.

Growing Your Achievement Flower Petals

Satisfaction with Your Achievements

I would like to kindly invite you to practice recognizing your achievements. All of them. Acknowledging your successes, even the small ones, is a form of **self-care**. As much as we are usually trained by society to acknowledge when we fail and do something wrong, it is equally important to **recognize and appreciate all that you have done well** too. Take some time to reflect.

Let me take you back to the last exam you took when you did not feel the best about how it turned out. Try to name what did not go well and what you wish you had done better. Great. This was easy. But let's flip it now. Try to recall objectively what went well about that exam and what you did properly at that time. Did you recall something you found difficult to remember? Did you do a good job of writing down your thoughts? Did you overcome your fear and manage your nervousness well? Or did you invest your free time to prepare for the exam? If it feels hard to find something positive you have done that particular day, imagine that you are assessing not yours but the performance of a dear friend of yours. What would you help them to see by pointing out what they have done well? Say it out loud, write it down, or just pay attention to the thoughts for a moment. See? There was a lot you managed to do well, too. Even though you have concluded that this particular exam was a failure. **There are always things we manage well.** Mostly everything we do. It is just about the practice of noting the good parts too.

Track your progress and reward yourself with positive acknowledging self-talk **every time you accomplish a goal.** Call your loved ones and share with them how well you have done! Journal about how good it feels and appreciate what you have done to achieve what you want. Celebrate your successes like you would celebrate others doing well. Revel in your achievements. Treat yourself to a good lunch or dinner, or buy yourself something that will remind you of your accomplishment. **Well done!**

Recognition and Enjoyment of Others' Achievements

Sharing positivity is a beautiful thing. Seeing your classmate, friend, or a family member succeed can bring joy to both of you. Not only does it feel good to see others happy about their achievements, you can learn to **draw inspiration from others' success,** too! You can learn from their strategies and get motivated, along with genuinely celebrating others. Keep your eyes open and become more attentive to moments of excellence, joy, excitement, and honor. Acknowledge others when you see them doing good by simple phrases like "I know you worked hard to prepare for this," "I am happy for you," "You deserve this," or just a simple, honest "Congratulations!"

I would also like to invite you to **listen** if someone close to you shares good news with you. Let them **relive the experience** by asking open questions such as: "How did it feel to make it?" "How did they react when you did well?" "How did they acknowledge you?" "How did you do that?" "What was your favorite part?" You will help your loved ones and people around you to **relive the great moment again**. You will both feel great, and you will connect through this shared positivity resonance even deeper.

Next time you see someone celebrating, don't turn your head away. **Join them**. Acknowledge them. Recognize their **effort and perseverance** and tell them. You both will enjoy the moment, and you, personally, will lean into the inspiration that will help you **succeed, too!**

Recognition and Use of Your Character Strengths

It can be fulfilling to realize that your character strengths are not only for you. They are meant **to be shared** with others.

There is a hero within all of us. We all have a unique portfolio of character strengths and a very special way of **sharing them with others** around us. Your character strengths are a group of positive traits you can possess that enable your **growth, flourishing**, and **moral excellence**. They also impact how you think, feel, and behave.

VIA Institute on Character (2022) points out that we all were given some **unique positive personal traits** that not only serve us but that mainly serve those around us. Others see them as inspirational and useful and they appreciate us acting on them! But your character strengths are different from your other personal strengths (your skills, talents, interests, and other resources). They reflect **the true you**. Who you are naturally, at your core. How you express yourself with **no need to push yourself into it**. Being aware of your character strengths and using them in your everyday life will help you to boost your **confidence**, increase your **happiness**, strengthen your **relationships**, manage **problems**, reduce **stress**, accomplish **goals**, build **meaning** and **purpose**, and improve your **work** and **school performance**. So how can you start using your character strengths in your everyday life?

STEP 1: Identify Your Character Strengths

What are the criteria for character strengths?

The authors of research on character strengths, Chris Peterson and Martin Seligman (2004), listed the following criteria for recognizing your character strengths. When you perform your strengths, you have:

- a sense of **ownership and authenticity** when exercising a particular strength ("This is really me right now!")
- a sense of **inevitability** ("Nothing will stop me from expressing myself like this.")
- a feeling of **excitement** when a strong side is shown, especially if it's the first time ("This feels amazing!")
- **internal motivation** to use your strength and the **desire to behave** in accordance with it ("I really want to behave this way right now!")
- **a steep learning curve** as a strength is tested and reinforced in a new situation ("Wow I can really learn this quickly!")
- **preference for activities** that are related to our strengths ("I want to do this because I sense I could succeed!")
- a feeling that applying your character strength **does not lead to exhaustion** but on the **contrary is empowering** ("I want more of this!")

So how can you identify your superpowers? Ask yourself these questions:

In what activity do I experience an increase in energy?
What can I do better than others?
What is it that I enjoy and at the same time do it with ease?
What do I do on my own initiative and what does no one need to remind me twice about?
What job would I choose if money didn't matter?
What do I talk about when my voice gets louder, clearer, resonant, and full of energy and enthusiasm? (Linley, 2008)
And
What am I usually praised for at home, school, or work?
What does my partner appreciate about me?
For what reason do my friends like me? (Slezáčková, 2012)

Also, get to know the framework for character strengths to identify yours:

Professor Peterson and Professor Seligman (2004) gave birth to the framework of character strengths and virtues, that offers:
- cognitive strengths (under the virtue of wisdom)
- emotional strengths (courage)
- social and community strengths (humanity and justice)
- protective strengths (temperance) and
- spiritual strengths (transcendence)

Under these **six virtues** they have identified **24 character strengths** that you have the capacity to express (see Figure 6.4).

Figure 6.4 The VIA classification of character strengths and virtues.

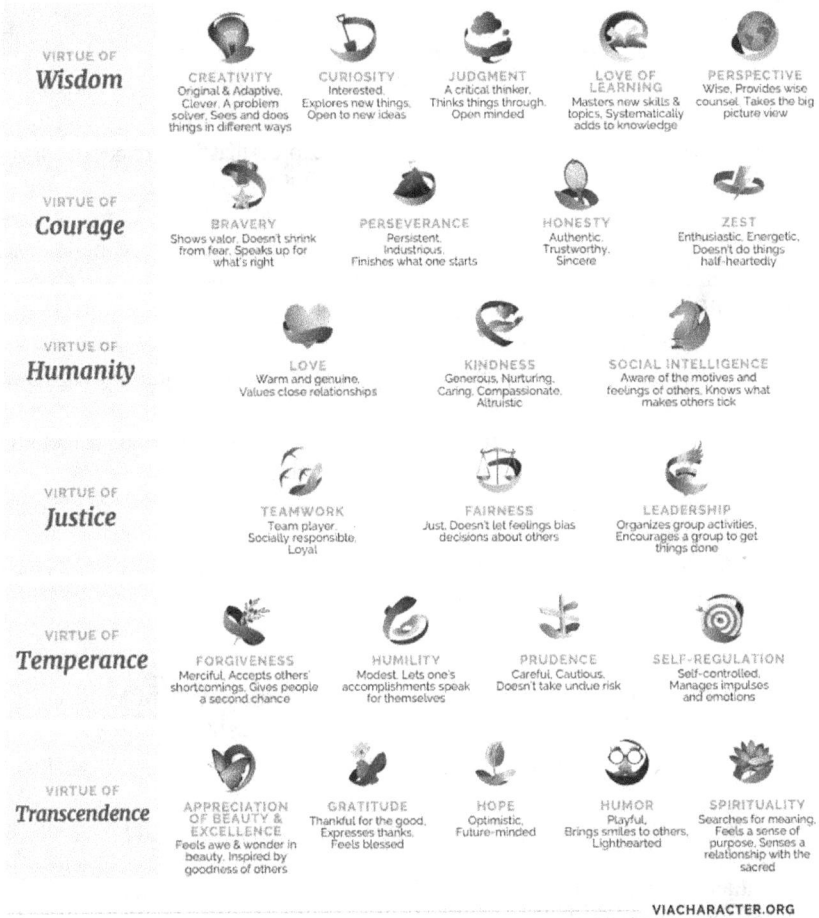

Look at the list of individual character strengths created by the VIA Institute on Character (2022) and read the statements about what it feels like to own them. **Observe what strengths you may identify with and that may feel like yours!**

- Appreciation of Beauty and Excellence: "I recognize, emotionally experience, and appreciate the beauty around me and the skill of others."

- Bravery: "I act on my convictions, and I face threats, challenges, difficulties, and pains, despite my doubts and fears."
- Creativity: "I am creative, conceptualizing something useful, coming up with ideas that result in something worthwhile."
- Curiosity: "I seek out situations where I gain new experiences without getting in my own or other people's way."
- Fairness: "I treat everyone equally and fairly and give everyone the same chance applying the same rules to everyone."
- Forgiveness: "I forgive others when they upset me and/or when they behave badly towards me, and I use that information in my future relations with them."
- Gratitude: "I am grateful for many things, and I express that thankfulness to others."
- Honesty: "I am honest to myself and to others, I try to present myself and my reactions accurately to each person, and I take responsibility for my actions."
- Hope: "I am realistic and also full of optimism about the future, believing in my actions and feeling confident things will turn out well."
- Humility: "I see my strengths and talents, but I am humble, not seeking to be the center of attention or to receive recognition."
- Humor: "I approach life playfully, making others laugh, and finding humor in difficult and stressful times."
- Judgment: "I weigh all aspects objectively in making decisions, including arguments that are in conflict with my convictions."
- Kindness: "I am helpful and empathic and regularly do nice favors for others without expecting anything in return."
- Leadership: "I take charge and guide groups to meaningful goals and ensure good relations among group members."
- Love: "I experience close, loving relationships that are characterized by giving and receiving love, warmth, and caring."
- Love of Learning: "I am motivated to acquire new levels of knowledge or deepen my existing knowledge or skills in a significant way."
- Perseverance: "I persist toward my goals despite obstacles, discouragements, or disappointments."
- Perspective: "I give advice to others by considering different (and relevant) perspectives and using my own experiences and knowledge to clarify the big picture."
- Prudence: "I act carefully and cautiously, looking to avoid unnecessary risks and planning with the future in mind."
- Self-Regulation: "I manage my feelings and actions and am disciplined and self-controlled."
- Social Intelligence: "I am aware of and understand my feelings and thoughts, as well as the feelings of those around me."
- Spirituality: "I feel spiritual and believe in a sense of purpose or meaning in my life; and I see my place in the grand scheme of the universe and find meaning in everyday life."
- Teamwork: "I am a helpful and contributing group and team member and feel responsible for helping the team reach its goals."
- Zest: "I feel vital and full of energy, and I approach life feeling activated and enthusiastic."

Do it **Discover Your Unique Character Strengths Profile!**

You possess each of the 24 character strengths in different degrees, giving you a unique character strengths profile. But you don't have to rely only on your gut to reveal what strengths might be your top strongest. **Take the VIA survey** and discover your unique character strengths profile! Knowing and applying your highest character strengths is the key to **feeling good** and **showing up to the world better than before**.

You can test yourself for free at https://www.viacharacter.org/. Take a free survey, identify your character strengths, and think of how to use your natural superpowers in your everyday life to thrive.

While your character and your character strengths are relatively stable over time, they can and often do gradually change throughout the course of life. **It is worth it to reflect on your current personality** every now and then and update your understanding of yourself throughout your current character strengths analysis.

STEP 2: Strengthen Your Superpowers (and love your weaknesses)!

Once you identify your character strengths and assess those that really feel like you, invest a bit of effort to develop them, stretch them, use them in new ways, and **fulfill the potential of your superpowers**.

No idea how to do that? Get inspired by a list of more than 300 ways to use your VIA Character Strengths (Rashid & Anjum, 2005) and look for the article "340 Ways to Use VIA Character Strengths." Pick and choose from the suggested activities and master your strengths to the fullest.

But what about our weaknesses? What about the character traits we feel like we struggle with? Guess what. We all have them. And they are as valuable a part of ourselves as our strengths. They make us who we are, they complement our personalities, and sometimes we were even able to develop some of our strengths only thanks to them. What if you could not be so beautifully zesty without your lower prudence or what if for your kindness, lovingness, and empathy you struggle telling people what to do and you cannot see yourself managing a team? We all have unique personalities that are often well balanced. And if you feel like it, you can always also focus on your weaknesses to grow all your character traits by practicing, challenging them, and getting out of your comfort zone. Or you simply don't. You truly don't need to change anything if you don't feel like it. Remember. Even though we all have some room to grow and to change for the better, you are perfect the way you are. You are unique, valuable, and worthy as you already are. And if you don't feel like challenging yourself now or pushing yourself into anything and would rather relax and contemplate, please do so. Learning to listen to your inner voice is a valuable skill too!

STEP 3: Share Your Superpowers with the World!

Knowing your strengths and maximizing their potential is a beautiful thing. But now comes the most important part. Your character strengths are not only for you, remember? They are meant to be **shared with the world**. Be creative! Think of ways to use your superpowers to feel more natural, confident, successful, and to better serve others **in your everyday life**!

Strengths Profile Supported by Alex Linley

Founded in 2005, Cappfinity has spent many years designing new and better ways of assessing people's strengths. At the heart of their product offering is our "Strengths' methodology", which has been developed by their CEO Alex Linley, the leading expert in the field of Positive Psychology.

You can discover your top three realized strengths, three unrealized strengths, two learned behaviors, and one weakness in the Free Starter Profile. Use it to start your strengths journey, gain self-awareness of what you love to do, and support any job applications.

Get your free starter profile here:

https://strengthsprofile.com/en-GB/Products/free?mc_cid=0ae2a237b0& mc_eid=ea0705810a

---

Harnessing our character strengths

Maximising the potential of our character strengths can bring many benefits. But while we become more and more conscious of our behavior, you might also benefit from learning how to harness them. What am I trying to say? Let me share a story with you. A student of mine once came to me after our class on identifying our character strengths and learning how to use them in our everyday lives. "What if my character strengths are hurting me?" She asked. "What do you mean by that?" I was slightly confused and curious. And my student responded, "I am very empathetic, and I end up giving myself to others most of the time. I often forget about myself. I do everything for others, and I sometimes feel like I don't even live for myself." "Wow, what an important insight." I thought to myself. "What would help you feel better about that, and what do you need?" I asked her. And my student responded immediately. "I need to learn how to focus more on myself and less on others." "Thus, becoming clearer on your own values, creating a vision for yourself, and perhaps practicing setting boundaries could be a good start." I thought out loud. "Yes." She responded. "It sounds scary, but I want to learn how to say no more often." She reflected.

Advising my student to cultivate her top strengths and use them as often as possible (which was the main message of our class) could have been draining for her and not exactly what she needed. I am so glad she listened to her feelings and that she came to discuss her thoughts. And the same rule applies to you, dear students. I still believe that cultivating our character strengths is a very powerful skill, but self-awareness and listening to yourself are as well. Assess your strengths profile, reflect on your results, respect your weaknesses, use your superpowers, but also pay attention to what you need at the moment.

Responsibility

Responsibility is a personal trait that reflects your **inner tendencies to keep** your **word, promises**, and **deadlines** not only towards your own plans but especially towards what you promised to others. Responsibility means that **you take the things you do seriously**. You make an effort and show up even when things get tough. This makes you accountable and easy to work with. But what if you feel like these strengths of yours might deserve a bit of your attention and practice? Start small! Set realistic, smaller goals for yourself. **Acknowledge** every time you keep your word. Search for **meaning** in everything you do to keep your motivation going. But responsibility can also be practiced socially! Help your neighbors when you can (if you have the extra energy). Participate in cleaning your neighborhood. Separate trash. Support local organizations. Donate old clothes, and volunteer to help kids at school or the elderly who might feel lonely. Be creative! Find the right way of becoming more responsible.

Moving forward towards your life goals can also be done by taking responsibility for your everyday life decisions, facing your issues, and solving your problems. To make both easier for you, it might be very useful to adopt critical thinking.

Students who are critical thinkers stretch my teaching skills the most. They often think of themselves as active learners rather than passive recipients of information. And they act on it. Students who have the ability to think critically tend to question my ideas and assumptions rather than accept them as facts to see whether the presented ideas and facts represent the whole picture. And if not, we think together about what needs to be included to make "the picture," complete. My critically thinking students often expand my thinking as well and I am grateful for that. The truth is, many of us have been raised to do the exact opposite. Accept the information as it is, rather than raising questions about it.

Critical thinking is related to both problem-solving and decision-making. It always has a goal – usually, to solve a problem or come to a decision. For example, you might apply critical thinking in your Healthy Lifestyle class when putting together ideas on what health promotion project to assign and how to make it all happen. What health project to choose is the **decision to make**, and how to make it all happen is the **problem to solve**.

Your group needs to make decisions such as who (and when) will do the research, who will organize the information, who will put together the project, and who will present it in front of the class. You also need to solve "the problems," such as when will you meet, where will you work together, how will you make time for this throughout the semester, and what to do when someone does not collaborate.

So how to become a decision-making master?

You don't probably even realize it, but you already get through your days by making one decision followed by another one. Just by entering a school building, you need to decide whether you use an elevator or whether you walk up the stairs. On your way to your classroom you quickly think about whether you go straight to the bathroom or whether you put your jacket and backpack in the classroom first. On your way to the coffee shop you try to decide whether you want coffee or soda and whether you will pay with a credit card or cash. When you get back to the class you wonder whether you deserve a break to scroll through Instagram or whether you will go say hi to some classmates to socialize. These decisions can seem small but the series of our decisions is more or less never-ending. But what if you need to decide something larger, something that can impact your life big-time? Learning decision-making skills to **make your own choices** helps you feel more confident and be more independent and responsible. As a student at school, at work and in your personal life. It also provides you with room for self-exploration and helps you to crystalize your core values. Being able to decide gives you a sense of control over your life, which can significantly reduce your anxiety and stretch your resilience. So how do you expand your decision-making skills?

I would like to invite you to (drums…) practice. By taking baby steps. Almost every conflicting situation in your life can be an opportunity to slow down and to:

- Name it: identify the problem or conflict you would like or need to solve
- Learn about it: gather as much relevant information as you can
- Brainstorm about it: think of any possible solutions, the realistic ones and the (apparently) non-realistic ones
- Think through it: identify any potential consequences, the good ones and even the bad ones
- Decide it: make a choice that resonates the most with you
- Do it: once you decide, trust your decision and take action on it

Let's imagine that you need to decide **whether you want to take an extra nutrition class or you take this semester easy** so you can make some room for yourself to slow down.

- Name it: *yes or no to the extra class* – do I expand my knowledge on how to eat healthier or do I save some time for myself that I desperately need
- Learn about it: I can study the syllabus to see how much I would be interested in the class but I can also read the comments from previous students on Facebook to see how much they enjoyed the course
- Brainstorm about it: (a) I can do something for my health long term by learning about proper eating. (b) I can prevent myself from having burnout when I don't

slow things down. (c) I can just not attend the classes but I can study myself when I feel more energized by reading some cool books about nutrition. (d) I can take some online nutrition courses on Coursera.org for free and I can adjust the pace of my learning to my current capabilities
- Think through it: (a) Not taking the course won't cause me any issues at school. (b) I might look like I gave up. (c) I can actually gain more from some practical courses online than from attending a course that has a lot of chemistry in it. (d) I can finally prioritize myself and give myself the well-deserved rest this semester
- Decide it: I will do the online course, once I feel like I have the energy
- Do it: I am not signing up for the course and I don't even feel bad about it

Congratulations! You are already practicing your decision-making skills. But how about problem-solving? Let's solve your problems by learning how to problem-solve!

Problem-solving can be seen as a skill **to identify and solve problems by applying appropriate strategies in a systematic matter**. Problem-solving is a process. There are series of actions or steps that need to be taken in order to achieve a desirable result – solving your problem. In this process you work with what you know to discover what you don't know. Yet.

There are five essential stages for solving the problem. Problem solving is the act of:

- defining a problem and the cause of it
- identifying possible solutions
- evaluating the possible solutions and prioritizing one
- after choosing a solution, moving to an implementation of the solution
- reflecting and evaluating whether you are satisfied with this solution or not

What the five essential stages can look like:

- defining a problem and the cause of it
  - ➢ *e.g. I am not ready for tomorrow's class since I haven't read the chapter I was supposed to. I simply did not find time to do it.*

- identifying possible solutions
  - ➢ *e.g. I can read it overnight but I would cut my sleep. I can ask some classmates if they can share a bottom line with me. I can watch some book summary on YouTube. Or I can read a few pages in the morning before the class.*

- evaluating the possible solutions and prioritizing one
  - ➢ *e.g. I don't want to compromise my sleep. Nor do I want to look bad in front of my classmates. I can watch some short videos online tonight and I can try to read a few pages before the class tomorrow.*

- after choosing a solution, moving to an implementation of the solution
  - ➢ *e.g. I will watch the video tonight and I will read a few pages in the morning*

- reflecting and evaluating whether you are satisfied with this solution or not
  - ➤ e.g. *The video was actually really helpful. Reading only a few pages made me confused and even more nervous. I will watch some video again next time before my readings, but I would rather find time to read the whole chapter.*

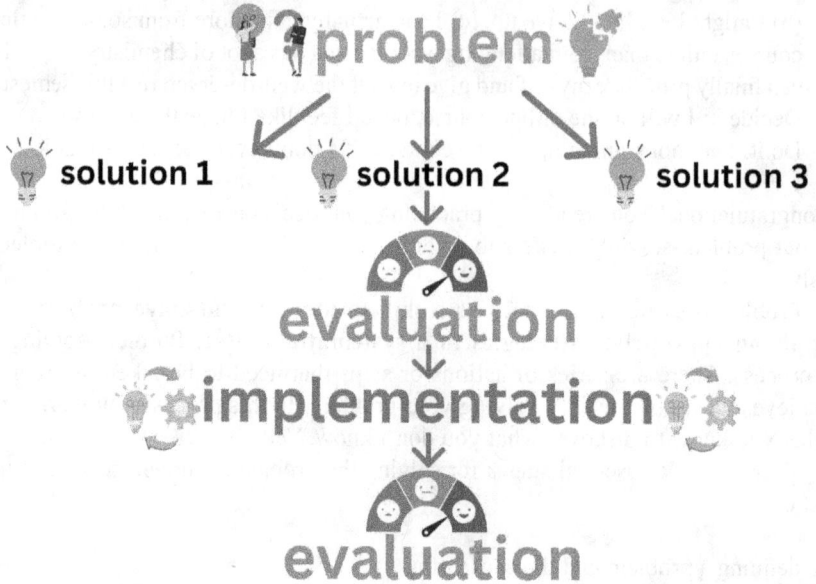

Figure 6.5 Stages of problem-solving.

Willpower

Willpower is another personal trait that can be of great help when trying to **"stay on track"**. It is a **driving force** that helps you **stay focused**; keep the things you want to achieve **in mind**. Whether it is to avoid something or to do, build, or create something. Can we practice our willpower? Absolutely yes! First, get rid of the negative, unsupportive self-talk and **don't say that you have no willpower**. Even if you believe that your willpower is not well-developed, change your self-talk, and start acknowledging your effort. Express your desire to improve. Secondly, search for meaning in everything you do. **When things make sense to us, we tend to stick to them.** Also, visualize the outcome. Having a clear picture of what you desire to do or have strengthens your motivation and gives you the energy to keep going and live the way you want. But also, take it easy on the days you feel low on energy. Be kind to yourself and please know that it is ok and even necessary to take a break from your duties from time to time.

Grit

Do you want to be successful in your life and get things done? Grit is a must have. But what exactly is Grit and how can we build it? Grit is **a combination of passion**

and perseverance for long-term goals that are meaningful to you and that are aligned with your values (Duckworth et al. 2007). Grit creates the energy we need to keep going and research (Duckworth, 2016) indicates that the ability to be gritty – **to stick with things that are important to you and bounce back from failure** – is an essential component of success independent of and beyond what talent and intelligence contribute.

We already know that Grit has two components. Passion and perseverance. But how do we awaken and strengthen them?

Perseverance for Long-Term Goals

As Angela Duckworth (2022) says, "Grit is not a talent. Grit is not luck. Grit isn't how intensely you want something in the spur of a moment." Instead, grit is about having what some researchers call an **"ultimate concern."** A goal that you care about so much that it gives meaning to almost everything you do. And grit is holding steadfast to that goal. Even when you fall. Even when you mess up. Even when progress towards that goal is halting or slowing down.

But what about talent? Talent absolutely matters for success. Our intelligence matters too. And some luck plays a role too. But with no practice, effort, and us showing up again and again talent might end up only as **unfulfilled potential.** A beautiful one, but never realized. So, how do you persevere? **Manage your self-talk** and support yourself when you feel like things are not going your way. **Change your attitude** towards failing and obstacles. Making mistakes helps you grow! **Be hopeful** and **trust yourself endlessly**. You can do anything you want! Eventually.

Passion for Long-Term Goals

We all know that feeling. When we are interested in something, we **get excited every time we talk or hear about it**. Something **we never get tired of**! We are all passionate about certain things in our lives. Some of us follow our passions more; some of us put them aside and focus on things that seem more important to work on right now. But **denying our passion** can, in the long run, reflect a **lack of energy, a decrease in inner motivation**, and a **loss of meaning**. On the contrary, doing what you are passionate about leaves you energized, motivated, and hopeful. Going after our passions makes us feel very authentic and true. It makes us feel like we are in the right place and have the right purpose. But what if your current job, school, or things you do in your free time don't align with your passions? Don't quit your job yet! Get creative. Craft! **Look for ways to bring what you are passionate about into what you are already doing.** Release your passion in your everyday life more. But what if you still feel like the goals you set for yourself are not the right ones? Well, it is important not only to know **when to grit**, but also to know **when to quit**. If you feel like your way of life sucks the energy out of you, does not make sense to you, and is not aligned with your values, let it go. **It is ok to update your life journey.** Reflect on your goals every now and then and focus on what is really, truly important to you.

How do you build your grit?

- Identify your values and reflect on them once in a while.
- Discover what excites you. What are you interested in?
- Assess your personal strengths. What are you naturally really good at?
- Think of what gives your life meaning and find your purpose.
- Generate your goals and strategies to get there.
- Practice, practice, practice!
- Seek feedback to learn from mistakes and to get better next time.
- Practice self-compassion and optimistic self-talk. Champion yourself!
- Join a gritty culture to get inspiration and motivation and to get things done.

Skills of Achievement

TIME MANAGEMENT

Time management should be one of your top management skills. Know what is important to you and find time for such activities. Discern your priorities and start saying no to those that are not on your list of importance!

IDENTIFYING YOUR VALUES

Check your "to-do" lists.
If possible, prioritize what is aligned with your values.
Start making a **"not to-do"** list too.

NO COMPARISON

Successful people only compare themselves to who *they* were yesterday. They understand that we all have our unique goals, journeys, and rhythms. Focus on **your own personal goals** that reflect what is important to you right now in this stage of life. Use your own strategies and reflect on your personal progress.

TAKING BABY STEPS AND SETTING MILESTONES

Successful people know how to dream big, how to strategize, and how to turn a dream into a plan. But some plans, especially those long-term ones, may seem almost unachievable at first. It can be very helpful to learn how to break your goals into smaller ones, set your milestones, and find comfort in taking small steps. Be satisfied with small steps and keep your eyes on the prize – even though it may be hard to see from all the distance. Successful people are those who show up repeatedly. Adapt the mindset of an achiever and trust the process. **Small steps lead to big dreams.**

MAKING PUBLIC COMMITMENTS (ONLY IF YOU FEEL LIKE IT)

Communicating your goals publicly and standing up for your visions generates confidence, responsibility, and inner motivation to reach your goals. **Share and discuss your goals** with your friends, co-workers, and family for an element of public commitment to the goal. You can even make a post with a statement on social media to communicate your goals to the world! But remember. Only if you feel like it. Don't push yourself into anything that does not feel right to you.

SMART GOAL-SETTING

SMART goal-setting is a strong tool too. You can read more about "SMARTly" setting your goals in the previous chapter on meaning, but just to remind you:

Make goals that are:

- **Specific** (clearly defined and focused on one target, knowing what you expect to achieve and knowing what strategies will help you reach the goal)
- **Measurable** (so you can clearly say you reached expected quantity and quality, and you can track your progress)
- **Achievable** (knowing that you have the skills and capacity to actually obtain the goal. Students usually have a lot on their plate. It is perfectly healthy to move forward with your goals step by step to make them achievable!)
- **Relevant** (the goal is aligned with your values and will help you to reach your personal and academic growth)
- **Time-based** (you are able to set a deadline and milestones for your journey to reach the goal to make it easier to stick with your plan!)

Finals are around the corner and your nervousness is increasing? Look at the following tips for what to do (and what not) before your exams in Figure 6.6 and pick what suits you the best. Good luck! You got this!

TEN COMMANDMENTS
BEFORE AN EXAM

SLEEP ON IT!

DON'T PUSH IT ANYMORE.

EAT WELL.

CHANGE YOUR MINDSET AND PERSPECTIVE.

SET A REALISTIC GOAL.

CREATE AND VISUALIZE AN IDEAL SCENARIO.

ACTIVATE YOUR SOCIAL CAPITAL.

DRESS UP COMFORTABLE, NOT NICE.

REFLECT ON WHAT WENT WELL.

REWARD YOURSELF.

Figure 6.6 Ten commandments before an exam.

How Can Grit and Self-Control Help Us Achieve Good Study Results

Research and Psychologist Angela L. Duckworth talks about Will Power: Grit, Self-control, and Achievement for Family Action Network (FAN) on November 29, 2012.

https://www.youtube.com/watch?v=7ALmzoWRQMo

Ten Empowering Questions to Support My Achievement Flower Growth

1   What is the smallest step I can take today to move forward towards my goals?
2   What do I need to say yes to today to move forward towards my goals?
3   What do I need to say no to today to move forward towards my goals?
4   What are my character strengths and what am I naturally good at or even better than others?
5   How can I use my character strengths today to move towards my goals?
6   What are the biggest achievements of my life?
7   What inspires me in others?
8   What am I passionate about?
9   How can I recharge and devote more time to my relaxation?
10 What went well today?

Ten Tips to Build My Achievement Flower

1   Change your self-talk and start praising yourself. Celebrate your big and small achievements. Whether you passed your exam successfully or just woke up and attended the early morning class.

2 Track your successes. Look back in time and sincerely acknowledge your achievements. And remember, achievement does not necessarily have to be a big career or school accomplishment. It can be your recovery from a breakup, going to the gym regularly, or the realization of some big step like moving to a different city.

3 Look around you for excellence. Get inspired by your colleagues, family members, and friends and learn from them!

4 Acknowledge the efforts of people around you and congratulate them for their accomplishments. Whether it is your mom's promotion, your friend ran a half marathon, or your classmate presented a really interesting project you liked.

5 Assess your character strengths and use them to your advantage. Think of what you are naturally good at and what makes you feel confident. Whether it is your humor, spirituality, prudence, vitality, bravery, curiosity, or ability to be thankful.

6 Train your willpower. To be successful, many tasks ask for resistance to short-term temptations in order to meet long-term goals. Focus on the desired outcome and what your willpower will bring you.

7 Persevere. You will get where you want!

8 Feed your passion. Talk about what you love. Don't stop learning. Watch TED Talks about related topics. Be around people who share your interests. Study the lives of people who reached what you are aiming for. You will find your way.

9 Look back in time and remind yourself your bigger but also smaller achievements in life. What was the last thing you accomplished?

10 Be aware of your everyday life achievements. Did you manage to get up early today? Did you make yourself a healthy lunch? Did you say no to some activity you really did not feel like doing? And did you manage to find time to rest this afternoon? Great! Those all are achievements as well!

Tips to Achievement Snacking

Building your achievement does not have to be complicated nor time demanding. Look at Figure 6.7 and try some of the tips right now!

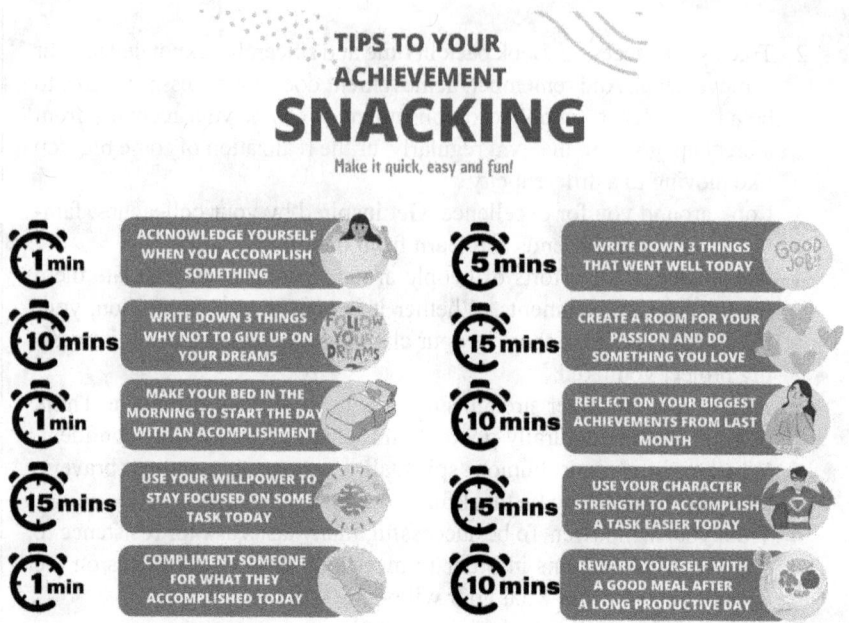

Figure 6.7 Tips to achievement snacking.

It does not matter how fast or slow you are going. It does not even matter how much or little you are accomplishing. What is important is your consistency. Working on your dreams and goals day by day, week by week. Keep working (but also relaxing!) and your desired outcome will happen. But what is the one thing that can help us accomplish any success we desire? Physical health. Our physical well-being is an elementary ingredient for every other aspect of our life. Engaging in regular body movement, eating a balanced diet, sleeping well, practicing relaxation to recharge properly, proper breathing, and limiting risky behaviors such as excessive alcohol and tobacco use, dangerous driving, and social media overuse. But do you feel more confused than wise from all the conflicting advice and restrictions that pop up at you from every direction you look? I would like to invite you to explore with me some current evidence-based recommendations and practices that will be presented in the next chapter focused on your physical health building blocks. Upcoming pages are aimed to make your life easier and to make you feel good rather than overwhelmed and confused. See you there!

References

Donaldson, S. I., Van Zyl, L. E., & Donaldson, S. I. (2022). PERMA+4: A framework for work-related well-being, performance and positive organizational psychology 2.0. *Frontiers in Psychology*, 12, 817244. https://doi.org/10.3389/fpsyg.2021.817244

Duckworth, A. (2016). *Grit: The power of passion and perserverance*. New York, NY: Simon & Schuster.

Duckworth, A. (2022). FAQ. Available at: https://angeladuckworth.com/qa/

Duckworth, A. L., Peterson, C., Matthews, M. D., & Kelly, D. R. (2007). Grit: Perseverance and passion for long-term goals. *Journal of Personality and Social Psychology*, 92(6), 1087–1101. https://doi.org/10.1037/0022-3514.92.6.1087

Govindji, R., & Linley, P. A. (2007). Strengths use, self-concordance and well-being: Implications for strengths coaching and coaching psychologists. *International Coaching Psychology Review*, 2(2), 143–153.

Koci, J., & Donaldson, S. I. (2022). *Zdraví a mentální well-being studentů distančního vzdělávání*. Prague: Charles University. ISBN: 978-80-7603-357-3

Linley, A. (2008). *Average to A+: Realizing strengths in yourself and others*. Coventry: CAPP Press.

Linley, P. A., Nielsen, K. M., Gillett, R., & Biswas-Diener, R. (2010). Using signature strengths in pursuit of goals: Effects on goal progress, need satisfaction, and well-being, and implications for coaching psychologists. *International Coaching Psychology Review*, 5(1), 6–15.

Peterson, C., & Seligman, M. E. P. (2004). *Character strengths and virtues: A handbook and classification*. New York: Oxford University Press and Washington, DC: American Psychological Association.

Proctor, E. K., Landsverk, J., Aarons, G., Chambers, D., Glisson, C., & Mittman, B. (2009 January). Implementation research in mental health services: An emerging science with conceptual, methodological, and training challenges. *Administration and Policy in Mental Health*, 36(1), 24–34. https://doi.org/10.1007/s10488-008-0197-4. Epub December 23, 2008. PMID: 19104929; PMCID: PMC3808121.

Rashid, T., & Anjum, A. (2005). 340 ways to use VIA character strengths by University of Pennsylvania. Available at: https://robertson.ms/wp-content/uploads/2020/04/340_ways_ to_use_character_strengths.pdf

Slezáčková, A. (2012). Průvodce pozitivní psychologií: nové přístupy, aktuální poznatky, praktické aplikace. Vyd. 1. Praha: Grada. 304 s.

VIA Institute on Character (2022). Character strengths. Available at: https://www.viacharacter. org/

7 Building Your Physical Health

To keep the body in good health is a duty… otherwise we shall not be able to keep our mind strong and clear.

— Buddha

It is Sunday morning at the beginning of January and you feel in your bones that this year is THE year. The year when you change everything you want and finally start living the way you deserve. You will get in really good physical shape and your whole life will improve as a result. To be sure that everything goes as planned, you wrote down your goals.

- Cooking my own healthy meals at home.
- No chips.
- Losing 14 pounds.
- Running every day.
- No naps.
- Meditating every morning.
- Cutting down on coffee.

You looked at the list one more time and you decided to update a few things:

- Cook my own ~~healthy~~ meals at home.
- No chips. (Can I switch to the healthy vegetable chips??)
- Losing ~~14~~ 7 pounds.
- Run ~~every day~~.
- No naps. :-(
- Meditate ~~every morning~~. I will download the Calm App to my phone.
- Cutting down on coffee. (No way I can do this if I won't take any naps.)

All right. You are still confused about what diet to follow so you will probably just ask your friend Katie if she could give you the meal plan she downloaded online. She hated it but she managed to lose a few pounds. You put your running shoes on

DOI: 10.4324/9781003378365-8

and you pushed yourself to run for almost a full hour around the neighborhood. You did not die! But you were really close. *"It felt so awful. There is no way I can do this tomorrow again." "Oh God, this is going to be a terrible month."*

This story reflects strategies we usually think are necessary when we are planning a lifestyle change. But all this above can, and often does, lead to resistance and a decrease in motivation over time. Which only deepens our false belief that we cannot do this. But how should we know what is the right way when there has never been so much conflicting information online on how to become healthier? Everything we usually wish for can be, in fact, very doable. There are a few simple approaches that can significantly increase the quality of our lives and can leave us feeling really good. First, our changes have to be sustainable. Thus, finding ways to enjoy them (or at least not hate them) helps and taking baby steps at the beginning will also increase the probability that you won't give up so easily. Second, it can be really helpful to study some fundamental recommendations that are based on science. Third, respect your individuality and make the changes according to your individual, unique needs. Create a simple game plan that you can incorporate into your everyday life. We all can get some sunlight first thing in the morning. We all can start a day with a quick cold shower (or at least the last 30 seconds of it). We all can drink more filtered water during the day, eat more real foods, and make sure we eat enough protein. We all can find more ways to move naturally during our days. How to relax after a long day and we all can think of a few changes that would help us sleep better. This upcoming chapter focuses on simple general physical health recommendations. Find your own unique way and enjoy the process of caring for yourself. You do deserve the lifestyle you want. And it does not even have to be the beginning of January. :-)

Introduction to Physical Health

Physical health has been traditionally defined as the absence of disease or serious illness. However, in recent years, modern science has expanded this limiting viewpoint. In 2008, Professor Seligman proposed a new field of **Positive Health,** promoting a state **beyond the mere absence of disease,** which is definable and measurable. Positive health can be operationalized by a combination of excellent status on biological, subjective, and functional measures. Thus, being physically healthy not only means the absence of disease or infirmity, it also means finding ourselves in a state of **complete physical prosperity**.

The World Health Organization defines health as *a state of complete physical, mental, and social well-being and not merely the absence of disease or infirmity.* State of the overall well-being of a person – physical, mental, and social. These dimensions of health are intricately interlinked, and the health of an individual encompasses all of them. Physical health is **closely linked** to your mental and social well-being. If your physical health strengthens, it often leads to strengthening in the mental and social dimensions too. But what are the main strategies to strengthen the important domains of our physical health?

A physically healthy student typically engages in regular body movement, has a balanced diet, sleeps well, and practices relaxation and proper breathing. Students also tend to limit risky behaviors such as excessive alcohol and tobacco use, dangerous driving, and social media overuse.

Benefits of Physical Health for Students' Well-being

Feeling physically healthy is a **key building block** for your well-being. Students who report experiencing better overall health tend to have higher levels of energy, learn easier, and study more effectively during their college experience than those with lower levels of physical health. If poor physical health or unhealthy behaviors are dragging down your well-being, addressing these issues is the best way to start building your physical health strengths back up to boost your positive functioning.

Physical health strengths often reduce the risk of illness later in life but also enhance how you feel, think, learn, and make judgments in **your everyday life at the current moment.** Therefore, it can be important for you to learn how to build physical health strengths such as **regular body movement, proper body posture, optimal nutrition, quality sleep, activities to improve your cognitive wellness such as relaxation and deep breathing, and risky behavior reduction**. Develop a unique routine that fits you and try to stick to it until it becomes a part of who you are. Dream big – but start small. By incorporating simple, specific changes into your daily student life, you can increase your life satisfaction, support your cognitive skills, uplift your academic achievements, and strengthen your well-being step by step.

Your Physical Health Flower Assessment

We have learned in Chapter 1 that physical health is one of the **nine essential building blocks** for generating well-being. It can be very useful to reflect on and think about your personal **physical health strengths**. Understanding the importance of physical health for your well-being, you will be provided with an opportunity to assess your physical health strengths!

In this exercise, you will be asked to fill out your own **flower diagram**. You will be provided with a wheel that represents **seven different strengths** building your physical health. These include adequate body movement, good body posture, optimal nutrition, high-quality sleep, regular relaxation, proper breathing, and the avoidance of risky behavior such as alcohol consumption, risky sexual behavior, or social media overuse. There is also room for your own choice of another physical health strength you might feel the need to be reflected in your life as well.

Here is a **set of statements** that will help you to assess how well you feel about each physical health strength. You might find it helpful to reflect by reading the descriptions of ideal states of all seven of your strengths and assessing where you stand.

Adequate Body Movement

I **enjoy** moving my body naturally during the school day and after. I care about the maintenance of my muscle and cardiovascular health by finding time for regular **aerobic, strength**, and **flexibility** activities and **balance** movements.

Proper Body Posture

I am aware of my body posture throughout the day. I am capable of **correcting my posture** properly when **moving, standing,** and **sitting,** even **while studying**.

Optimal Nutrition

I **enjoy** good nutrition in a regimen that fits me. My diet is **balanced**, it is full of **natural foods** rich in **nutrients** (vegetables, fruits) and **healthy fats,** and it includes **high-quality protein** in every meal.

High-Quality Sleep

My sleep quality is **good** and **consistent**. I wake up feeling **refreshed** and ready for school. I **care** for my sleep by sticking to a regular sleep **schedule, avoiding** large meals and alcoholic drinks before bed, **relaxing** before bedtime, and managing my **sleep environment**.

Regular Relaxation

My body feels **relaxed most of the time.** When I notice my body getting stiff after a stressful situation at school or in my personal life, I am **able to relax my body**. I practice relaxing my body intentionally during the day and especially before sleep.

Proper Breathing

My breathing is **slow** and **deep,** and I breathe into my **belly** most of the time. When I notice myself breathing shallowly in moments of school or personal stress, I can regulate **my breath** and **balance myself** back into calmness with **breathing exercises** if needed.

Avoidance of Risky Behavior

I limit exposing myself to the potential risk of harm by avoiding **substance abuse**, heavy **alcohol consumption, unprotected** sexual intercourse, **reckless driving**, practicing **extreme** sports, or **overusing social media**, as I care for my health.

Other Physical Health Strengths

Are there any other physical health strengths on your mind you would like to assess? If yes, please scale them as well as the previous strengths.

So how do you actually assess your strengths? **Please imagine a ladder with steps numbered from 0 at the bottom to 10 at the top.**

The top of the ladder represents the best result (I feel very confident in this particular strength), while the bottom of the ladder represents the worst (I would like to build this particular strength better).

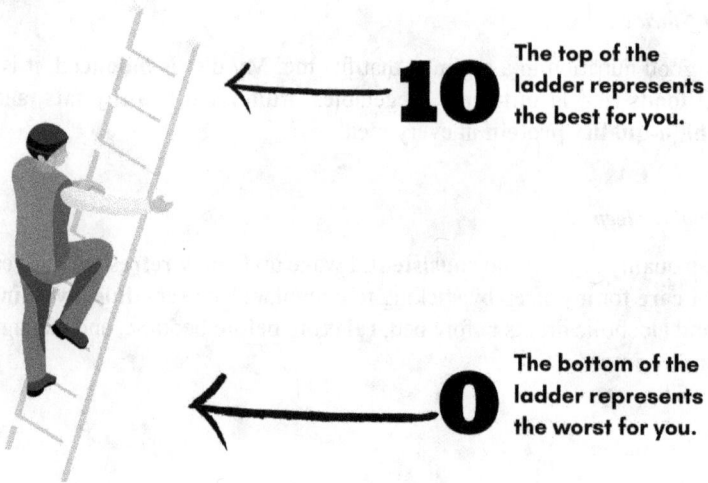

The top of the ladder represents the best for you.

The bottom of the ladder represents the worst for you.

Figure 7.1 Your well-being assessment ladder.

On which step of the ladder on a scale of 0–10 would you say you personally feel you stand at this time in terms of:

- adequate body movement
- good body posture
- optimal nutrition
- high-quality sleep
- regular relaxation
- proper breathing
- avoidance of risky behavior
- other physical health strengths

After you assess all your physical health strengths, draw your very own physical health flower! Circle the resulting numbers of your strength on the physical health wheel ladders. Then draw the petal shape from the center of the wheel through all the numbers on each ladder to create your own flower (see Figure 7.2 for an example of the flower diagram).

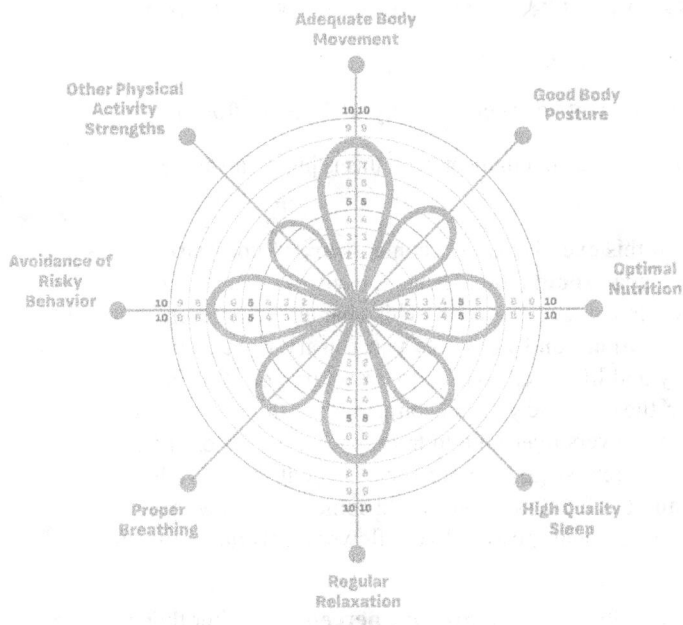

Figure 7.2 Example of your physical health flower diagram.

Let's assess your **physical health strengths** and later you can reflect on them and learn how to build particular strengths (if needed) in the upcoming chapter.

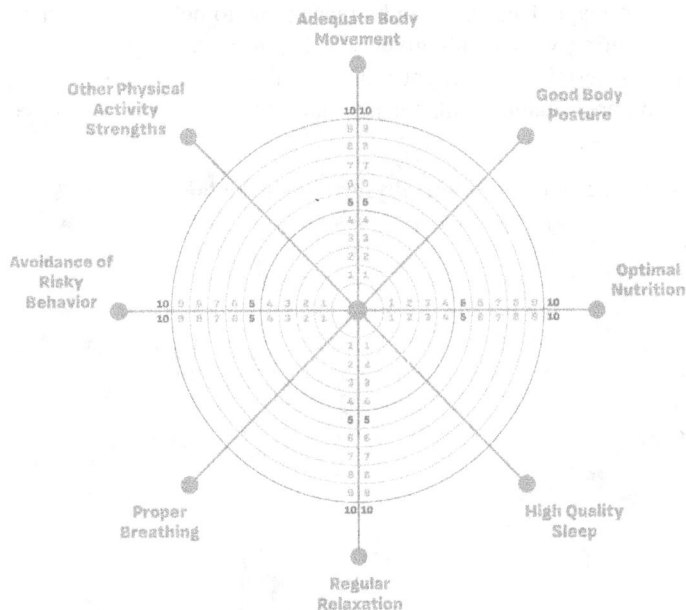

Figure 7.3 Your physical health flower assessment.

YOUR PHYSICAL HEALTH FLOWER REFLECTION

Great job! How do you feel?

Let's have a look at your personal **physical health flower**.

Remember, there is no judgment here; this is just an awareness exercise.

The goal of this exercise is to become **aware of your situation and decide what your next goal should be**. Then you will have a chance to think about what you can do to achieve said goal. This chapter will present some **evidence-based recommendations and activities** you can try right away to see if they fit your personality and lifestyle. It is fun to reflect on your flowers with your friends, but remember, the only one you can compare your flowers to is yourself. Enjoy checking on your flowers over time to track your progress or changes reflecting certain events in different stages of your life. The goal shouldn't be to have perfect, long petals in all your flowers – you should come to terms with imperfection. Invite the possibility of gradual growth of your flower petals rather than unhealthy overnight perfection.

Each flower reflects your **subjective perception** rather than your objective state. You might rate your *Optimal Nutrition* petal lower while caring for your nutrition. Why do people do that? Well, our perception of ourselves is rarely objective. Sometimes, this can be caused by having a certain idea or vision of what our ideal *Optimal Nutrition* should look like. Sometimes, the *Optimal Nutrition* petal is disturbed by indulging in certain unhealthy foods and drinks during vacations and holidays. Hence, it can be reasonable to believe we still have room for growth. Rating your petals gives you **the opportunity to reflect on** your current state in certain areas of your life. It will also make you think about what strengths you are satisfied with for now and what strengths you might like to focus on. :-)

Let's see how you can **grow your physical health petals**.

Growing Your Physical Health Flower Petals

Physical health is operationalized as a combination of high levels of **biological**, **functional**, and **psychological** health assets. The aim of this chapter is to inform you about certain ways that might help you build your physical health strengths by focusing on your **body movement, body posture, nutrition**, and **sleep** while being able to **relax, breathe properly**, and successfully **avoid risky behaviors**. But again, please remember that one size does not fit all. Pick and choose what fits you or interests you. Don't force yourself and be patient while trying to change your lifestyle.

Adequate Body Movement

Regular physical activity is one of the **greatest contributors** to the well-being of students. The World Health Organization (2020) states that adequate body movement benefits your body and heart, helps you sleep better, boosts your mood, and makes you feel more energized. Moving your body supports your mind and cognitive health by enhancing your thinking, learning, and judgment skills. It can also reduce the symptoms of stress, anxiety, and depression that each of us experiences from time to time. In addition to all of this, being physically active can make you more prosocial – thus, it can strengthen your relationships, too!

Moving your body regularly will make our daily life better. Choose **your way to move**, get more active throughout your school day and start immediately feeling better.

The World Health Organization recommends moving your body for at least **150–300 minutes** of moderate-intensity aerobic physical activity or at least **75–150 minutes** of vigorous-intensity aerobic physical activity each week. An equivalent combination of moderate and vigorous-intensity activity throughout the week might be your best fit as well. Greater health benefits can be seen with **more than 300 minutes** of exercise weekly. We all should also do **muscle-strengthening activities** at moderate or greater intensity that involve all major muscle groups on two or more days a week, as these provide additional health benefits. The World Health Organization also recommends **limiting the amount of time spent being sedentary**. Replacing sedentary time with physical activity of any intensity (including light intensity) provides health benefits. Also, to help reduce the detrimental effects of high levels of sedentary behavior on health, it is recommended for all adults and older adults to aim to do more than the recommended levels of moderate (e.g., walking, dancing, and biking) to vigorous intensity exercise (e.g., brisk walking, jogging, fast swimming, running, and fast cycling).

This means getting **at a minimum 150 minutes** of any movement that gets your heart beating faster while being able to talk without having trouble breathing. Such an effect can be achieved by walking briskly to school or around the campus, swimming after classes, walking your neighbor's dog, or cleaning up your room (while listening to music of course! :-)). You can substitute that with at least 75 minutes of moving while breathing faster, finding it hard to talk. Vigorous-intensity aerobic activity will get your heart rate up quite a bit and will make you sweat. Biking up a hill, running, or playing basketball can help you get there!

You might want to cut the 150 minutes down to 20 minutes of "exercise snacks". It might be especially desirable to move during your highly sedentary study day to avoid sitting for many hours in a row.
Your weekly schedule of exercise could look like this:

• Biking to school and back 2 times a week (20 minutes each way, 80 minutes in total)
• Taking a short yoga class on YouTube twice a week right after you get back to the dorms from school (40 minutes total)
• 10 minutes of brisk walking around the campus (e.g. walking to the library, walking around the campus to stretch your body, going to get your coffee at your favorite coffee shop…) 3 times a week (30 minutes total)

Find something that can be easily included in your routine, sounds fun and doable, and you are good to go!
The best way to incorporate some physical activity into your life is to find something that **you enjoy**. Explore different types of exercise, move your body in a variety of ways, and see what works for you. To maintain your health and balance your body movement benefits, devote your time to different types of exercise.

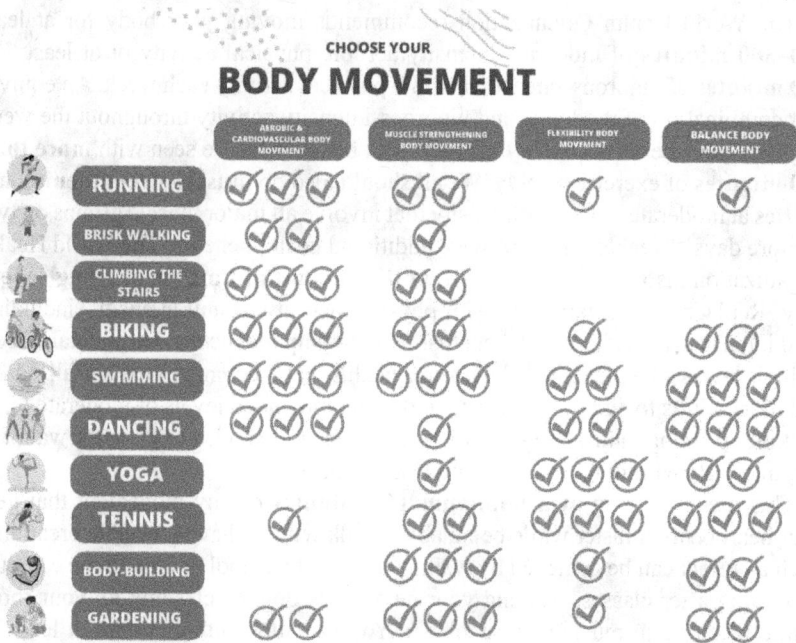

CHOOSE YOUR
BODY MOVEMENT

	Aerobic & Cardiovascular Body Movement	Muscle Strengthening Body Movement	Flexibility Body Movement	Balance Body Movement
RUNNING	✓✓✓	✓✓	✓	✓
BRISK WALKING	✓✓	✓		
CLIMBING THE STAIRS	✓✓✓	✓✓		
BIKING	✓✓✓	✓✓	✓	✓✓
SWIMMING	✓✓✓	✓✓✓	✓✓	✓✓✓
DANCING	✓✓✓	✓	✓✓	✓✓✓
YOGA		✓	✓✓✓	✓✓
TENNIS	✓	✓✓	✓✓✓	✓✓✓
BODY-BUILDING		✓✓✓	✓	✓✓
GARDENING	✓✓	✓✓✓	✓	✓✓

Figure 7.4 Body movement activity throughout different types of exercise.

Simply move to become more active. And move it the way you like it. The U.S. Department of Health and Human Services (2022) asks – what is your move? Walk. Run. Dance. No matter who you are, you can find safe, fun ways to get active – **to move your way**.

You don't have to spend long hours at the gym to be healthy. Dan Buettner's research on Blue Zones, the places in the world where people live the longest and are healthiest – shows that these people moved over their lives **mostly naturally**. They walk to grocery stores; they bike to work or across the neighborhood to visit friends. They spend a lot of time out in nature and do all the housework such as cooking, cleaning, and gardening by themselves. All of this helps to stretch your body, strengthen your muscles, and burn calories. So, get creative and move your way! Walk to the library every day, bike around the campus, park farther from the building where your class is, and stretch your legs with a brisk walk every morning. Remember, the natural way of moving counts!

Move Your Way!

Walk. Run. Dance. Play. What's your move? Everyone needs a physical activity to be healthy. Explore the Move Your Way® tools, videos, and fact sheets with tips that make it easier to get a little more active.

Learn more at https://health.gov/moveyourway

Physical Activity Snacking

Research shows (Mental Health Foundation, 2022) that **even a short burst of ten minutes' brisk walking** increases our mental alertness, energy, and positive mood. Participation in regular physical activity can increase our self-esteem and resiliency – our capacity to bounce back from life difficulties.

Physical activity "snacking" is a suitable way to incorporate brief exercises spread throughout your school day. It is an easy way to break **long hours of sitting down**. What does it look like? It can be something as small as stretching on your chair between classes, walking while on the phone with your loved ones, or doing a few squats at home while taking a break from studying.

**TIPS TO YOUR
PHYSICAL ACTIVITY**

SNACKING

Make it quick, easy and fun!

1 min STRETCH YOUR BODY ON THE CHAIR BETWEEN CLASSES		**5 mins** WALK WHILE BEING ON THE PHONE WITH YOUR LOVED ONES
10 mins WALK TO A SNACK SHOP TO GET YOUR REFRESHMENT		**4 mins** VACUUM YOUR ROOM
1 min USE STAIRS IN STEAD OF ELEVATOR		**1 min** TAKE YOUR COFFEE TO GO AND WALK AROUND CAMPUS
15 mins BIKE TO SCHOOL AND AROUND THE CAMPUS		**15 mins** PARK YOUR CAR A BIT FARTHER AND WALK
3 mins DO SQUATS EVERY TIME YOU TAKE A BREAK FROM STUDYING		**3 mins** WALK NEIGHBOR'S DOG AFTER SCHOOL

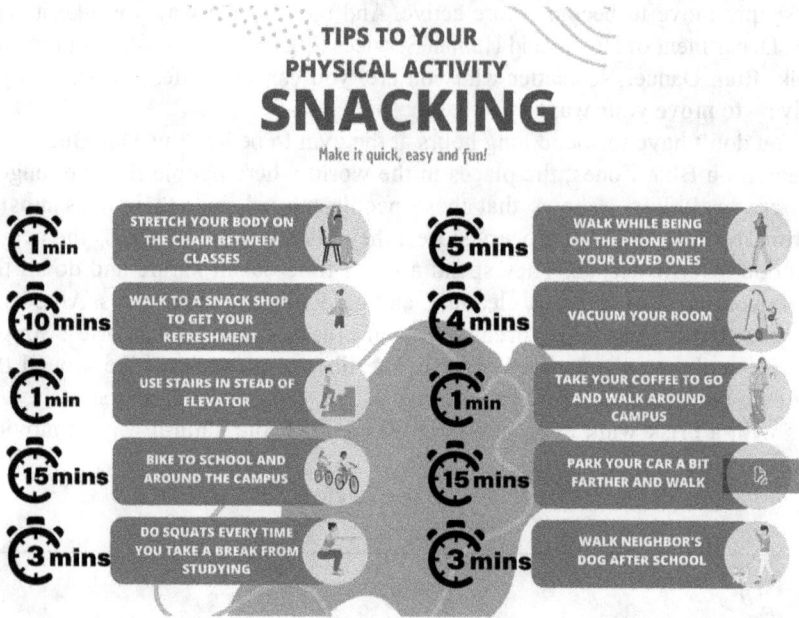

Figure 7.5 Physical activity snacking board.

Ten Tips to Get Your Body Moving!

1 Put planned exercise on your calendar and treat it with the same level of **priority** as any other event, meeting, or class. Remember, what is not planned does not happen :-) if it's necessary to cancel it, reschedule your exercise immediately.

2 **Track** your movement with up-to-date apps, smart watches, or phones. Celebrate your progress and encourage yourself to continue with your movement.

3 **Use any chance to move.** Step out of the bus one stop sooner and walk the rest to stretch your legs. Walk around the campus anytime you have a chance. Go and talk to your teacher in person instead of writing them an email.

4 **Find a buddy** to join or create a group with your classmates. Ask your friend to walk to school with you, create a group of friends who are on the same page as you, and enjoy weekend trips together. Add your classmates to your Garmin account and track each other's success.

5 Make it fun! Buy some pretty, colorful running shoes that you will be **excited to put on**. Join a friend you enjoy being with for a gym session. Or if you feel like being alone, make the time for yourself and go to the Rec Center alone. Put your headphones on and play your favorite music. Do anything that makes you more excited to move and enjoy it!

6 Fake it till you make it!" Any time you go to a practice, imagine how skilled "your ideal version of yourself" already is. Imagine how mastering this new skill **would feel**. Take this identity on and walk like you already are the master!

7 Take the first small step. If you decide to start swimming regularly, check the opening hours of swimming pools in your neighborhood. Buy yourself

swimming goggles. Check the condition of your swimsuits. Do anything that is easily doable and that will help you get started. **Think big but start small!**

8 Visualize. If you decide to go for a run tomorrow, sit down for a minute today and **imagine every step** you must undertake to make it happen. Prepare the sports clothes and running shoes, and charge your smart watch. After that, you just open the door and run out of the dorms. Having your brain experience the action in your mind first significantly increases your chance of really doing it!

9 **Work with your schedule** – take advantage of a window in between your classes. Sign up for dancing lessons. Jump on a treadmill at the campus recreation center or go for a swim regularly.

10 Use your **student benefits**! Check your possibilities as a student; many sport facilities offer cheaper entries, universities offer special events only for students; and many campuses offer healthy student life coaching.

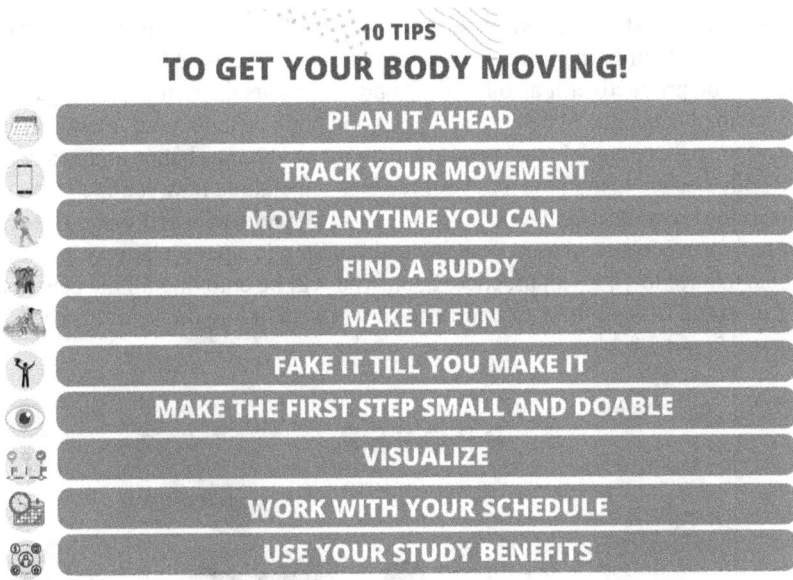

10 TIPS
TO GET YOUR BODY MOVING!

- PLAN IT AHEAD
- TRACK YOUR MOVEMENT
- MOVE ANYTIME YOU CAN
- FIND A BUDDY
- MAKE IT FUN
- FAKE IT TILL YOU MAKE IT
- MAKE THE FIRST STEP SMALL AND DOABLE
- VISUALIZE
- WORK WITH YOUR SCHEDULE
- USE YOUR STUDY BENEFITS

Figure 7.6 Ten tips to get your body moving!

Get Your Body Moving

Are you ready to get your body moving? Use the U.S. Department of Health and Human Services' interactive tool to build your activity plan here:

https://health.gov/moveyourway/activity-planner

Do it **Fifteen Minutes Morning Yoga Practice**

Do you feel like you could use some short and complex morning stretches to start your day right? Sun salutation can be a great fit for you. Try this simple yet very effective Sunrise Yoga with Adriene:

https://www.youtube.com/watch?v=r7xsYgTeM2Q

Good Body Posture

A proper body posture influences not only how well your body **functions** but also how **you feel**. Your body posture impacts your energy levels and your capability to focus and be productive. It also helps you prevent yourself from getting injured or even having headaches. When maintaining good body posture, your internal organs have more space to work better; hence, you digest and breathe better, and as a bonus, good body posture also influences your feelings – including how confident you are.

Learning to walk, stand, and sit properly **may feel awkward** at first because your body has become so used to sitting and standing in a particular way, but it will become natural to you with practice. Soon, you will be enjoying all the benefits of good posture! To learn how to stand and sit while attending the lectures, checkout Figures 7.7 and 7.8.

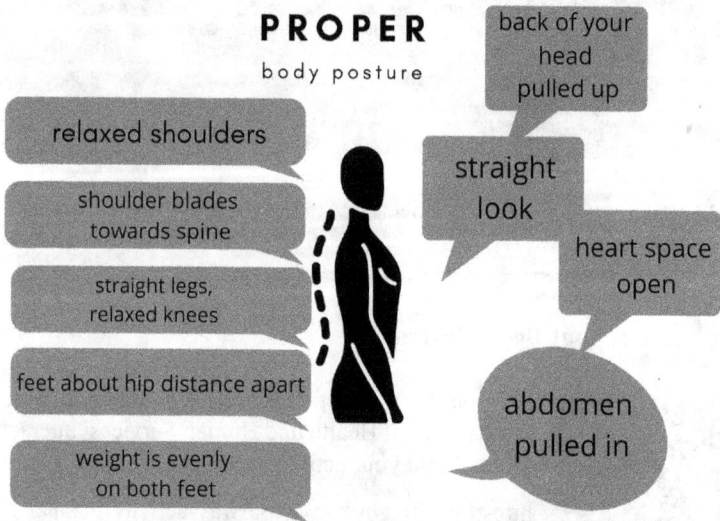

PROPER

body posture

relaxed shoulders

shoulder blades towards spine

straight legs, relaxed knees

feet about hip distance apart

weight is evenly on both feet

back of your head pulled up

straight look

heart space open

abdomen pulled in

Figure 7.7 Tips to stand properly.

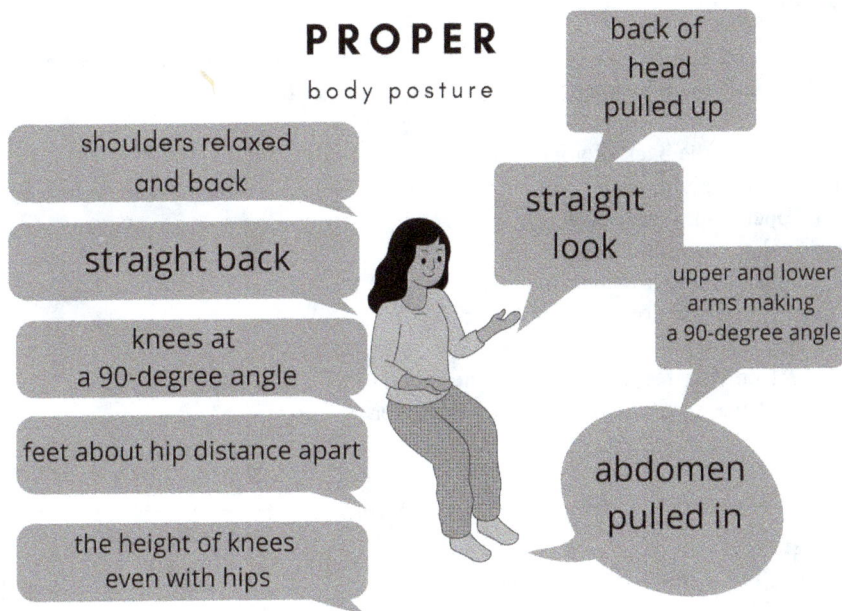

Figure 7.8 Tips to sit at school properly.

To Learn More about Benefits of Proper Body Posture Watch the Video from Ted-Ed Production!

Has anyone ever told you, "Stand up straight!" or scolded you for slouching at a family dinner? Comments like that might be annoying – but they're not wrong. Your posture is the foundation for every movement your body makes and can determine how well your body adapts to the stresses on it. Murat Dalkilinç gives the pros of a good posture.

https://www.youtube.com/watch?v=OyK0oE5rwFY

Proper Standing Practice

Think of an activity you do every day (such as brushing your teeth) that could be a great opportunity to practice proper body posture. Tie correcting your body posture by brushing your teeth. Try not to forget (place a sticky note on the mirror at first if it helps) to practice your proper body posture every day to make it a natural part of who you are.

- pull up the back of your head
- look straight
- open your heart space
- relax your shoulders
- push shoulder blades towards your spine
- pull your abdomen in
- straighten your legs and keep your knees relaxed
- place your feet about hip distance apart
- balance your weight evenly on both feet

Do it **Proper Sitting Practice**

Every time you start a class, use it as a reminder to correct your sitting. Use any tricks to not forget (remind your friends to sit well and have them to remind you as well) practicing your proper body posture every day to make it a natural part of who you are.

- pull the back of your head up
- look straight
- straighten your back
- relax your shoulders and pull them back
- have your upper and lower arms make a 90-degree angle
- pull your abdomen in
- place your knees at a 90-degree angle
- feet about hip distance apart
- balance height of your knee with the height of your hips

Power Poses

Believe it or not, the way you carry your body can **influence how you feel** and may even increase the possibility of **performing better** during high-stakes so- cial evaluations, such as giving a speech or presenting your project to your class. As Harvard's professor Amy Cuddy says, your body posture and body language may **shape who you are**. Professor Cuddle and her team had their research par- ticipants adopt expansive, open (high-power) poses or contractive, closed (low- power) poses and had them prepare and deliver a speech as a part of a simulated interview afterwards. As predicted, high-power posers performed better and were more likely to be hired (Cuddy et al., 2012). Professor Cuddle says that **as little as two minutes in a power pose** can make you feel more powerful and perform better. Try to check your body posture every morning and every night while brushing your teeth in front of the mirror and create a new habit of walking and sitting confidently. Spend as little as 2 minutes in a power pose (see Figure 7.9) before you leave the dorms to write a test or to present in front of your classmates. It is really a negligible time investment that brings about wonderful results.

Figure 7.9 Power poses to adopt.

Learn More about the Power of Power Poses

Amy Cuddy's research on body language reveals that we can change other people's perceptions – and perhaps even our own body chemistry – simply by changing body positions.

To learn more, watch Amy Cuddy's TED Talk here:

https://www.ted.com/talks/amy_cuddy_your_body_language_may_shape_who_you_are

Optimal Nutrition

Your body deserves to be provided with the **highest quality nutrition** in order function positively. But also to be capable of peak performance to keep up with your student lifestyle.

Eating well – having a balanced diet full of natural foods rich in nutrients (dark leafy vegetables, fruits of all colors), healthy fats, and high-quality protein in every meal – can improve your sense of mental well-being, your current mood, and cognition. Your ability to think, concentrate, and remember.

Healthy Eating Plate

Learn to work with the Healthy Eating Plate (Figure 7.10) created by nutrition experts at the Harvard T.H. Chan School of Public Health and editors at Harvard Health Publications. The Healthy Eating Plate is a simple, understandable, and practical guide, teaching you **how much of what you eat should come from each food group** to achieve a healthy, balanced diet. Practice composing your nutrition throughout your day in accordance with Harvard's guidelines. Healthy Eating Plate can help you maintain a balanced diet and discover what works best for your body. This practical tool was created based on the most up-to-date nutrition research, and it is not influenced by any food industry or agriculture policy.

To maintain a healthy body weight, energy intake (measured in calories) should be in balance with energy expenditure. But a healthy diet is much more than tracking your calories. It is **more about the quality than the quantity of the food**. Navigate your daily nutrition with the Healthy Eating Plate (2011) recommendations and focus on the quality of your diet:

- Eat and snack on plenty of vegetables and fruits (half of the plate) of various colors every day. Always prioritize them over processed sweets in the dining hall.
- The carbohydrate type is, according to the Healthy Eating Plate, more important than the amount of said carbohydrate in the diet. This means that some sources of carbohydrates – such as vegetables (other than potatoes), fruits, whole grains, and beans – are more beneficial than others. See the list of "foods to prioritize" below.
- Drink plenty of still, pure water from the fountains in school halls. Make some green tea at home while studying or have a cup of coffee while taking a break between classes. Try to ignore the vending machines around the campus and avoid sugary beverages, a major source of calories in our everyday diet.
- Go for whole grains for a quarter of every plate you make yourself in the dining hall.
- Include healthy protein in every meal you eat at school or at home.
- Use healthy oils, limit butter, and avoid trans fats as much as possible.

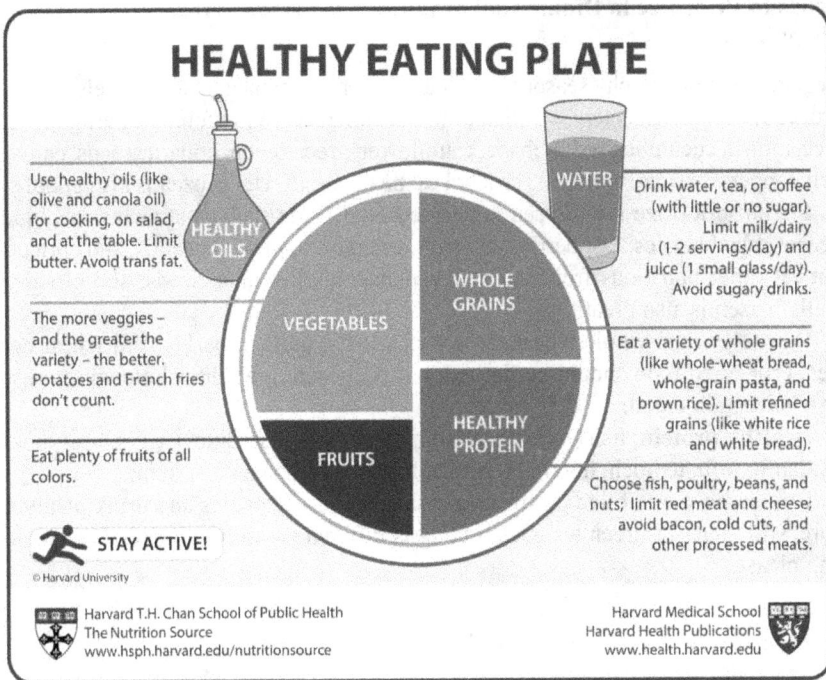

Figure 7.10 Healthy eating plate (Harvard, 2011).

Learn more about the Harvard Medical School's resources and access their downloadable tools, including over 25 translations of the Healthy Eating Plate: hsph.me/hep20

Foods to Prioritize in Dining Hall or to Look for While Grocery Shopping for Home

Vegetables: non-starchy seasonal vegetables such as spinach, kale, brussels sprouts, broccoli, asparagus, celery, eggplant, mushroom, zucchini, onion, leek, arugula, lettuce, radish, cucumber, red cabbage, cauliflower, green onion, collard greens, endive, bell peppers, carrots, tomatoes, artichokes, beats, herbs, etc. Frozen is also good!

Fruits: prioritize low-glycemic and seasonal fruits such as strawberries, blueberries, blackberries, raspberries, cherries, oranges, apples, avocados, and apricots, but eat other nutritious fruits such as bananas, apples, nuts, seeds, and olives as well. Frozen is also great!

Whole grains: whole wheat, brown rice, oats, quinoa, barley, and wheat berries. Processed food should be limited, but if chosen, grab the whole wheat pasta or whole grain bread.

Healthy protein: fish (such as salmon, mackerel, or sardines), eggs, beef, poultry, lamb, tofu, tempeh, hummus, lentils, beans, nuts, yogurt, or kefir.

Drip some virgin olive oil over your salads and vegetables and drink plenty of pure, still water or green tea. Celebrating is fun, but try to limit alcohol consumption please.

Brain Foods

Research suggests that a healthy, balanced diet can help **you do better at school**! A 2015 study from UCLA (Arab & Ang, 2015) linked higher walnut consumption to improved cognitive test scores. These significant, positive associations between walnut consumption and cognitive functions among all adults, regardless of age, gender, or ethnicity, suggest that **daily walnut intake may be a simple beneficial dietary behavior**.

Maintain good brain health by eating high-quality foods (vegetables, fruits, legumes, and wholegrains that are rich in vitamins, minerals, fiber, and antioxidants) that nourish the brain and protect it from oxidative stress to keep it in peak condition.

Enrich your diet with some of the favorite brain foods below that also, according to research, protect your heart and blood vessels:

- fatty (oily) fish (salmon, cod, mackerel, tuna including canned light tuna, sardines, and pollack)
- nuts and seeds (walnuts, almonds, pumpkin seeds)
- green tea or coffee
- berries (blueberries, strawberries, blackberries, raspberries)
- avocado
- turmeric and other spices and herbs
- broccoli and green (leafy) vegetables (spinach, kale, collards)
- eggs
- dark chocolate
- fermented foods
- oranges

Mindful Eating

Mindful eating and focusing on incorporating brain foods into your diet can also really help eliminate stress and increase your academic performance and life satisfaction. Thus, boost your mental well-being and overall health in the process.

Check and practice these seven strategies of mindful eating in your everyday life (originally published in the book SAVOR: Mindful Eating, Mindful Life by Thich Nhat Hanh and Dr. Lilian Cheung):

- with every meal you eat, honor the food
- engage all senses
- serve in modest portions
- savor small bites and chew thoroughly
- eat slowly to avoid overeating
- don't skip meals
- eat a plant-based diet for your health and for the planet

Let Harvard T.H. Chan – School of Public Health Help You to Adopt a Healthy and Balanced Diet!

Eat real food. That's the essence of today's nutrition message. Our knowledge of nutrition has come full circle, back to eating food that is as close as possible to the way nature created it. Based on the solid foundations of current nutrition science and Harvard's Special Health Reports, the school of public health presents freely accessible Guides to Healthy Eating: Strategies, tips, and recipes to help you make better food choices, which describes how to eat for optimum health.

Healthy Living Guide 2020/2021: A Digest on Healthy Eating and Healthy Living

https://www.hsph.harvard.edu/nutritionsource/2021/01/19/healthy-living-guide-2020-2021/

Healthy Living Guide 2021/2022: A Digest on Healthy Eating and Healthy Living

https://www.hsph.harvard.edu/nutritionsource/2022/01/06/healthy-living-guide-2021-2022/

High-Quality Sleep

Good Night's Sleep

Every living organism on the planet needs sleep, even if only a small amount of it. Just like diet and exercise, a good night's sleep is essential for our good health, for keeping us alert and energetic, and for building our body's defense against infection, chronic illness, and even heart disease (Harvard Medical School, 2019).

Sleep is an **integral component of human health**, and sleep loss can adversely affect the way we function in our everyday lives – including our academic performance. According to the sleep expert, Professor Matthew Walker from the University of California, Berkeley, rapid eye movement (REM) sleep **boosts learning and memory** and **affects our mood**. Getting enough REM sleep can improve recall and memory consolidation and help our brain regulate the synapses associated with some types of motor learning as well.

Walker (2018) explains that our sleeping patterns have a direct influence on our waking behavior (mood, ability to focus during classes and to recall what we learned), but our daytime activities influence our sleep right back (larger evening meals, exercising in later hours, or accumulated stress throughout the day can affect the quality of your sleep).

Sleep also plays a fundamental role in the recovery process from fatigue, but other functions can be dependent on it as well. Sleep is important because it can help students physically heal, recover from illness, deal with stress from school, solve problems in our daily lives as well as during our learning processes at school, consolidate memories, and improve our motor skills. However, be aware that a good night's sleep isn't just about how many hours of sleep we get, but also **the quality of that sleep** (Walker, 2018).

Both sleep deprivation and poor sleep quality are prominent in today's society, especially in university student populations. Research is very clear in associating poor sleep quality with lower academic performance (Gilbert & Cameron, 2010; Lee et al., 2021; Peach et al., 2016; Schlarb et al., 2017; Walter et al., 2002).

University students are one of the top at-risk groups for chronic sleep loss and poor sleep quality, which can have deleterious effects on their health. The university student population is also notorious for poor sleep hygiene or modifiable behaviors that promote insufficient sleep quantity and quality.

Students face many challenges and experiences that may lead to sleep difficulties. To name a few, these university students' difficulties include:

- varied and changing schedules every few months
- repeated deadlines that are stressful
- increased freedom that puts a higher demand on self-responsibility to care for student's health by e.g. not sleeping in too often
- group living arrangements that often cause higher levels of noise or other sleep disturbing
- high levels of perceived stress, including lifetime traumatic stress

The quality of university students' sleep really matters. On average, most university students only get 6–6.9 hours of sleep per night, and college students are notoriously sleep-deprived for years due to an overload of activities. Up to 60% of all college students suffer from poor sleep quality, and 7.7% meet all criteria for an insomnia disorder. Sleep problems have a great impact on the students' daily life, including their grade point average. Recent research on university students and sleep indicates that insufficient sleep also impacts the health of our students, their moods, their GPA, and their safety.

As students, due to irregular daytime routines, chronotype changes, part-time jobs, and exam periods, you need an **individualized approach** for improving your sleep. It can be very beneficial to create your own strategy for better sleep. Explore the following tips to fall asleep more quickly and see what works for you the best.

Tips for Better and Healthier Sleep

Do you have trouble sleeping? Try the following 12 tips for a healthy sleep originally published by the NIH Medline Plus in Walker (2018) adapted for university students:

1   Stick to a sleep schedule. As creatures of habit, people have a hard time adjusting to changes in sleep patterns. Sleeping in on weekends won't fully make up for the lack of sleep during the week and will make it harder to wake up early on Monday morning. Also, as strange as it sounds, learn to set an alarm for your bedtime. Often, we set an alarm for when it's time to wake up but fail to do so for when it's time to go to sleep. We know how hard it can be for a student who has an irregular schedule and how tempting it is to sleep in on the days when the classes start later. But if there is only one piece of advice you should remember and take from these 12 tips, Walker says that it should be this: **go to bed and wake up at the same time each day**.

2   Exercise is great, but not too late in the day. Try to exercise for at least 30 minutes on most days but **not later than 2–3 hours before bedtime**. Be your own time manager and plan your exercise in accordance with your class schedule – each week in advance.

3   I know this one can be hard for students, but avoid caffeine and nicotine. Coffee, many soda drinks, certain teas, and chocolate contain a stimulant called caffeine. And its effects can take **as long as 8 hours to fully wear off**. Keep in mind that a cup of coffee in the late afternoon can make it hard for you to fall asleep at night. If you are meeting your classmates for a study group in the afternoon, order yourself a cup of herbal tea or decaffeinated coffee instead of coffee. Nicotine is also a stimulant, often causing smokers to sleep only very lightly. In addition, smokers often wake up too early in the morning because of nicotine withdrawal.

4   **Avoid alcoholic drinks before bed.** I know that having a nightcap or alcoholic beverage before sleep may help you relax, but heavy use robs you of REM sleep, keeping you in the lighter stages of sleep. Heavy alcohol ingestion may also contribute to impaired breathing at night. You also tend to wake

up in the middle of the night when the effects of the alcohol have worn off. Be especially mindful of cutting off your alcoholic beverages over the examination period, when a good night's sleep can really help you perform at your best.

5   **Avoid large meals and beverages late at night.** A light snack is okay, but a large meal can cause indigestion, which interferes with sleep. Schedule your meals in advance to fit them between your classes to avoid hunger and overeating at night. Also, drinking large amounts of fluids at night can cause frequent awakenings to urinate.

6   If possible, avoid medications that delay or disrupt your sleep. Some commonly prescribed heart, blood pressure, or asthma medications, as well as some over-the-counter and herbal remedies for coughs, colds, or allergies, can disrupt sleep patterns. If you have trouble sleeping, talk to your health care provider or pharmacist to see whether **any drugs you're taking might be contributing to your sleep disturbance** and ask whether they can be taken at other times during the day or early in the evening.

7   Don't take naps after 3 p.m. Naps can help make up for lost sleep, but **late afternoon naps can make it harder to fall asleep at night**. If you feel tired after a long day at school, take a power nap: lie down for 10 minutes to rest and recharge, but try not to fall asleep.

8   Relax before bed. Don't overschedule your day so that there is no time left for **unwinding**. A relaxing activity, such as reading or listening to music, should be part of your bedtime ritual. But by reading I do not mean studying. This is your time to relax, which means that no studying before bed is allowed. Instead, please try the mindfulness meditations or relaxing exercises presented in this chapter.

9   Take a hot bath before bed. The drop in body temperature after getting out of the bath may help you feel sleepy. **Taking a bath can help you relax** and slow down so you're more ready to sleep. Plus, you deserve some relaxation after a long day of learning and studying.

10 Dark bedroom, cool bedroom, gadget-free bedroom. **Get rid of anything in your bedroom that might distract you from sleep,** such as noises, bright lights, an uncomfortable bed, or high temperature. You sleep better if the temperature in the room is kept on the cool side. Any TV, cell phone, or computer in the bedroom can be a distraction and deprive you of much needed sleep. If you need your phone to use an alarm to get up for your morning classes, buy yourself a regular alarm clock. Having a phone in our bedroom is tempting for us to check social media or emails before bedtime or even during the night when we wake up. Having a comfortable mattress and pillow can help promote a good night's sleep. Individuals who have insomnia often watch the clock. Turn the clock's face out of view so you don't worry about the time while you're trying to fall asleep.

11 Have the right sunlight exposure. Daylight is key to regulating daily sleep patterns. Try to **get outside in natural** sunlight for at least 30 minutes each

day. Any time you can do so, go out for a short brisk walk. Or eat your lunch outside on the grass or on the bench in front of your house. If possible, wake up with the sun or use very bright lights in the morning. If you have problems falling asleep, sleep experts recommend that you get an hour of exposure to morning sunlight and turn down the lights before bedtime.

12 **Don't lie in bed awake.** Many students like to do so in the morning while still having some time to get ready for classes. I assume that many students also like watching movies in their bed. Who does not, right? However, try to watch your favorite show somewhere else other than your bed to prevent associating your sleeping place with awake time. Ideally outside of your bedroom, if possible. If you find yourself still awake after staying in bed for more than 20 minutes or if you are starting to feel anxious or worried, get up and do some relaxing activity until you feel sleepy again. The anxiety of not being able to sleep can make it harder to fall asleep.

Regular Relaxation

Being relaxed is our very **natural state**, even though our hectic and fast life-style makes us believe the exact opposite. Being in tension can keep us **alert** and **focused**, so we can **memorize things better** and be more **productive**. But only for a certain period of time. We don't want to be tense long-term and cause ourselves more harm than good. Unchecked tension in our bodies and minds can contribute to many health problems, including **high blood pressure, constant nervousness** and **worrying, increased anxiety, sleep problems, back pain, headaches**, and much more. Paying attention to our bodies, starting to notice when we are in tension, and developing the skill to relax can be crucial strengths to develop to care for your well-being. But how do we do that? Practice. As with any other skill, you will become better and better over time, and you will be able to relax quickly enough after finding yourself in tension eventually.

Relaxation and Meditation among Students

The *Healthy Minds* program (2017) is an organization based in the United Kingdom that teaches life tools and techniques for well-being. It is a strong promoter of the importance of good mental health in young people and in university students within education and life in general.

Studies conducted on over 1,800 students from all around the world have found that meditation improves mental **well-being, academic skills**, and **social abilities** in students. Youngsters who were taught meditation in school reported better concentration on their tasks. They were also more self-confident and had a more positive outlook on life. Meditation has been shown to promote a stronger self-identity and higher optimism.

The *Healthy Minds* program states these benefits of relaxation and meditation:

- increases happiness
- reduces stress and anxiety
- boosts confidence and motivation
- improves self-awareness and relationships
- more memory recall
- increases intelligence
- clear, sharp mind
- better decision-making and life choices
- turning negative thinking into positive thinking
- time-out for children and young people to relax and learn to still their minds and calm their bodies

---

Do It Mindfulness Meditation

Have you ever tried mindfulness meditation? If not, listen to a guided loving-kindness meditation created by scientist Barbara Fredrickson with current knowledge on how to regulate your emotions.

To listen to the meditation, go to: https://www.positivityresonance.com/meditations.html.

You can practice this in the morning before you head to school, between your classes to calm down, or before bedtime to get relaxed and prepared for a good night's sleep.

There's an App for That! Get Your Own UCLA Mindful!

With this easy-to-use app, you can practice mindfulness meditation anywhere, anytime, with the guidance of the UCLA Mindful Awareness Research Center. Scientific research shows mindfulness can help manage stress-related physical conditions, reduce anxiety and depression, cultivate positive emotions, and improve overall physical health and well-being.

https://apps.apple.com/us/app/ucla-mindful/id1459128935?ls=1

There's Another Cool App for That! Download Your Calm App – The #1 App for Meditation and Sleep

Do It

Their goal is to help you improve your health and happiness.

What can Calm help with today?

To improve sleep quality, reduce stress or anxiety, improve focus, self-improvement, and more.

https://www.calm.com

Facilitating Mindfulness

Are you interested in the research behind mindfulness to release stress? Or are you looking for some practical tips to train your awareness and learn how to relax your body, heart, and mind? UCLA Mindful Awareness Research Center is here for you!

The mission of the Mindful Awareness Research Center (MARC) is to disseminate mindful awareness across the lifespan through education and research. You can learn more about the research behind mindfulness as well as find many practical tools to release tension and relax your body, heart, and mind with free classes, workshops, or guided meditations!

https://www.uclahealth.org/marc/default.cfm

Proper Breathing

We could spend some time discussing what came first – the egg or the chicken. There is a similar relationship between our bodies and our breathing. We don't know what affected the other first, but what we do know is that the state of our body affects our breathing and vice versa – **our breathing affects our body**. As a result, our breathing impacts our mood, cognition performance, and the brain itself. Learning how to control your breath can help you manage your mood and alertness, which can be handy in both stressful times before exams or oral presentations and when getting tired while studying for too long when a little waking up would come in handy. Generally, extending your exhales compared to inhales can help you **to calm down**, and deepening your breaths in compared to breaths out can help you to oxygenate your brain and **to become alert** again!

Proper breathing can be a gamechanger for students, especially considering that most students sit slouched at school for hours. Hunching over gets your chest and rib cage in a position which is less favorable to your lungs. It results in making air delivery and carbon dioxide exhalation harder. Consequentially, you get sleepy and less able to focus and memorize the information – the exact thing we want to avoid while learning and studying!

So, how do you know whether your breathing is proper or not? If you're breathing effectively, your breaths are relaxed, smooth, controlled, and expend your whole core. Your breath should feel easy and satisfying.

Belly Breathing:

You can practice belly breathing basically anywhere. In your bed right after you wake up in the morning, during classes at school, or in line while waiting for your coffee at your favorite coffee shop. Let's have a look at what **good belly breathing** looks like while sitting on a chair.

Properly relaxed belly breathing to practice while sitting in classes or by computer:

- sit up straight, but relaxed, with your knees bent and feet hip-width apart (check the proper sitting body posture exercise)
- let consciously go of any tension in your body, shoulders, neck, and core (imagine the tension leaving your body like a steam)
- put your hands on the sides of your rib cage so you can feel the movement of your diaphragm
- inhale slowly through your nose primarily into your belly and lower back, feeling your stomach expand into the rib cage (breathe into an imaginary circle around your central body), and exhale using pursed lips
- you can check your back expansion by placing your hands there
- do not eliminate your chest breathing completely, you should also feel gentle activity in here
- focus on gentle inhales and try to extend breaths out to slow down your breathing rhythm

---

Try a Breathing Exercise to Reduce Stress

Headspace shares how to try breathing exercises to reduce stress when we have to give a big speech, hear some disappointing news, or get a case of the Sunday scares. So we'll know what to do to feel better next time: breathe.

https://www.youtube.com/watch?v=OXjlR4mXxSk

Do It   **Physiological Sight to Reduce Anxiety**

"Stress is an inevitable part of life and if you are a student and you are serious about your studies, you're going to experience stress. That's just the reality." Professor Andrew Huberman from Sandford University says. Let Professor Huberman teach you a super quick and easy pattern of breathing called physiological sighs that will help you relax anytime you get stressed in your everyday life. "Just one to three of those physiological sighs can bring you from a state of intense anxiety and stress to very very calm." Dr. Andrew says.

Learn physiological sighs with Professor Huberman here: https://www.youtube.com/shorts/9JhTMTksk9s

Avoidance of Risky Behavior

Risky behavior is such behavior that **increases** the chance of **injury or illness or social problems in** our lives. It can potentially do more harm than good to us and may prevent us from reaching our full potential in life.

The World Health Organization defines such behaviors as *"behaviors that increase the likelihood of a negative health outcome, now or in the future – for example, excessive alcohol use."*

To strengthen your **avoidance of risky behaviors strength**, try to:

- eat a mindfully balanced diet in the most suitable regimen that fits your way of living
- be mindful of your alcohol consumption; avoid drinking alcohol or consume it in moderation to prevent binge drinking and heavy drinking
  - The Centers for Disease Control and Prevention (2019) define binge-drinking in women as four or more drinks consumed on one occasion (one occasion = 2–3 hours). For men, binge drinking is five or more drinks consumed during one occasion. Heavy drinking for women is eight drinks or more per week. For men, heavy drinking is 15 drinks or more per week
- avoid smoking, vaping, and tobacco consumption
- protect yourself in sexual encounters
- use social media wisely and in moderation
- say no to illegal substance use
- drive safely, wear a seatbelt, and be responsible while crossing streets (look both ways before crossing the street)
- do adrenaline sports safely while having a professional to assist you
- protect yourself while doing sports by wearing a helmet and other protection
- avoid illegal activities like trespassing or vandalism
- be mindful while processing your negative emotions such as anger and don't fight
- prevent truancy in students by always looking for meaning in your study activities
- fill up your free time with meaningful activities you enjoy doing

If you choose to drink, do so in moderation:

- up to one drink a day for women
- up to two drinks a day for men
- don't drink at all if you are under age 21, pregnant or may be pregnant, or have health problems that could be made worse by drinking (CDC, 2019)

U.S. standard drink sizes (CDC, 2019):

- 12 ounces of 5% ABV beer
- 8 ounces of 7% ABV malt liquor
- 5 ounces of 12% ABV wine
- 1.5 ounces of 40% ABV (80-proof) distilled spirits or liquor (examples: gin, rum, vodka, and whiskey)

Please remember that the potential health benefits of alcohol consumption are NOT BASED ON EVIDENCE.

Do it   **My Leisure Time Physical Health Activity Boost**

Identify physical activities related to your student lifestyle that help you fill your time valuably and sneak them into your student way of living.

What is your favorite way to enjoy your free time while moving? What activities help you have fun with friends? How do you like to calm down after a stressful day, what helps you recharge your batteries? Write down a list of all the fulfilling activities you like to do to rest from school, your work, and personal life duties. Analyze your list and highlight activities supporting your physical health that can be incorporated into your everyday life and carry them out in the upcoming week.

Do it   **Ten Empowering Questions to Support My Physical Health Flower Growth**

1   What is the smallest thing I can do to make my nutrition more balanced today?
2   What always makes my body and mind feel relaxed?
3   What positive effect do I feel when standing/sitting properly?
4   What helps me sleep better?

5   What works well for me when I desire to avoid or limit risky behavior?
6   What kind of movement does my body love?
7   What healthy foods do I really enjoy?
8   When can I stop to enjoy one deep breath in and out today?
9   What is my main reason to treat my body right today?
10   What else can I do to support my physical health today?

Do It   **Ten Tips to Build My Physical Health Flower**

1   Maintain your sleep schedule even though your school schedule can be very irregular sometimes. Get sunlight first thing in the morning, if possible.
2   Care for your body by eating real food (whole foods, healthy fats, protein, and low-glycemic foods) and drinking more filtered water or green tea.
3   Do body movement snacking in between long sittings at school or while studying at home. Find time to do some cardio or weight training during your week.
4   Take a break from social media during your day and be fully in the moment wherever you are.
5   Find a few moments for activities that help you relax every day. Enjoy a cup of coffee between classes, spend some quality time with loved ones after school, or take a relaxing walk somewhere in nature, whenever you have a chance.
6   Pay attention to your breath and calm yourself down by extending your breath, especially in times of accumulated stress such as exams or class presentations.
7   Use every opportunity to move more naturally during your school day. Move your way in at least 150–300 minutes of moderate-intensity aerobic physical activity for at least 75–150 minutes of vigorous-intensity aerobic physical activity (or an equivalent combination of moderate and vigorous-intensity activity) throughout your week.
8   Eat high-quality protein in every meal (e.g., meat, fish, and seafood, eggs, tofu, tempeh, dairy, or hummus).
9   Slow down on your evenings. Listen to some music, take a bath, or relax with a non-school book.
10   Cut your risky behavior in half. You can do it and your life will improve in every way.

Tips for Physical Health Snacking

Building your physical health does not have to be complicated nor time demanding. Look at Figure 7.11 and try some of the tips right now!

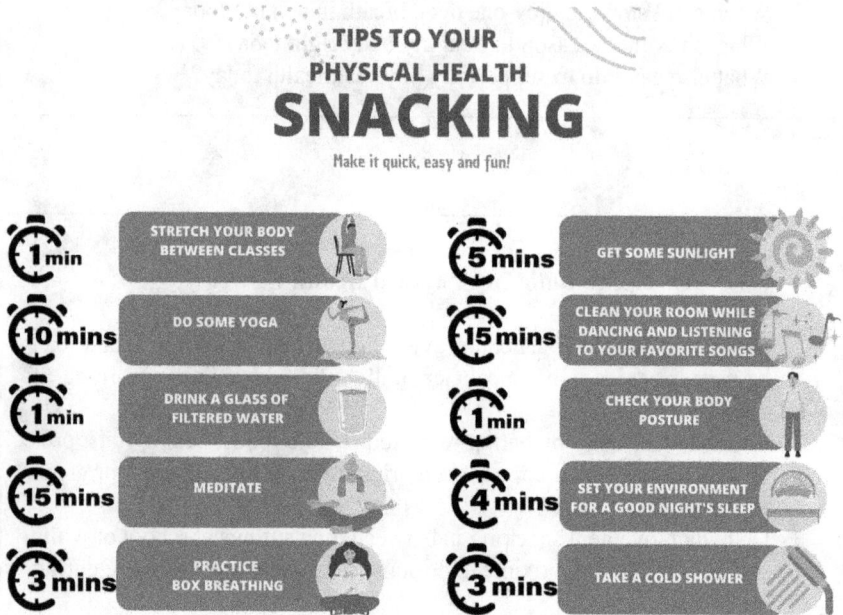

**TIPS TO YOUR
PHYSICAL HEALTH
SNACKING**

Make it quick, easy and fun!

1 min	STRETCH YOUR BODY BETWEEN CLASSES	**5 mins**	GET SOME SUNLIGHT
10 mins	DO SOME YOGA	**15 mins**	CLEAN YOUR ROOM WHILE DANCING AND LISTENING TO YOUR FAVORITE SONGS
1 min	DRINK A GLASS OF FILTERED WATER	**1 min**	CHECK YOUR BODY POSTURE
15 mins	MEDITATE	**4 mins**	SET YOUR ENVIRONMENT FOR A GOOD NIGHT'S SLEEP
3 mins	PRACTICE BOX BREATHING	**3 mins**	TAKE A COLD SHOWER

Figure 7.11 Tips to physical health snacking.

Building our physical health, day by day, is probably the best investment we can make for ourselves. But what if we see physical activity as something we "have" to do rather than something we "enjoy" doing? What if we see a good night's sleep as something "we are naturally bad at" rather than something we "can get better at"? What if we see balanced nutrition as something that is "not our thing" rather than something that "I choose to do to care for myself"? These slight shifts in perspective can make a big difference and impact our everyday lives significantly. Everything starts with our mindset. The tricky part is that most of our mindsets were already installed in our subconscious when we were children. We picked up on mindsets that our parents lived by, that our family members modeled for us, that our friends showed us, or that our teachers taught us. The whole culture's and society's common beliefs are imprinted in us and we often do not even realize that. It is time to reflect on your beliefs. To eliminate those that don't serve you anymore and to choose the beliefs you want for yourself. I would like to invite you to explore the upcoming chapter with me. You and I will look at the theory and science behind mindset to deepen your understanding and you will have a chance to pick and try some activities to build your growth and positive and healthy mindset day by day to live the life you choose for yourself.

References

Arab, A., & Ang, A. (2015, March). A cross sectional study of the association between walnut consumption and cognitive function among adult US populations represented in NHANES. *Journal of Nutrition, Health Aging*, 19(3), 284–290. https://doi.org/10.1007/s12603-014-0569-2.

Buboltz, W. C., Soper, B., Brown, F., & Jenkins, S. (2002). Treatment approaches for sleep difficulties in college students. *Counselling Psychology Quarterly*. Routledge, 15(3), s. 229–237. ISSN 0951-5070. https://doi.org/10.1080/09515070210151788

Cuddy, A., Wilmuth, C. A., & Carney, D. R. (2012). The benefit of power posing before a high-stakes social evaluation. Harvard Business School Working Paper, No. 13-027.

Gilbert, S. P., & Cameron C. W. (2010). Sleep quality and academic performance in university students: A wake-up call for college psychologists. *Journal of College Student Psychotherapy*. Routledge, 24(4), s. 295–306. ISSN 8756-8225. https://doi.org/10.1080/87568225.2010.509245

Harvard University (2011). Healthy eating plate. [Cited August 8, 2022]. Available at: https://www.hsph.harvard.edu/nutritionsource/healthy-eating-plate/

Harvard Medical School Special Health Report (2019). Improving sleep: A guide to a good night's rest. 53 pgs. Available at: https://www.health.harvard.edu/staying-healthy/improving-sleep-a-guide-to-a-good-nights-rest

Lee, H., Rautas, M. E., & Rachel A. (2021). FUSCO. Perceived stress and sleep quality among master's students in social work. *Social Work Education*. Routledge, 0(0), s. 1–17. ISSN 0261-5479. https://doi.org/10.1080/02615479.2021.1910231

Mental Health Foundation (2022). How to look after your mental health using exercise. [Cited August 1, 2021] Available at: https://www.mentalhealth.org.uk/sites/default/files/2022-07/How-to-exercise.pdf

Peach, H., Gaultney, J. F., & Gray, D. D. (2016). Sleep hygiene and sleep quality as predictors of positive and negative dimensions of mental health in college students. *Cogent Psychology*. Cogent OA, 3(1), s. 1168768. ISSN null. https://doi.org/10.1080/23311908.2016.1168768

Schlarb, A. A., Friedrich, A., & Claßen, M. (2017). Sleep problems in university students – An intervention. *Neuropsychiatric Disease and Treatment*, 13, 1989–2001. https://doi.org/10.2147/NDT.S142067

Stanlake, M. in Healthy Minds Relaxation Programs (2022). Benefits of meditation and relaxation sessions on mental health. Available at: https://www.healthyminds.org.uk/healthy-minds-program

U.S. Department of Health and Human Services (2022). Move your way. [Cited December 9, 2022] Available at: https://health.gov/moveyourway

Walker, M. (2018). Why we sleep. Penguin Books.

World Health Organization (2020). Physical activity. [Cited August 1, 2021] Available at: https://www.who.int/news-room/fact-sheets/detail/physical-activity

World Health Organization (2022). Unpacking "risk". https://apps.who.int/adolescent/second-decade/section/section_5/level5_5.php

8   Building Your Mindset

Whether you think you can, or you think you can't – you're right.

— Henry Ford

Two students are sitting close to you in the dining hall and you overhear their discussion. *"We are supposed to meet downtown so I don't even know where we will go. If we will go to have some dinner or if we will just walk around. So I have no idea what to wear. Gosh. I am just so nervous."* The first girl spoke with a certain frustration in her voice. The other girl looked at her smiling and said, *"Then don't go on a date! Go to a dinner or for a walk with some cute guy who reads the same books as you. You said you met him in a library, right?"* Now you get curious and you look at the girl who is supposed to go on a date tonight wanting to know more. *"I did,"* said the first girl. *"But what do you mean when you say don't go on a date?"* She looked back at her friend like she really needed an explanation. *"Well,"* started her friend. *"I am not dating. I am meeting new friends and if someone, someday turns into something more, great. But I am not seeing it as a date. That would make me nervous and I would not even be me. I don't want to put that kind of pressure on myself."* Her friend said this and smiled again. *"Oh!"* The first one stopped. *"I have never thought of that, but just the idea of seeing it as a walk with a new friend sounds more fun and relaxing. Thanks!"* she said. Yes thanks, you think for yourself too. I hadn't ever thought of that either, but I am going to use this strategy!

This is what a shift in your mind looks like in the real world. This is how easy it is and how powerful it can be. We all have our own viewpoints on different things, situations, and people in our lives.

Just changing our perception and setting our mind differently can strongly change how we feel about the situation which, as a result, helps us to behave in a more desirable way. Sound interesting? Then let's dive deeper into this chapter.

Introduction to Mindset

Do you believe in the power of a positive mindset and the value of seeing opportunities within challenges? Do you believe that confidence in your abilities impacts your success tremendously? And do you believe that our minds can influence our

DOI: 10.4324/9781003378365-9

health? I do too. Luckily, we don't have to rely only on our gut feelings anymore. This chapter will focus on the science of mindset, on understanding how mindsets can be changed, and on what can be done to positively affect our physiological and psychological well-being through the setting of our minds. You will learn what a growth mindset is and how to redirect a fixed mindset. And you will also be invited to practice tools to adopt beliefs that will serve you the best in a playful and fun way.

But what is mindset and how does it shape our lives?

Alia Crum, an associate professor of psychology at Stanford University, defines mindsets as **our core assumptions that we make about the things and processes in the world that orient us to a particular set of expectations, explanations, and goals (2019)**. For example, "aging is an inevitable decline," "failing at school means that I am not smart enough," and "healthy foods taste bad."

Professor Crum says that the world is complex and uncertain and yet we need to predict what will happen in order to act. **Mindsets are our human way of simplifying and understanding a complex reality**. The mindsets we adopt are not right/wrong, true/false, but they **do have an impact**. Mindsets can change our reality by shaping what we **pay attention to, how we feel, what we do, and what our bodies prioritize and prepare to do**. Mindset can be understood as the way our mind is set when it comes to our assumptions, beliefs, expectations, explanations, and goals. We shall explore how to apply some of the most rigorous science focused on the importance of developing a growth mindset (Dweck, 2007) and your positive psychological capital (PsyCap; Luthans & Broad, 2022) below.

Benefits of Right Mindsets for Students' Well-being

Are you **the type of person** who avoids challenges and gives up easily when running into an obstacle or do you get excited and persist when facing challenges and even thrive by overcoming them? Are you a person who perceives effort negatively or do you see effort as a gateway to mastery? Do you see the glass half empty or do you see it half full? Do you believe things will be well even though you don't have any assurance?

Well, research shows that things are not just "black and white" and neither are humans. Yes, we do have certain tendencies, but we also have different mindsets towards different aspects of our lives. Those areas of our lives that we do well in are usually supported by good mindsets and those in which we struggle are usually weakened by beliefs that don't serve us well. The bottom line is, we are "one type of a person" in one area of our life and a "different type of a person" in another life domain.

Whether we are aware or not, all the beliefs, attitudes, and mental habits above shape **how positively or negatively we see the world around us**. What we experience on a daily basis, how fast we **learn**, how **healthy** we are, and even how quickly we **heal**. It is important to become aware of your mindsets, how much they serve us, and if they don't, we can always decide to adopt the ways of thinking that will serve us better.

You will be introduced to different areas and determinants of your mindset, so you can reflect on your mindset as a building block of well-being. After that, you will be presented with theories on mindsets and you will be invited to try out some practical tools that could help you to unlearn what no longer serves you and to adopt beliefs you would like to have. Enjoy!

Your Mindset Flower Assessment

We have learned in Chapter 1 that mindset is one of the **nine essential building blocks** of generating well-being. One of the things that can be very useful is to reflect and to think about your personal **mindset strengths**. Understanding the importance of mindset for your well-being, you will be provided with an opportunity to assess your mindset strengths!

In this exercise you will be asked to fill out your own **flower diagram**. You will be provided with a wheel that represents **six different strengths** for building your mindset. These go from hope, confidence in yourself (efficacy), resiliency, optimism, future orientation, and growth mindset, and there is also room for your own choice of another mindset strength you might feel needs to be reflected in your life as well.

Here is a **set of statements** that will help you assess how well you feel about each mindset strength. You might find it helpful to reflect by reading the descriptions of ideal states of all six of your strengths and assessing where you stand.

Hope

I choose to stay **hopeful**. I **trust that my expectations and desires** will happen, even though I don't know exactly how yet. I feel hopeful about my future, motivated, and confident about achieving my goals through proactive planning and taking action.

Confidence in Yourself (Efficacy)

I know my weaknesses but I am also well aware of my **skills, abilities,** and **character strengths**. I use them in my everyday life to reach my goals and it helps me feel confident. I show myself self-compassion if needed.

Resiliency

I have the ability to spring back into shape and I **recover quickly from difficulties**. I have the mental capacity to bounce back and to even bounce forward after recovering from difficulties. I learn from my experiences and in some cases, I feel like I even **recover beyond the original level of my well-being**.

Optimism

I often feel like things will be well and I choose to **stay hopeful**. If I fail, I know there is something I can do about it. I don't see my failures as entirely my fault.

I know I generally do well, and failures are just an exception. I am aware that my failures are temporary and will be replaced by successes again.

Future Orientation

Knowing that being here and now is where life is, I also **look forward to the future rather than ruminating on my past**. **I anticipate good future** consequences. I **plan** before acting. **I set** my goals and I choose strategies to reach what I am aiming for. I show compassion to myself when things don't go exactly the way I would like them to.

Growth Mindset

Challenges often make me excited and obstacles make me want to **try again**. **Effort** is my way to success. **I choose to learn** from mistakes and practice constructive criticism. The success of others inspires me.

Other Mindset Strengths

Are there any other mindset strengths on your mind you would like to assess? If yes, please scale them as you did the previous strengths.

So how do you actually assess your strengths? **Please imagine a ladder with steps numbered from 0 at the bottom to 10 at the top.**

The top of the ladder represents the best result (I feel very confident in this particular strength), while the bottom of the ladder represents the worst (I would like to build this particular strength better).

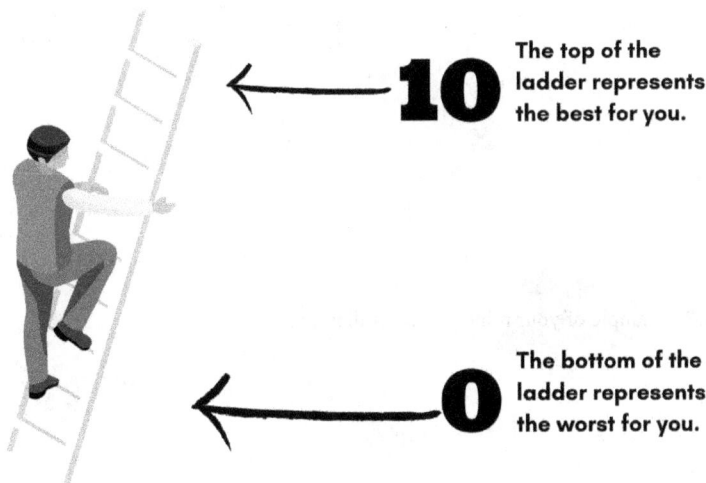

10 ← The top of the ladder represents the best for you.

0 ← The bottom of the ladder represents the worst for you.

Figure 8.1 Your well-being assessment ladder.

On which step of the ladder on a scale of 0–10 would you say you personally feel you stand at this time in terms of:

- hope
- confidence in yourself (efficacy)
- resiliency
- optimism
- future orientation
- growth mindset
- other mindset strengths

After you assess all your mindset strengths, draw your very own mindset flower! Circle the resulting numbers of your strength on the positive mindset wheel ladders. Then draw the petal shape from the center of the wheel through all the numbers on each ladder to create your own flower (see Figure 8.2 for an example of the flower diagram).

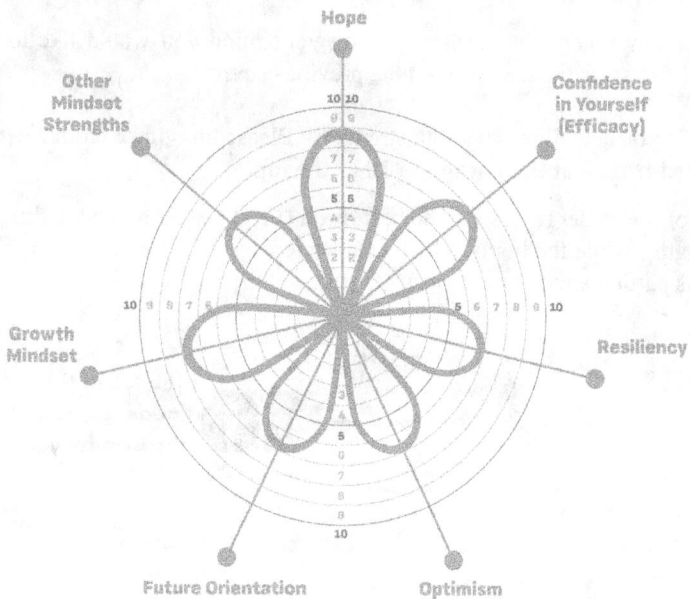

Figure 8.2 Example of your mindset flower diagram.

Let's assess your **mindset strengths** and later you can reflect on them and learn how to build particular strengths (if needed) in the upcoming chapter.

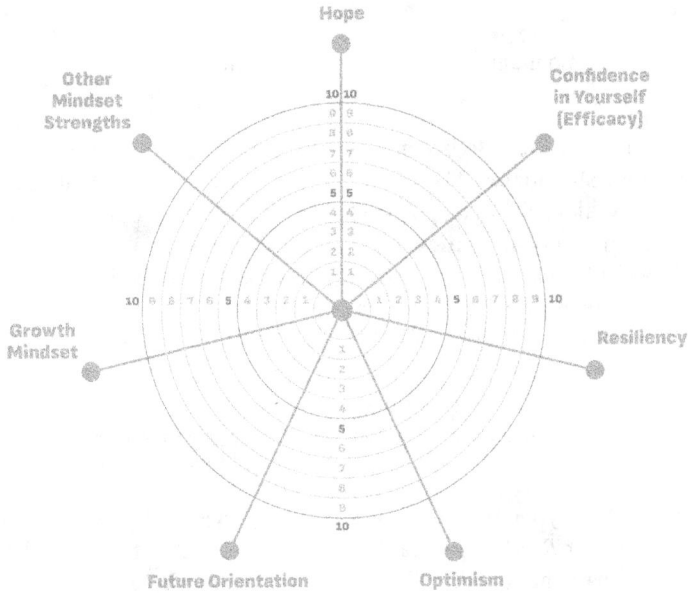

Figure 8.3 Your mindset flower assessment.

YOUR MINDSET FLOWER REFLECTION

Great job! How do you feel?

Let's have a look at your personal **mindset flower**.

Remember, there is no judgment here; this is just an awareness exercise.

The goal of this exercise is to become **aware of your situation and decide what your next goal should be**. Then you will have a chance to think about what you can do to achieve said goal. This chapter will present some **evidence-based recommendations and activities** you can try right away to see if they fit your personality and lifestyle. It is fun to reflect on your flowers with your friends, but remember, the only one you can compare your flowers to is yourself. Enjoy checking on your flowers over time to track your progress or changes reflecting certain events in different stages of your life. The goal shouldn't be to have perfect, long petals in all your flowers – you should come to terms with imperfection. Invite the possibility of gradual growth of your flower petals rather than unhealthy overnight perfection.

Each flower reflects your **subjective perception** rather than your objective state. You might rate your *Resiliency* petal lower while being able to bounce back from difficult situations rather quickly. Why do people do that? Our perception of ourselves is rarely objective. Sometimes, this can be caused by having a certain idea or vision of what our ideal *Resiliency* petal should look like. Sometimes, the *Resiliency* petal is disturbed by final exams that might weaken your resiliency temporarily or by some challenging event going on in your life right now. Hence, it can be reasonable to believe we still have room for growth. Rating your petals gives you **the opportunity to reflect on** your current state in certain areas of your life. It will also make you think about what strengths you are satisfied with for now and what strengths you might like to focus on. :-)

Let's see how you can **grow your mindset petals**.

Growing Your Mindset Flower Petals

Would you like to adopt a growth mindset and to be able to see challenges or setbacks as opportunities for growth? Would you like to endorse your optimistic and future-oriented view of life better? And would you like to even learn how to lower your expectations and the importance of your task results so you can live more freely from stress? If you said yes at least once, this topic is for you. This chapter will introduce you to embracing the right mindset and building your psychological capital. Let's have a closer look at what are the components that can help you care for mindsets that serve you and what are the ways to support them.

Psychological Capital

We understand traditional **financial capital** as wealth in the form of money or other assets available for purposes such as unexpected payments or investing. It is, simply put, what financial wealth one has at the moment. **Human capital** can be understood as what we know. What are our experiences, what education we have, and what skills and knowledge we have obtained. But there are other very important forms of capital for us. For example, **social capital**. This one can be seen as who we know. Who are our friends, what is our social network like, and what relationships do we have? And last but not least, psychological capital. Looking back at all the capitals available to us, **psychological capital** is basically a reflection of who we are. How hopeful we are, how confident we are, what our resilience is like, and what level of optimism we have adopted.

Psychological Capital can be defined as *"an individual's positive psychological state of development"* which is characterized by having high levels of HERO (Luthans & Broad, 2022). Hero is an acronym for four psychological traits that are fundamental to our positive functioning. Those are the four elements of:

- hope
- (self-)efficacy
- resilience
- optimism

Psychological capital (also known as PsyCap) was first introduced at the beginning of this century and since then, it's been empirically researched with groundbreaking findings of its impact on performance and well-being (e.g., see Luthans & Broad, 2022; Luthans & Youssef-Morgan, 2017). Let's have a closer look at what the individual elements are and how you can grow them in your everyday life.

Hope

Oxford Languages defines hope as a **feeling of trust**, a feeling of **expectation**, and a **desire for a particular thing to happen**. Hope motivates us to perceive our goals, to plan proactively, and to take action.

Exploring the process of building PsyCap, learning about and developing hope makes us feel empowered. This can be easily accomplished by learning how to set **realistic goals**, identifying your **specific strengths** and **weaknesses**, and actively **taking actions** towards your goal achievement.

The Psychological Capital Intervention (Luthans & Broad, 2022) suggests a three-pronged strategy in a goal-oriented framework – (1) goal design, (2) multiple pathway generation, and (3) overcoming obstacles. This can look in your day-to-day life like:

- learning to generate **pathways** and **assess inventory resources** that will help you to reach your goal
- **identifying subgoals** as milestones and stepping stones to your desired accomplishments, thus taking **small steps** towards your goals
- creating an **imaginal, implicit**, and **successful experience** to give yourself a taste of what it will be like to accomplish what you want to accomplish through visualization and imagination
- making **"what if" plans**, thus when designing your goals, trying to come up with **plan B** and **plan C**, ideally both as satisfying to you as goal A was
- using your superpowers – your **character strengths** and skills you master well to reach your goals *(more on your character strengths in the previous chapter on the achievement building blocks of well-being)*

Confidence in Yourself – Efficacy

World-renowned social psychologist Albert Bandura is credited with the theoretical foundation and developmental process of **building efficacy** and **confidence**.

Bandura's widely recognized taxonomy of sources of efficacy includes:

- task mastery or success
- modeling or vicarious learning
- social persuasion and positive feedback
- physiological and/or psychological arousal

In order to build your PsyCap and self-efficacy, you should be proactive in goal-orientation and achievement framing, as Bandura likes to emphasize! Bandura also asserts that the perceived expertise and relevance of models are key to determining the magnitude of influence.

> **Do it**   **Practice Self-Awareness**
>
> To build your PsyCap efficacy, focus on strengthening your **self-awareness**. Observe how you think and feel – but also why you think and feel that way. Self-awareness, among other things, includes an understanding of how you react to stress and what your coping mechanisms are. This will let you **assess your current state of being** and work on making **desirable behavior** changes. You can support yourself by using appropriate coping skills and changing your inner negative voice into a positive one. You can also shift your fixed self-talk from "I cannot do it" to "I cannot do it YET!" From "I always fail" to "I will do better next time." And from "I cannot do this" to "I can learn this."

Resiliency

Resiliency of university students is a widely desirable state nowadays. Schools realize the importance of helping their students to be more resilient and provide support from positive education to well-being coaching or healthy lifestyle designing. But how do we actually understand what resiliency is?

Oxford Languages define resiliency as the capacity to **recover quickly from difficulties**. Our toughness and mental elasticity. Our ability to spring back into shape after life challenges.

Being resilient means having the mental capacity to bounce back and bounce forward when difficulties arrive. It also means learning from our experiences. In some cases, even **going beyond the original level of our well-being**!

Exploring the process of **building your resilience** and **PsyCap** (Luthans & Broad, 2022), identifying your **strengths** and **weaknesses** can be a valuable investment of your time! When adversity does strike, it is helpful to learn how to quickly deploy previously identified assets and assess which factors are currently **within** and **outside of your control**. Choosing to focus on what is within and letting go of what is not is a great skill. Finally, it is helpful to try to mitigate the bumps on your road and proactively **strategize** how to deal with obstacles. **Identifying risk factors** that could hold you down in your bouncing back and beyond will help too.

Unwinding and Managing Stress

University students report **experiencing stress almost on a daily basis**. This can, on the one hand, help you to become resilient and strong for the future, but you can also often feel overwhelmed, tired, and unmotivated. We are facing a radical increase in the prevalence of anxiety and depression which can increase your risk of weakening your immune system and increasing the risk of chronic diseases. Therefore, learning how to relax deeply and finding time to do activities that make you feel **calm** and **at peace** is so important. Slowing down helps to lower your blood pressure and blood cortisol (the stress hormone) levels. Relaxation also helps you to lower your heart rate, to slow your respiration (breathing) rate, decreases your anxiety, and increases your feelings of well-being. It helps you to recharge and to gain your energy back so you can face challenges better equipped. Finding time to contemplate can also help you to get to know yourself deeper and it can help strengthen your sense of your identity. But slowing down can be different for each and every one of us. It can be done through meditation, breathwork, spending time with loved ones, walking in nature, coloring, taking a bath, or journaling. **You name it.** How do you manage pressure and what helps you connect to yourself?

Do It **Stress Management**

We all deal with stress differently, as well as we all choose different coping strategies. Take a moment and look at the following figure. Choose the strategies that you know will help you calm down or relax, and write them down. You can also note them for example on your phone so you have inspiration on how to recharge next time you feel drowned!

Figure 8.4 Stress management techniques and activities to choose from.

Caring for You Emotional Well-being

Harvard Medical School (2013) offers several steps you can take to improve your emotional well-being, no matter what state you're in. Those can be easily applicable in your everyday life as I propose below:

1 **Live in the moment**, even while working on school tasks and projects. When you're fully engaged in activities (e.g., lecture, project design, discussion with your teacher), you will enjoy them more and be less preoccupied by concerns about the past and the future.
2 **Be grateful for the things in your personal and school life.** Keeping a daily gratitude journal promotes positive feelings, optimism, life satisfaction, and connectedness with others. Practice being thankful for how positively your studies impact your life and see the improvement in your well-being!
3 **Do things for others.** Happiness comes from connecting with others and not being overly self-focused. Try to do things that also benefit your classmates, school friends, teachers, or your loved ones who support your studies!
4 **Take inventory of your strengths**, then apply them in new ways in your daily life, including your studies. For example, if you count curiosity as a strength, read about a new subject. If you consider yourself brave, try something that makes you nervous, such as public speaking in front of your online class.
5 **Savor pleasure.** Reminisce about good times, celebrate good moments with others, and be happy and proud of yourself when you accomplish something, especially at school.

Optimism

How would you define optimism? And how would you describe an optimistic person? Perhaps there is an optimist in your close circle. Someone who always charges you with energy, someone who makes you feel hopeful and optimistic about your life, your plans, and someone who brightens your day? If yes, keep that person close. Research shows that **optimistic people have a positive effect on people around them**. We feel more hopeful, resilient, and even more confident in their presence. So yes, keep optimistic people around and keep building your HERO within.

Martin Seligman (2006) defines positive thinking *as the notion that if you think good thoughts, things will work out well. Optimism is the feeling of thinking things will be well and being hopeful!*

Some of us are "naturally" optimistic and some of us tend to be more pessimistic. But what if we decide to be more of an optimist ourselves? And can we even learn to be optimists? Professor Seligman wrote a book focusing on ways of training oneself to think like an optimist and what benefits it might have for their life satisfaction, success, and even health (read the book *Learned Optimism: How to Change Your Mind and Your Life*, 2006). Let's have a closer look at the mindset of an optimist and try to act more like one. You can adopt a new way of thinking as well as any new skill you are trying to learn. With a little bit of effort, you can make positive changes.

So, how to assess whether you are an optimist or a pessimist? Let's have a look at the personal traits of optimists and pessimists in Figure 8.5.

When it comes to optimism, we draw from an expectancy-value orientation. Related to goals and their realization, the adoption of a positive attributional, explanatory style, with realistic optimism being the ideal, is beneficial for us as well.

OPTIMIST VS. PESSIMIST
EXPLANATORY STYLES

NOT PERSONAL
"WELL, THIS IS NOT ENTIRELY MY FAULT."

PERSONAL
"IT IS ME! IT IS ALL MY FAULT."

LOCAL
"IT ALL RELATES ONLY TO THIS ONE SITUATION. I WILL DO BETTER NEXT TIME."

PERVASIVE
"I CANNOT DO ANYTHING RIGHT! I ALWAYS MESS UP!"

TEMPORARY
"THIS WILL PASS."

PERMANENT
"THIS WILL LAST FOREVER!"

CONTROL
"THERE MUST BE SOMETHING I CAN DO ABOUT IT!"

POWERLESSNESS
"THERE IS NOTHING I CAN DO ABOUT IT."

Figure 8.5 Explanatory styles of optimists and pessimists.

In the eyes of an optimist:

* a failure is not the result of their personality
  * *"Well, not passing the exam was not entirely my fault. There were other factors that contributed to this result – the topic is generally so hard and the teacher did not ask clear questions."*
* just like success is always praised where praises are due to your effort
  * *"I passed because I studied really hard!"*

- in failures, optimists tend to see the unfortunate situation objectively
  - *"Well, it's ok I did not pass the exam, my results are normally great. I will sleep better next time, and I will pass as always."*
- they own and generalize successes
  - *"I am a great learner, I usually do great at tests!"*
- optimists see misfortune as temporary
  - *"Next exam will be better!"*
- optimists tend to take at least some control over the situation
  - *"I can ask someone to help me to understand this better before next exam."*

How to boost optimism at school:

1 Engage in small, daily rituals to increase positivity and optimism. This means doing specific things at specific times that generate positivity for you. Such a ritual could be **a walk to your favorite coffee shop to get a coffee with a friend** to connect and get some movement in. Create your own school rituals – boost your optimism daily!
2 Another example would be identifying **positive emotions that occur daily** (e.g., enjoying eating lunch together with a classmate, playing games in between classes, engaging in active listening, and talking to family members).
3 Take **moments to reflect** on your daily optimism. Reflect on your personal plans, too, and share your reflections with classmates or family members. They can also benefit from such activities by engaging in positive future planning with you and getting inspired while doing that!
4 Write down three things that you are thankful for that relate to your school and make you work toward your goals. If you feel like sharing your gratitude, tell people what you are thankful for and why.

If you yourself don't feel naturally optimistic and you don't desire to make any changes, don't put any pressure on yourself. You can still serve others very well, too. Talking about our life plans and goals with an optimist can show a pessimist "what is possible." Pessimists can, on the other hand, open optimists' eyes and point out obstacles they might not have thought about. Pessimists can lead us to think of plan B, plan C, or even plan D and to think about the resources we might have to use on our way, such as family support, friends, or any possible material support.

I hope that you feel more capable of building your HERO within now. To summarize the activities you had a chance to try and to provide you with even larger inspiration, I would like to invite you to explore what to do to build your HERO within in Figure 8.6.

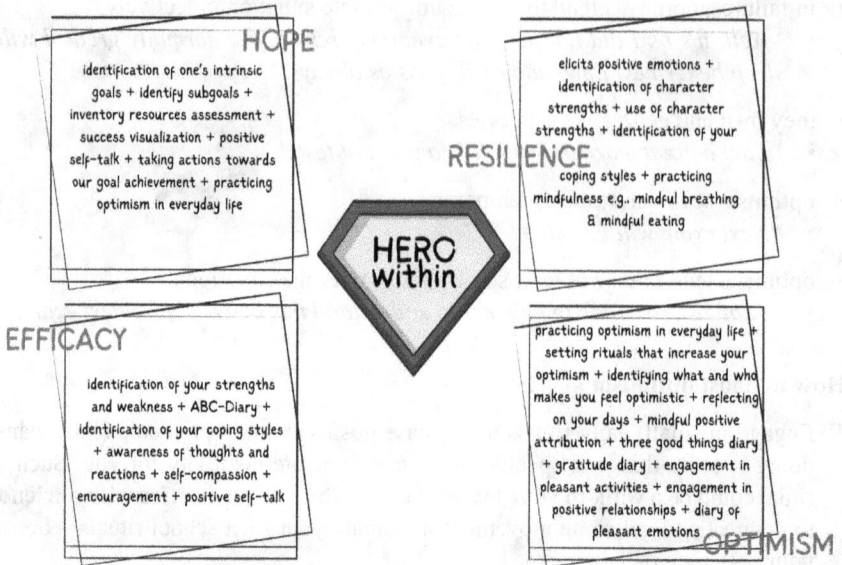

HOPE

identification of one's intrinsic goals + identify subgoals + inventory resources assessment + success visualization + positive self-talk + taking actions towards our goal achievement + practicing optimism in everyday life

RESILIENCE

elicits positive emotions + identification of character strengths + use of character strengths + identification of your coping styles + practicing mindfulness e.g., mindful breathing & mindful eating

HERO within

EFFICACY

identification of your strengths and weakness + ABC-Diary + identification of your coping styles + awareness of thoughts and reactions + self-compassion + encouragement + positive self-talk

practicing optimism in everyday life + setting rituals that increase your optimism + identifying what and who makes you feel optimistic + reflecting on your days + mindful positive attribution + three good things diary + gratitude diary + engagement in pleasant activities + engagement in positive relationships + diary of pleasant emotions

OPTIMISM

Figure 8.6 How to build your HERO within?

Future Orientation

While realizing that being in this moment is healthy for us, future orientation teaches us to focus on the future, rather than ruminating on our past. Being future-oriented is closely related to successfully reaching our goals, being hopeful and optimistic. We think about the future, anticipate (ideally good) future consequences, and plan ahead.

Being a future-oriented person results in a desire to plan for the short-term and long-term future. Focusing on the future supports you in achieving your goals. If you can mentally visualize the steps of the process, you can also predict possible obstacles and envision your success as it has already happened.

We can substitute future orientation with a beautiful term – **prospection**. The action of looking forward to the future – the opposite of retrospection, an act of looking back and assessing events in our past. Prospection or future orientation is a part of the so-called "big eight," along with:

- high positive effects
- low negative effects
- high optimism
- resilience
- innovation
- social skills
- meaning and importance

According to Professor Seligman (2022), these "big eight" represent the best documented factors underlying our learning, success, and health. Learn from the past, appreciate what you have learned and experienced, but also be prospective.

> (Do It) **Your Possible Future**
>
> Journal or at least think for a moment about your possible future by answering the following questions:
>
> * what is important in your life
> * what is it you love and enjoy to do in life
> * what would your ideal future look like
> * what kind of people would you love to have in your life
> * what would your ideal intimate relationship look like
> * what would your ideal job look like
> * what is your ideal income
> * what vacations would you love to take
>
> also:
> * formulate your goals
> * prioritize your goals
> * strategize how will you fulfill your visions
> * identify and describe ways to overcome possible obstacles
> * create a plan B and a plan C
> * reflect on your progress toward your life goals

Growth Mindset

Psychologist and Stanford University researcher Carol Dweck says that success comes from having the right mindset rather than intelligence, talent, or education. She defines two different mindset tendencies that co-create different lives – **fixed mindset** and **growth mindset**. She says that when you change your way of thinking, you change your life.

People with a fixed mindset believe that they're born with certain skills, intelligence, and abilities that they cannot change. "**I can't do it**," they often say.

People with a growth mindset believe that skills can be cultivated through effort, and they thrive on challenges. When they fail, they often say "**I can't do it yet**". It is important to realize that we all have fixed mindsets in particular areas of our lives (usually where we struggle) as well as growth mindsets (usually where success comes naturally to us). So, how do we define our mindset tendency in a particular area of our life and how do we change it? First, **be aware** of how you think, feel, and talk. Do you often think:

* I rather avoid challenges. What if I lose?!
* When I see obstacles, I give up easily. Losing does not feel good.
* Effort means that I am not good enough, as I must try hard.
* I don't like negative feedback. Ouch!
* I feel uncomfortable when I see others succeed.

If yes, no worries! This is the first step to changing that. Let's look at how people with a growth mindset think and change their self-talk and behavior to following:

- Challenges make me excited. Challenge accepted!
- Obstacles make me want to try over and over.
- Effort is my way to success and achievement.
- Negative feedback helps me to get better and to grow.
- Success of others is inspirational.

Figure 8.7 Fixed mindset traits versus growth mindset traits.

Carol Dweck (2007) says that students who have adopted the growth mindset believe that hard work, perseverance, and learning from mistakes give them the ability to learn and continually develop their knowledge and skills. Practice self-compassion every time you perform not as well as planned. Use your inner voice to repeat your compassionate wish and learn how to grow from your own mistakes!

A growth mindset, proposed by Stanford professor Carol Dweck, describes students who believe that their success is dependent on time and effort. Students with a growth mindset feel their skills and intelligence can be improved if they are persistent enough.

Your goal, according to the author Carol Dweck, should always be to seek a **growth mindset in all areas of your life**. To do this, always focus on the solution and not on the problem. Embrace all challenges and situations as opportunities for your personal and educational growth.

If you are studying, understand that a grade is the result of a variety of situations at a given time and does not determine who you are. If you want to improve, keep studying, keep trying, and keep growing. But please, don't be hard on yourself. We all make mistakes, we all fail, and we all need to rest without feeling guilty to recharge. Including you. Finding time for your well-being is also about self-growth.

Also, seek to stimulate the thought of growth in your classmates and the people around you. This means valuing the effort and not the result, rejecting limiting and judgmental thoughts, and focusing on learning opportunities.

Do It **How to Practice a Growth Mindset in Your Everyday School Life?**

1 Notice your saboteur when learning and failing in something and dissociate from the negative thoughts. See them for what they are, the products of your mind that can be either used or not. You are not your thoughts :-)
2 Change your self-talk and champion yourself with words like "I can do it," "I can learn it," and "I will get better with some effort."
3 View school challenges as opportunities.
4 Replace "I am failing" with "I am learning."
5 Try different learning tactics.
6 Focus on the process over the result. Appreciate you trying.
7 Try to have fun when learning new things and overcoming obstacles.
8 Do things for yourself rather than for approval of others.
9 Value your effort and the effort of others, not accomplishments.
10 Celebrate growth with others.
11 Learn from criticism and celebrate your growth!
12 Learn to reveal purpose in everything you do.
13 Set intentions before any school activity.
14 Use the word "yet" and change your self-talk from "I can't do it" to "I can't do it YET."
15 Practice self-compassion. It is ok to fail. It is important not to give up!

Do It **Self-Compassion**

Schotanus-Dijkstra et al. (2017) also suggest training **self-compassion** to develop a positive mindset in order to generate our mental well-being. How can such activity be implemented into university students' lifestyles? When failing at school or not performing as planned, show yourself some self-compassion. Think to yourself phrases like: "I have tried and that is success too," "I did what I could and that is a win too," "I have learned where can

I improve," or come up with phrases that feel more natural to you yourself. Talk to yourself. Look in the mirror and tell yourself something kind, something you would say to someone you love. It might seem odd doing it for the first time, but you deserve your attention and kindness as much as people around you.

Do it　**Ten Empowering Questions to Support My Mindset Flower Growth**

1　What would it feel like if I really believed that I could do it?
2　What have I learned from my last failure?
3　What do I find inspiring in my classmates?
4　What would I do knowing I cannot fail?
5　What would my ideal future look like?
6　What would a realistic optimist think about this?
7　What does true hope feel like?
8　What is my next step to get closer to fulfilling my dreams?
9　What have I achieved in my life thanks to my constant effort?
10　What kind of self-talk would support and encourage me?

Do it　**Ten Tips to Build My Mindset Flower**

1　Be aware of your current beliefs. Don't judge, just listen to your inner voice. What does your inner saboteur tell you?
2　Be kind to yourself. Don't beat yourself down when you notice you are operating based on beliefs that no longer serve you (e.g. "There is no way I can learn all this," "This is going to be so embarrassing when I fail," "I cannot change.") Acknowledge yourself for becoming more sensitive to the beliefs you are running on!
3　Manage your self-talk. Disagree with your saboteurs when they show up. For example, when your self-talk tells you, "This is too much, I cannot learn this in a week" pause for a second and support yourself by responding, "Actually I have done this in the past. I can do this."
4　Try to think as an optimist. If you catch yourself being negative about some situation, think to yourself what a realistic optimist would think about this. You might even think of a certain person you really know who is optimistic most of the time and ask yourself, what would they think about this?

5　Appreciate your learning from your mistakes. There is no learning without mistakes and there is no growing without learning.

6　Be playful when facing challenges. Try to be like a little kid that is trying to learn to walk and gets up every time it falls. Just smile, laugh, or even release your frustration verbally if it helps but always try one more time.

7　Be hopeful. Try to put on a coat of a feeling of true hope. Even when you don't know how to solve the situation yet.

8　Try to change your perspective a bit and look at challenges as your vaccination by stress. You can bet that you will handle the same situation with more ease next time.

9　Trust yourself. Be your biggest supporter. Always think of why could this work out rather why not. Look for evidence from the past and remind yourself that you have skills and abilities to handle it.

10　Remind yourself that there is always something you can do. Always. Ask yourself, what can I really do here? And listen for answers.

Tips to Mindset Snacking

Building your mindset does not have to be complicated nor time demanding. Look at Figure 8.8 and try some of the tips right now.

TIPS TO YOUR MINDSET SNACKING
Make it quick, easy and fun!

1 min — ACKNOWLEDGE YOURSELF FOR YOUR LATEST SUCCESS

10 mins — WRITE DOWN ALL YOUR SUCCESSES, THE BIG ONES AND THE SMALL ONES!

1 min — REMIND YOURSELF THAT YOU CAN DO IT!

15 mins — WRITE DOWN THE STEPPING STONES YOU NEED TO TAKE TO ACHIEVE YOUR GOAL!

3 mins — REMIND YOURSELF OF YOUR DREAMS

5 mins — REFLECT ON: WHAT DO YOU FIND INSPIRING ABOUT PEOPLE IN YOUR LIFE?

4 mins — WRITE DOWN THREE THINGS YOU ARE THANKFUL FOR AND WHY

1 min — BREATHE MINDFULLY - OBSERVE YOUR BREATH FOR ONE MINUTE

5 mins — VISUALIZE YOUR SUCCESS

3 mins — REMIND YOURSELF OF YOUR STRENGTHS

Figure 8.8 Tips to mindset snacking.

Having a good mindset is the baseline for living a good life. But it is not always only our choice what we believe in and how we perceive the world around us. There are many determinants that influence our mindset. Our beliefs are shaped by the culture we grew in, the current society we live in, beliefs our parents have or used to have, and what our family members, coworkers, and friends tell us every day. All the above influence our mindset. It all comes down to an environment we live in during our day-to-day lives. Healthy and supportive environments can dramatically impact our well-being. And even though it might seem like our environment is pretty much predetermined there is always something we can do to make our environment healthier for us. First we create our environment, then our environment creates us. I would like to invite you to explore how the strategy of life crafting can be used to influence your environment positively. You will learn about different environments and you will also have a chance to practice some tools and activities to create a healthier and more positive environment for yourself in the upcoming chapter.

References

Dweck, C. (2007). *Mindset: The new psychology of success*. Ballantine Books, New York, NY: ISBN: 978-0345472328.

Godmen, H. (2013). Your well-being: More than just a state of mind. Harvard Medical School. Harvard Health Publishing. [July 10, 2021; online] Available at: https://www.health.harvard.edu/blog/your-well-being-more-than-just-a-state-of-mind-201303065957

IPPA Positive Education Insight Series (2022, October). Positive Education Division (IPPAEd): The big eight, New Content for Education, Therapy, and **Coaching**.

Luthans, F., & Broad, J. D. (2022). Positive psychological capital to help combat the mental health fallout from the pandemic and VUCA environment.. *Organizational Dynamics*. https://doi.org/ 10.1016/j.orgdyn.2020.100817

Luthans, F., & Youssef-Morgan, C. M. (2017). Psychological capital: An evidence-based positive approach. *Annual Review of Organizational Psychology and Organizational Behavior*, 4, 339–366.

Schotanus-Dijkstra, M., Drossaert, C. H., Pieterse, M. E., Boon, B., Walburg, J. A., & Bohlmeijer, E. T. (2017). An early intervention to promote well-being and flourishing and reduce anxiety and depression: A randomized controlled trial. *Internet Interventions*, 9, 15–24. https://doi.org/10.1016/j.invent.2017.04.00

Seligman, M. E. P. (2006). *Learned optimism: How to change your mind and your life*. New York, NY: Vintage.

Somani, P. (2019). Mindsets: Q&A with Dr. Alia Crum, Stanford Psychology. Available at: https://www.parulsomani.com/post/mindsets-q-a-with-dr-alia-crum-stanford-psychology

Youssef-Morgan, C. M. & Luthans F. (2015, August). Psychological capital and well-being. *Stress Health*, 31(3), 180–188. https://doi.org/10.1002/smi.2623. PMID: 26250352.

UMass Memorial Health Center for Mindfulness (2021). Mindfulness classes. Available at: https://www.ummhealth.org/center-mindfulness

9 Building Your Environment

The truly healthy environment is not merely safe but stimulating.
— William H. Stewart

I would like to invite you to dream with me. Imagine what would your ideal environment look like? Would it be some place out in the nature? A garden, a place by the lake, the top of a mountain, or in the middle of a meadow? Or somewhere indoors? In a cozy old cottage? Are you sitting by the window on a sunny day or are you in your own room? What is the temperature there? Is it warm here? Or do you feel some cool air on your skin? And what about the light? Do you see a sunrise or candle flames? What do you smell? What is on the walls or around you if you are outside? And what does it feel like to be here? Does it feel safe? Exciting? Or freeing? Who is here with you if anyone? We could go on and on.

In this exercise, my students create empires in the middle of the ocean, spaceships floating around Mars, or secret Japanese gardens for themselves. It is your choice to decide what your ideal environment looks like and what it feels like to hang out here. You can come back to this anytime and you can keep designing your ideal environment in your visualizations while practicing relaxations, meditations, or in the middle of the night when you wake up and cannot fall back to sleep. This place is only yours and it is available to you anytime you wish.

Introduction to Environment

A high-quality environment is essential for good living conditions. Choosing and co-creating a good living environment can greatly impact your health and well-being (Koci & Donaldson, 2022).

What is a good environment for university students? It is a combination of positive physical, social, and learning environments. It refers to **home environment, family environment, the set of facilities that your university provides, work environment, community environment, and your online environment, but also access to and time spent in nature.** The physical and learning facilities provided by your university include campuses, classrooms, infrastructure, drinkable water availability, sanitation, the quality of lighting, etc. Psycho-social components are, for example,

DOI: 10.4324/9781003378365-10

the teacher-student relationships at your school, the long-term university atmosphere, the moral or social values and norms of the whole academic community, but also your family relationships, support in your community, and the culture you live in.

Healthy, joyful, and functional environments allow us to live our daily lives peacefully and they help to fulfill our basic needs. Positive environments make us feel safe and allow us to adopt healthy behaviors; they make us feel welcome, included, and connected to others. As a result, we can be creative; we can fully engage in learning, in our work, and in our hobbies. They also allow us to rest, recreate, and regenerate.

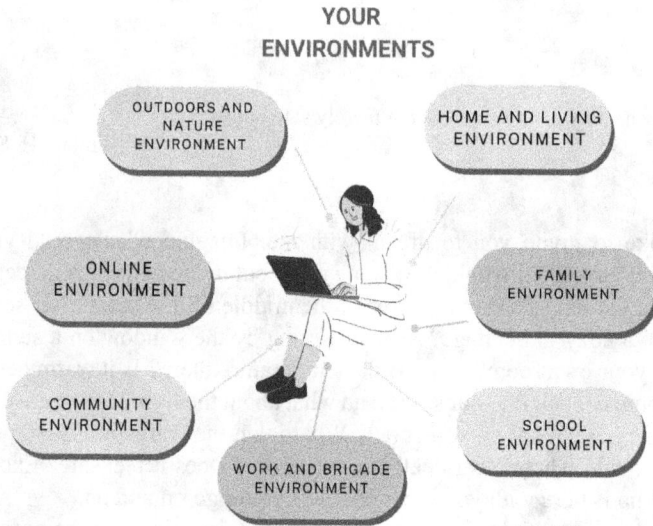

Figure 9.1 Your environments.

The environments you live in are:

- home environment
- family environment
- school environment
- work and part-time job environment
- community environment
- your online environment
- but also outdoors and nature

The World Health Organization (2022) states that healthier environments could prevent almost one-quarter of the global burden of disease. **A healthy environment provides:**

- clean air
- stable climate
- adequate water
- sanitation and hygiene

- safe use of chemicals
- protection from radiation
- healthy and safe workplaces
- healthy and safe schools
- sound agricultural practices

Health-supportive cities, built environments, and a preserved nature are all prerequisites of good health.

The individual environments we spend our time in are psychophysical systems, consisting of all objects, stimuli, and subjective evaluations of the environment.

The objects in our environments are people, animals, nature, air quality, buildings, building and room design, and equipment. **The stimuli** are the natural light, sounds, smells, ventilation, and temperature, and the **subjective evaluation** of the environment is how you perceive the physical safety, connectedness to others, and climate of the culture you live in – the so-called social climate or long-term atmosphere. We could say that environments have a physical component as well as a psycho–social component, both represented by our relationships with people and animals in specific environments.

Our overall environment connects both – the physical environments we find ourselves in and our personal perception of the individual environments. Thus, we must discern whether we **like them and feel comfortable** with them or not.

The **benefit** of a healthy environment is tremendous, as it greatly impacts our well-being. There is a lot we cannot control or change, but there is certainly a lot we can, let's say, **craft**. You can change the individual environments you find yourself in to make yourself feel good in them. But we should not forget to do our part to **help, too. We shall support all the environments we live in by co-creating a sustainable, healthy environment for all.** Because remember? First, we create our environment and then our environment creates us.

Figure 9.2 Healthy environment.

Benefits of Good Environment for Students' Well-Being

Given that you spend at least a **third of your day at the university** or engaged in studying and learning, a positive university environment may be one of the biggest contributors to your well-being and academic performance (Koci, 2023). Building **good environments** and a **positive university social climate** can potentially improve both your **health** and **your school results**.

Supporting and co-creating healthy environments can support the development of many of your competencies, such as **better focus**, **critical thinking**, **problem solving**, **decision-making**, **personal management**, and **a healthy lifestyle**. It can help improve your **academic achievement**, help you **adopt positive attitudes toward education**, enhance **learning engagement**, and improve participation in other **school activities, including overall school attendance**. Being active in making your environment healthier will help you appreciate the university environment better and enjoy learning more. Building healthy environments will also help you improve your home, family, and community surroundings, and you can become more likely to **engage in positive relationships**. You will be more motivated to **participate in building a healthy community environment** and you will care for nature too. And last but not least, you will become **more selective about the content of your online environment**.

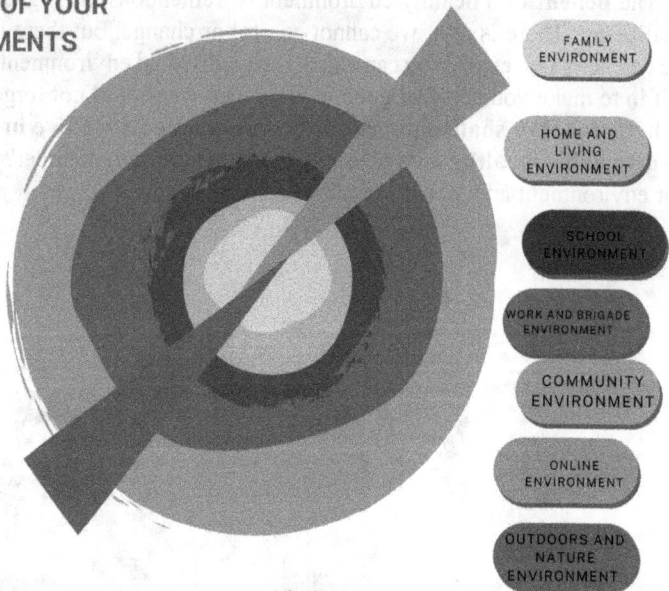

Figure 9.3 Proximity of your environments.

Your Environment Flower Assessment

We have learned in Chapter 1 that environment is one of the **nine essential building blocks** for generating well-being. One of the things that can be very useful is to reflect and think about your personal **environment strengths**. Understanding the importance of a positive environment for your well-being, you will be provided with an opportunity to assess your positive environment strengths!

In this exercise, you will be asked to fill out your own **flower diagram**. You will be provided with a wheel that represents **seven different strengths** for building a positive environment. These go from home environment, family environment, school environment, work and part-time job environment, community environment, online environment, time spent outdoors in nature, and there is also room for your own choice of another environment strength you might feel needs to be reflected in your life as well.

Here is a **set of statements** that will help you assess how well you feel about each environment strengths. You might find it helpful to reflect by reading the descriptions of ideal states of all seven of your strengths and assessing where you stand.

High-quality Home Environment

I **enjoy** spending time at home. I like the **design of my home** and I **actively co-create** good living conditions by keeping my home clean, filtering my tap water, limiting chemical-based products, letting the natural light in, and having plants at home. I ventilate regularly to have fresh air.

High-quality Family Environment

I **enjoy spending time** in the family environment that my family members and I help to build together. I actively **help to co-create** a healthy physical family environment and I try to contribute to a great psycho-social climate as well. I help to manage a **clean, healthy, and safe family environment** as much as I can.

High-quality School Environment

I find the **design of school** buildings beautiful, and I feel **safe, comfortable, and connected** to the school community. My university **promotes health and actively creates a healthy environment** for their students. I am actively co-creating a healthy school environment by **sorting my waste and not wasting water, paper, and energy**.

High-quality Work and Part-time Job Environment

I **enjoy my work environment** – its design, **clean** water, **fresh** air, **good** ventilation, **natural** light, **lack of** noise, **limited exposure** to chemicals, and **easy access** to nature (e.g., parks or trees around the building). I would also say that the psychosocial climate at my work is healthy and supportive.

High-quality Community Environment

I find my community environment **healthy and clean, especially** when it comes to the infrastructure, air, water, and community waste. I like the buildings; I feel **safe** and **connected** to others. I voluntarily **separate my waste** and help to **clean the neighborhood** when there is a chance to do so.

High-quality Online Environment

I feel good about the **quality of the online content** I expose myself to. I pay attention to the quality of the **media and the people I follow**. I **limit my exposure to commercials,** and I care for my online **identity safety**. I mostly use the online environment for education and to connect with my family and loved ones. I **limit** my time spent on social media and my overall screen time.

Time Spent Outdoors in Nature

I can access nature easily. I enjoy having **plants** in my home, in my workplace, and at school. I always make time for spending time in nature in the **sunlight, fresh air**, near **water**, or in the **woods**. I walk in nature or just sit there and enjoy the natural scenery.

Other Environmental Strengths

Are there any other environment strengths on your mind that you would like to assess? If yes, please scale them as you did the previous strengths.

So how do you actually assess your strengths? **Please imagine a ladder with steps numbered from 0 at the bottom to 10 at the top.**

The top of the ladder represents the best result (I feel very confident in this particular strength), while the bottom of the ladder represents the worst (I would like to build this particular strength better).

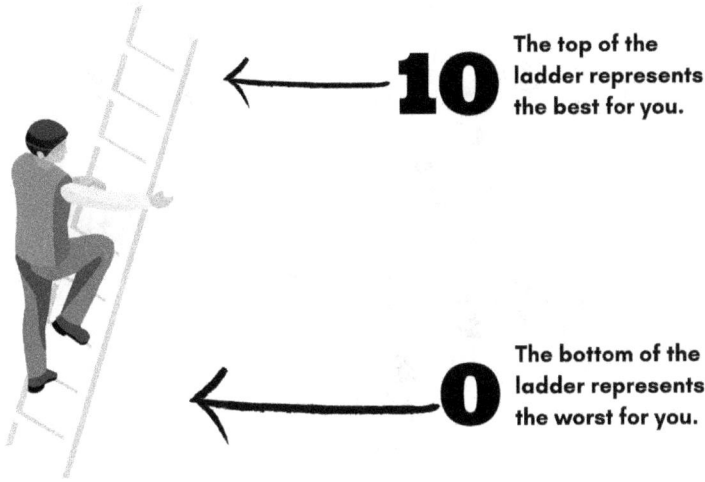

Figure 9.4 Your well-being assessment ladder.

On which step of the ladder on a scale of 0–10 would you say you personally feel you stand at this time in terms of:

- high-quality home environment
- high-quality family environment
- high-quality school environment
- high-quality work and part-time job environment
- high-quality community environment
- high-quality online environment
- time to be spent outdoors in nature
- other environment strengths

After you assess all your environment strengths, draw your very own environment flower! Circle the resulting numbers of your strength on the environment wheel ladders. Then draw the petal shape from the center of the wheel through all the numbers on each ladder to create your own flower (see Figure 9.5 for an example of the flower diagram).

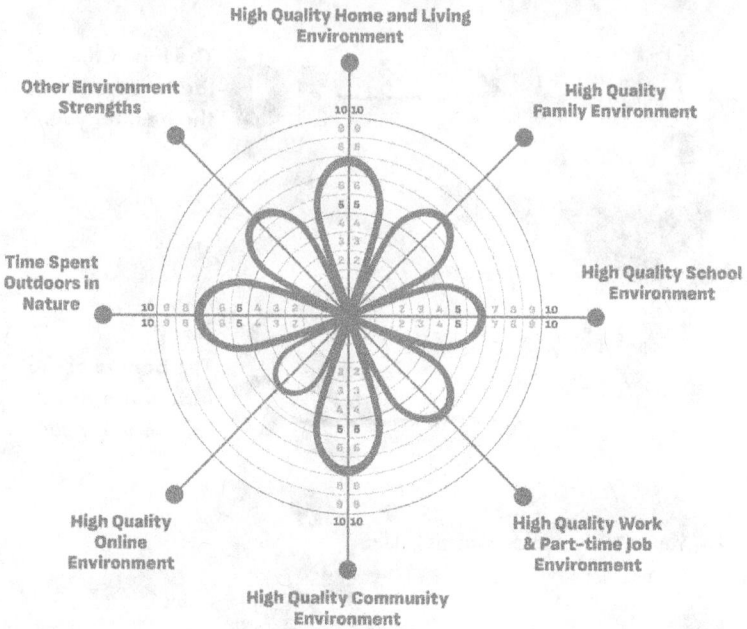

Figure 9.5 Example of your environment flower diagram.

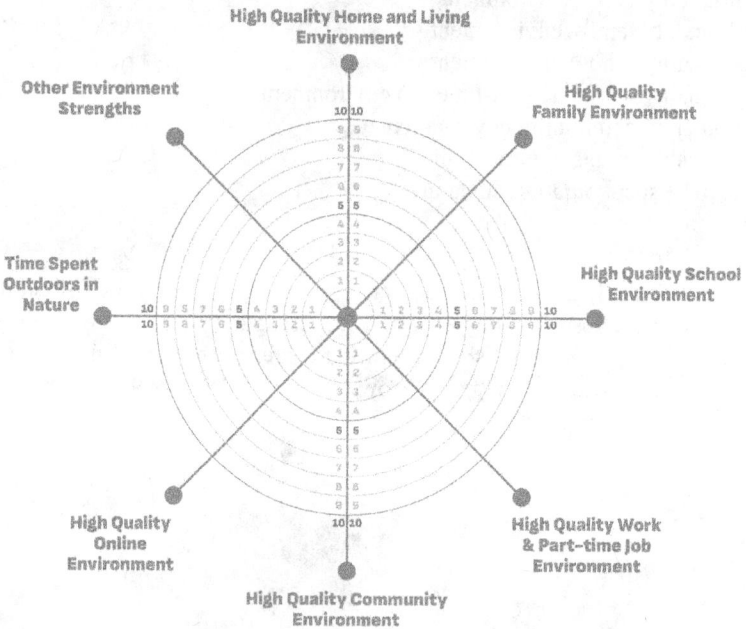

Figure 9.6 Your environment flower assessment.

YOUR ENVIRONMENT FLOWER REFLECTION

Great job! How do you feel?

Let's have a look at your personal **environment flower**.

Remember, there is no judgment here; this is just an awareness exercise.

The goal of this exercise is to become **aware of your situation and decide what your next goal should be**. Then you will have a chance to think about what you can do to achieve said goal. This chapter will present some **evidence-based recommendations and activities** you can try right away to see if they fit your personality and lifestyle. It is fun to reflect on your flowers with your friends, but remember, the only one you can compare your flowers to is yourself. Enjoy checking on your flowers over time to track your progress or changes reflecting certain events in different stages of your life. The goal shouldn't be to have perfect, long petals in all your flowers – you should come to terms with imperfection. Invite the possibility of gradual growth of your flower petals rather than unhealthy overnight perfection.

Each flower reflects your **subjective perception** rather than your objective state. You might rate your *High-Quality Community Environment* petal lower while living in a healthy environment and a good community. Why do people do that? Our perception of ourselves is rarely objective. Sometimes, this can be caused by having a certain idea, a vision of what our ideal *High-Quality Community Environment* petal should look like. Sometimes, the *High-Quality Community Environment* petal is disturbed by an unpleasant situation – the current outdoor concert that left a lot of trash in your neighborhood or an ongoing construction project. Hence, it can be reasonable to believe we still have room for growth. Rating your petals gives you **the opportunity to reflect on** your current state in certain areas of your life. It will also make you think about what strengths you are satisfied with for now and what strengths you might like to focus on. :-)

Let's see how you can **grow your environment petals**.

Growing Your Environment Flower Petals

The quality of your physical environment (which includes spatiotemporal elements, such as access to **natural light**, **fresh air**, **physical safety**, and a **positive psychological climate**) influences your engagement and productivity tremendously. This means that it is important to constantly choose healthy environments for yourself in the first place, but you should also **take responsibility** for the environments you live in to make them healthier, more positive, and stimulating. Let me say it one more time. First, we create our environments and then our environments create us.

The importance of choosing a healthy and joyful environment is undeniable. We spend approximately a **third of our life** in school and at work. We also spend a great portion of our time in our **home** and **living** and in our **family environment.** Well, at least we are there physically. We often slip in living mentally in our **online environment**, scrolling through social media, checking emails, or talking to people on messenger apps rather than talking to people we are physically present with. This relates to the fact that, until today, a society has never **spent less time outdoors** and the quality of our **community environment** has never been this important.

As we already discussed, there is a lot in our environment that we cannot change, but there is also a lot that we **can do** to co-create a positive environment to live in. Let's have a look at how you can support your individual environment to live a **more joyful** and **fulfilling life**.

High-quality Home and Living Environment

A high-quality home and living environment can contribute to our positive functioning. A good home and living environment provides us with certain benefits – a sense of safety, belonging, comfort, and the promotion of a healthy, high-quality life. Decorating one's home can be a way of self-expression. Whether you live with your parents or you live in dorms, make your room a place you enjoy spending time in. A place you consider yours. A place that makes you feel great every time you return to it.

How does one craft their home and living environment? Many environmental conditions are set quite firmly, but there is always a lot you can do to make your home and living environment a healthy, safe, and joyful place to be. First, take care of your physical environment. Eliminate the outside noise, keep your air clean and fresh, check your lights, and get rid of toxins. Have a special place where you can get your schoolwork done. Set your study environment in a way that will help you focus and be productive. Remove distractions. Keep things organized. Do it your way! Also, make a comfy, sleep-friendly bedroom your priority. Eliminate noise and bright lights before bedtime or use an air purifier if that is something that would help you sleep better. Create your own personal space. Whether it might be a sofa you like to read on or a simple pillow on the windowsill. Get creative! You probably already know what place in your home we are talking about right now. Purge, organize your closet and your computer, too. Yes, your computer. Browse through all of your devices and delete everything that only takes up space! And let me invite you to clean your car, too. Cleaning our space, in a certain sense, cleans our life, too. And you are worthy of a clean living environment.

How to help? As amazing as it is to make your place feel more like home, it also helps to make your living environment healthy. However, don't ever forget to take action please and help make the living environment healthy for those you share it with. Aim to make your home and living environment healthy for everyone. Be respectful of your roommates' needs, set some rules together, and do your best to stick to them. Communicate openly and please don't freak out if you disagree on things. That's actually where great communication starts sometimes. Make room for your significant other to have their own space at home, too. Let them express themselves in the space's design as much as you do. Help your parents with work around the house over weekends and show them you care. Be there for your sibling(s). Know your strengths and use them to not only aid yourself but also to aid others.

Do It — **Appreciate Where You Live!**

Scan your previous day (24 hours) and identify three good things that happened and enriched your life – especially those influencing your living or home environment. What do I mean by this? I would personally write down that I noticed my little eucalyptus tree is growing new leaves and it made me excited. I also had a fun chat with my neighbor this morning about her cat and she gave me a big smile when we were parting ways. And I am also thankful for my small yoga corner where I stretched my body before bedtime yesterday. Write your three good things related to your home and living space if you want. Monitor your days and start a diary.

Do It — **Make Your Home a Better Place: Let's Get to Work!**

Make a list of the things that you can do to make your home environment healthier, cleaner, better organized, or cozier!
   e.g.:

- organizing your closet
- cleaning your work desk
- getting rid of old skincare and cosmetics
- getting rid of chemicals
- buying yourself a new painting

- or painting one :-)
- and much more...

Look at the list and listen to your gut. What items make you excited or simply need to be done? If you can, do it right away. If not, check your calendar and create a reminder that will help you get your plan done!

Do It   **Do More of What You Love**

What do you love to do? What activities bring you joy while helping you create or experience a healthy environment? Perhaps it's **a joyful run in the nature space around your neighborhood** that brings more fresh air into your day. You could enjoy visiting your parents and playing with your dog as well! Or it can be something as simple as cleaning and organizing your work desk – an activity that leaves you feeling like you accomplished something. Write down a list of all the pleasant activities you love to do that also help you experience a healthier environment. Analyze your list and highlight activities that can be easily incorporated into your everyday life.

Do It   **Use Your Strengths!**

People who use their character strengths in daily life report greater life satisfaction than those not using their strengths. Identify your personal character strengths at VIA Character Strengths Survey (https://www.viacharacter.org/) and think of how specifically your strengths can help you support your healthy environment. For example, if creativity is your strength, you can cook some fun meals for your roommates and you can spend a nice evening together. Try to find joy in co-creating a healthy school and home environment for yourself and for others.

High-quality Family Environment

Not only does a high-quality family environment provide us with a sense of safety through physical means that create a shelter for us, but the family environment also represents a very strong psycho-social component of our lives. Each family environment is unique and has a different dynamic – that is often called a "family climate." A good family climate is a long-term group phenomenon created by good communication and respectful interaction among all family members and results in an overall long-term prospective mood.

A high-quality family environment brings many **benefits** to our lives. It provides a tremendous amount of physical and psycho-social safety and support and creates a space for joy, transparency, authenticity, and full expression. Family environments often let us experience lifelong, unconditional relationships. Family environments also generate life purpose for many of us.

How Can You Craft Your Family Environment to Make It Healthier and More Positive?

Express your love and care. It does not cost anything, and it changes everything.

Be open about what makes you feel good, express your needs, and ask your loved ones to help you meet them. And be there for them as well. Make decisions together. Support open and non-judgmental communication. Have a "teambuilding" session together as a family. Balance your school-family life. Set healthy boundaries. Find time to visit your family or call them every now and then to show you care. Make family dinners and eat together. Recreate and play together. Contribute to making your physical family environment healthy by sorting waste and composting if possible. If you feel like it, you can choose organic foods and toxin-free cosmetics and watch for high-quality light and air, as well as get rid of stuff you don't use.

And How to Help to Make Your Family Environment Healthy for All?

Communicate openly, care for your family, and let your family members express their needs. Respect their boundaries. Ask them how you can help with the household. Try your best to help fulfill the needs of your loved ones (but take care of your well-being just as much). Care for their well-being and help them build their well-being actively.

Do It　　**Acts of Kindness to Support the Environment**

Think of your **upcoming week and plan three acts of kindness** that also help you create or experience a healthy environment and plan on doing them. It does not matter if you want to demonstrate these acts of kindness supporting your health environment at school, at home, or in your community. What matters is to create a realistic and specific plan you can bring to life. Write down a list of acts of kindness that also support your healthy environment (e.g., you will sort the waste, you will help clean the neighborhood, or you will help your family to take care of their garden). Choose three acts of kindness that will help you experience or support a healthy environment that can be incorporated into your next week's schedule. Plan how you want to demonstrate them, why, and when. If you use a calendar, insert these engaging acts of kindness there and set a reminder.

High-Quality School and Study Environment

I teach at the School of Education. I have been blessed to work with students who decided to be teachers, who enjoy working with people, or who don't even plan to teach, but they choose their major simply because they love it. Our school of education has a very specific vibe and the environment is very friendly. Students walk to the building passing a flag saying, "*Welcome to the school of education family!*" When they walk in, there is a hall where you can find a Christmas tree and boxes for used clothing that students can bring to donate to people in need from our community in the winter, or small markets with cute souvenirs in the summer. There are some older books for free usually at the reception and as you walk the stairs, there are posters with big cloverleafs saying, "*Good luck with exams!*" prompting students to tear off a stripe with small cloverleafs saying, "*Put your luck in your pocket.*" There are also posters with pictures of our students who are sharing their stories about why they chose to be teachers all around the school. Other students get their daily dose of inspiration and I get my dose of joy seeing pictures of students I had the pleasure of spending last semester with during my leisure time education course. There are new posters, activities, and events every semester and everyone who enters the school says that this building is alive. Students feel safe, included, and seen and I feel like I am a part of something much bigger than individuals by themselves. Yes. Something like a "big school of education family."

The truth is your school environment **affects** your levels of achievement tremendously. But more importantly, a high-quality school environment positively impacts your well-being as well. Universities do their best to make their environment as healthy and as enjoyable for their students as possible. I also see students creating powerful "bottom-up" movements to change the school environment from a student's perspective at the university level with greater frequency. Organizing social events, starting university clubs, or even nonprofit organizations aimed to improve education. But there is still a lot **you can do by yourself** to make the most of it. Find a coffee shop you like and track the time you enjoy being there the most. Join a study group to make new friends. Becoming a member of school organizations will strengthen your sense of belonging. As well as the simple act of buying a hoodie with a school logo. Finding or creating a study place on campus where you feel comfortable and where you can focus effectively feels good too! As well as being an active co-creator of a healthy and positive school environment by sorting through your trash. I would also like to kindly invite you to explore options beyond your school. Sign up for a course at a different college or go study abroad! Many universities have great programs that will literally change your life. But it might also be beneficiat for you to contribute to feel included. **Actively help** with keeping bathrooms clean, respect your schoolmates, and model respectful behaviors such as being quiet in places set for studying. Help to organize students' events or learning communities Figure out what **you are good** at and **what you enjoy doing**. What would be the best way to contribute while enjoying it?

How to Set a Study Environment to Impact Your Study Achievement Positively

Most college students spend a significant amount of time studying – an average of 17 hours a week, according to USA Today (2021). Having the right study environment is key to your academic success. It's important to establish a space where you can be both productive and comfy! But how do you create a healthy and positive space you want to be in? Check out the tips from Herzing University to enjoy your study time while being productive!

https://www.herzing.edu/blog/6-tips-create-perfect-study-environment

Time out on Campus

I would like to invite you to spend as much time as you can out in nature. You can do it when spending time in or around campus by taking your lunch outside, walking around the park with your coffee, or sitting by the water fountain while reading a book. But try to do so at work or in your personal life as well. Appreciate and enjoy the moment of connection with nature during your school day.

High-quality Work and Part-time Job Environment

We all enjoy (and benefit from) a high-quality work and part-time job environment. A workplace you like can create a sense of meaning in your life. We are more productive in positive work environments. We are more engaged while working, more creative, and more motivated and we like investing our time in our work better. A high-quality work and a part-time job environment support your health and well-being significantly.

Do it **Job Crafting**

Is there anything you can do to craft your work and part-time job environment to make it healthier for you? Absolutely! Here are a few tips, see what fits your lifestyle the best:

- open your windows and let the fresh air in
- check your lighting and let some sun in
- make it safe and clean by getting rid of toxins

- following safety rules
- using proper storage for everything
- make it yours – bring a bit of home there if you feel like it would help
- make it joyful, funny, and cozy – play your favorite music, bring your pictures, buy a plant

Taking turns and doing your part to clean can **help** to make your work and part-time job environment healthy for all. Respect the space of others but also don't be afraid to initiate some group activity on the other hand. Have breakfast meetings with colleagues and share what you are currently working on. It is so nice to know what your co-workers are currently focusing on. Or don't talk about work at all :-) Eat lunch together and try the opposite. Talk about anything but work! Do coffee breaks at a local coffee shop and celebrate birthdays at a local restaurant. It will strengthen your relationships and create a positive work climate.

Use Your Character Strengths to Create a Positive Work Environment

As we know well, those of us who use our character strengths at work report greater job and life satisfaction and engagement than those not using their strengths. Identify your personal character strengths at VIA Character Strengths Survey (https://www.viacharacter.org/) and think of how specifically your strengths can help you build and maintain **a positive work environment**. For example, if humor is your character strength, make it a goal to make a colleague laugh at least once a day. Or if creativity is your personal strength, think of how you could decorate your workplace to make everyone feel better there! If gratitude comes naturally to you, speak openly with your coworkers about things you are thankful for at work and why you appreciate them for a week and watch your happiness increase!

High-quality Community Environment

A healthy **community environment** enables its residents to have access to quality education, transportation, adequate employment, and quality health care. Even people's physical activity is supported by community parks, playgrounds, and bike paths. Finding yourself in such an environment makes you feel included and supported, and a positive environment can also increase your meaning in life and health. Let's look at blue zones again. There are some principles in places where the healthiest and happiest communities live longer than the rest of the world. Those are, for example, **"people first"** designs which make social engagement easy by having a lot of walking pathways and natural spaces for recreating and doing sports.

So, what can you do to craft your community environment?

Browse, search, and go to events! Meet new people and join a school club if you feel like it. Participate in university life and support the student community. You will meet a lot of like-minded people to learn from and to simply enjoy their company. Find your favorite places in your community and around campus (parks, coffee shops, museums, etc.) and enjoy having them in your life. But what about your community beyond the school environment? Our relationships with our neighbors are important. Our neighbors often turn to our friends and we share our life with them beyond small talks in front of our doors. They contribute to our sense of belonging and safety and they are often there when we need them. Smile at them a second longer next time you take your trash out and you meet them at the hall.

Don't forget to do your part too. Join and support community transformation programs and participate in community events. Vote! Support local businesses. Become a member of a non-profit organization. Do voluntary work (but don't push yourself if you are short on time please). Students who volunteer report getting a regular dose of life satisfaction. Smile at strangers when your eyes meet on the street. Help your neighbors when they need you. No good deed ever goes wasted!

Do it   Sort!

Let me invite you to start sorting your waste. It is easy, fun, and it feels good. Think big but start small. Buy an extra trash can and separate plastic or paper. Separate your lunch waste in the dining hall properly or use the colorful cans around campus to separate the trash you produce. It feels right to take responsibility for your contribution to the community.

Do it   Use Your Personal Power to Help Your Community

Use your character strengths to support your community environment. By now, I am sure you have already identified your character strengths, but in case you did not – identify your personal character strengths at VIA Character Strengths Survey (https://www.viacharacter.org/) and think of how specifically your strengths can be beneficial to your community environment. For example, if curiosity is your character strength, you can expand your knowledge in a healthy community environment through books, journals, magazines, TV, radio, or internet for half an hour, three times a week. Acknowledge what new knowledge about healthy environment support you have gained and are ready to apply into your everyday life. Find joy in co-creating a positive community environment while using what comes to you naturally.

High-quality Online Environment

Managing and keeping your online environment healthy can have a lot of **benefits** (Koci, 2022). Many of us study online, stay connected to others through the internet, and stay updated by following high-quality informational sources. Many of us get daily doses of inspiration by following online content that relates to our interests and we can also build our network of work and study connections online easier than ever. But many of us could also use a bit of better management over the time we spend online and the content we absorb.

How do you Craft Your Online Environment?

Sort your online waste – delete content and applications that you haven't used for a certain period of time and download those that can have a positive impact on your life (Headspace, Calm, USLA Mindful, My Possible Self, Yoga Studio: Mind & Body, to mention a few). Surround yourself with content that makes you feel good (funny profiles, educative profiles, etc.). Avoid anyone and anything that makes you feel anxious. Don't be afraid to go through your list of friends and unfollow people you don't know or don't feel comfortable being connected to. Be authentic in your social media and simply search for what can help you grow and move towards what you want in your life. Set some rules for yourself (e.g., no internet browsing when learning) and balance your time online with real social interactions or time for yourself.

How do you Help Make Your Online Environment Healthy for Everyone?

Think twice before you share something online. Share valuable, funny, or inspiring content. Always be aware of why you are posting something and ask yourself, will I make others feel good when I share this? And always remember to keep your personal facts private.

Do it   **Time Off(line)**

Reduce your online time by blocking commercials, unwanted emails, and spam. Turn off all the notifications you can on both your phone and your computer. Avoid temptations to spend time on social media by regularly changing the location of your social media apps on your phone. This will prevent automatic logins and help you become conscious of your social media time. Check your screen time on your phone occasionally to be aware of your social media use. Set limits for your daily use and make healthy boundaries for yourself.

Time Spent Outdoors in Nature

Spending time in nature is the most natural thing you can do. Not only does getting fresh air feel good, spending time in nature helps us to turn the noise of our everyday life down and helps us to re-connect – not only to nature but also to ourselves. Despite that, humanity spends the least amount of time in nature now than in all of history.

What Can You Do to Spend More Time in Nature?

Acknowledge your physical and mental needs to spend more time in nature. Actively seek nature everywhere you go and everywhere you are!

What can get you closer to nature?

- go to parks
- visit botanical gardens
- sit near a lake or a river
- go for a hike
- sit outside when eating in restaurants to get some sun
- give plants as presents
- have plants yourself at home or at work
- buy natural skin products
- prefer to wear natural fiber clothing such as cotton, silk, linen, and wool
- eat natural foods
- paint your home with natural colors
- eat your snacks outside of the buildings
- go for a walk with a friend instead of meeting at a library
- buy your coffee to go and go for a walk with friends instead of sitting indoors
- plan a trip in a forest
- go fishing
- run around your neighborhood rather than running inside on a treadmill
- go for a walk while on the phone
- try gardening
- go camping

And how do you help to make your natural environment healthy for everyone? Separate waste. Change your cleaning supplies to be nature-friendly. Volunteer in gardening or trash picking. Be respectful, caring, and supportive of nature by not throwing waste on the ground, including chewing gum. Help cultivate parks and any nature around your home, school, and workplace.

Do it   **Nature Calls!**

Plan a trip into a nature. Either with friends you love to spend some time with or alone. Think of what you love doing, what nature speaks to you, take a weekend off from school projects, and disconnect in nature. Don't plan any work there. Don't even plan any big sight-seeing. Just be. You and nature.

Do It   Ten Empowering Questions to Support My Positive Environment Flower Growth

1   What is the smallest thing I can do to make my study environment more enjoyable today?
2   What can I do to make my home environment more positive and healthier?
3   What can I do for the community environment today?
4   What can I do to change my home environment to study more effectively?
5   What am I good at that can help co-create a positive school environment?
6   What would help me limit my time spent online?
7   What can I do to spend more time in or connected to nature every day?
8   What can I do to co-create a high-quality living environment for my family?
9   What do I like about my work environment the most and how can I support it?
10   What else can I do to support my positive environment today?

Do It   Ten Tips to Build My Positive Environment Flower

1   Make sure you always have access to fresh air. Open the window during the class break. Go out for a quick walk. Get your air conditioning filter changed in your car. Use air cleaner and air humidifier therapy at home.
2   Safety first! Always, in any environment. Limit consumption of foods grown with pesticides, and protect yourself from chemicals and any physical or mental harm. Follow the safety protocol for your work, if there is one.
3   Get clean and avoid or eliminate as many toxins as possible in your environment. Clean your home with natural products. Check the label of the cosmetics you use. Buy bio and natural foods.
4   Build and care for high-quality relationships in your communities, use your social skills and your character strengths to care for others.
5   Craft your environment to make it healthier and more positive.
6   Reduce screen and digital time.
7   Make your study environment as effective and cozy as possible.
8   Be respectful of the space of others.
9   Always contribute to co-creating a healthy environment.
10   Protect and care for nature.

Tips to Positive Environment Snacking

Building your environment does not have to be complicated nor time demanding. Look at Figure 9.7 and try some of the tips right now.

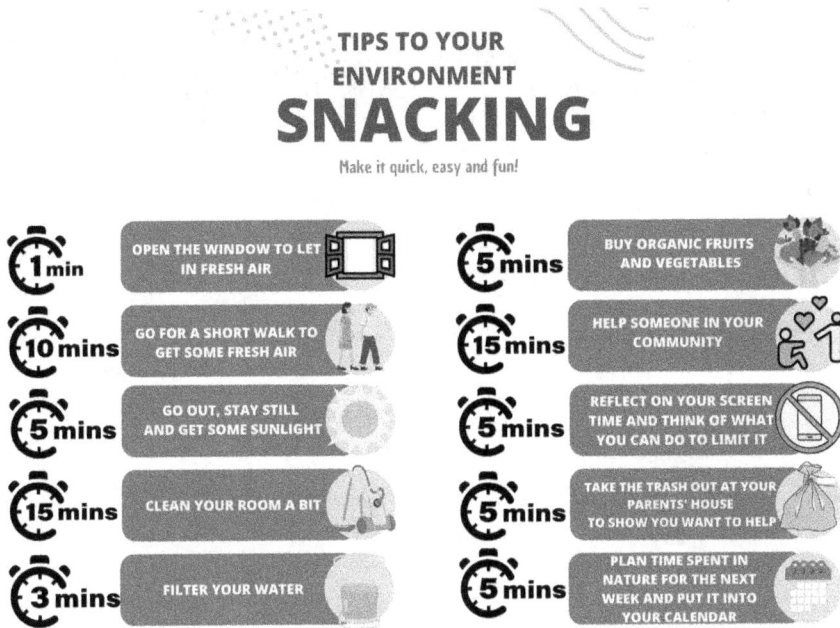

Figure 9.7 Tips to positive environment snacking.

Environments we live in can be very strong predictors of your health and well-being. There are some aspects of our environment we nurture, accept, or change. We can consciously choose healthy environments for us, we can craft to make some healthier, or we can even help to co-create positive environments. But good and healthy environments would not be enough for our well-being if we felt financially insecure. Money cannot buy happiness, we often hear. But economic security lets us feel safe, calm, and secured in general. So where is the line of "having enough" to feel secured, what is the economic situation among students, and what can be done to support your economic security building block of well-being? Let me invite you to our last chapter to make your well-being care complete!

References

Koci, J. (2022). Health and well-being tips for distance learning university students. Volume 6, Number 3, University Counseling – Current Challenges and Trends.

Koci, J. (2023). *How to build well-being in university and college students – Methodology of academic well-being promotion.* Prague: Charles University. ISBN: 978-80-87489-38-3

Koci, J., & Donaldson, S. I. (2022). *Zdraví a mentální well-being studentů distančního vzdělávání.* Prague: Charles University. ISBN: 978-80-7603-357-3

Pierre, K. 2023. USA Today: How much do you study? Apparently 17 hours a week is the norm. Available at: https://eu.usatoday.com/story/college/2014/08/18/how-much-do-you-study-apparently-17-hours-a-week-is-the-norm/37395213/

The World Health Organization (2022). Environmental health. Available at: https://www.who.int/health-topics/environmental-health#tab=tab_1

USA Tosay (2021). *How much do you study? Apparently 17 hours a week is the norm.* Available at: https://www.usatoday.com/story/college/2014/08/18/how-much-do-you-study-apparently-17-hours-a-week-is-the-norm/37395213/

10 Building Your Economic Security

> Your economic security does not lie in your job, it lies in your own power to produce –
> to think, to create, to learn, to adapt.
>
> — Stephen R. Covey

You are standing in line in a local coffee house and you are playing with a thought of whether you should pamper yourself with the fancy Frappuccino covered with whipped cream and caramel crunches all around or whether you should buy the regular coffee for $1.99 to save money. *"Gosh, will this ever end? Will I ever get to the point when I don't have to look at the price and I just buy myself what I really wish?"* We all have been there. Or at least I certainly have. But let's dream for a minute. Imagine that it is five years from now and you really got to the point when you buy yourself the fancy Frappuccino and you don't even check the price. You no longer try to save money by compromising yourself. What does it feel like? How much money do you have on you now? And how much do you have saved in your bank account? What is your job that lets you live this lifestyle and what is your monthly income? Now let's look at the past in between your future self and your current self. What happened in between? What was the point when you started to feel financially secured and what helped you to get there? Did you set some satisfactory income goals for yourself? Or did you start tracking your expenses and you also started setting some money aside every month? Did you learn about finances and even about investments? Or did you slowly combine this all along the way? Whatever it is that helped you to be your more economically secured future self, this chapter will help you to get a clearer idea about what and how you can start creating changes that can seem small at the beginning but that can have a great impact on your economic security in the long term.

Introduction to Economic Security

Your economic security is generated by a good income, having satisfactory savings, investments, and proper expense management. All that can be cared for thanks to your good financial literacy. Access to quality health care is also a big part of our economic security.

DOI: 10.4324/9781003378365-11

David S. Rosenthal Center for Wellness and Health Promotion at Harvard University Health Services defines care for your financial well-being as "*being mindful of your financial decision making.*" (2022).

Supporting your financial health can look like "*differentiating between needs and wants and living within your means, and managing short-term and long-term financial goals.*"

Before we differentiate between wants and needs, let's have a quick look at what students spend their money on the most often.

The student's total costs can be divided into **living costs** and **study-related costs**. Living costs include costs for:

- accommodation (rent or mortgage and utilities)
- food
- transportation
- communication (telephone, internet, etc.)
- health (e.g. medicine, medical insurance)
- childcare
- debt payment (except mortgage)
- social and leisure activities
- other regular living costs, such as clothing, toiletries, tobacco, pets, insurance (except medical insurance), or alimony

Study-related costs contain three sub-categories:

- university fees, including fees for tuition, registration, and administration
- contributions to student unions/associations/councils, for student services, or insurance (except medical insurance)
- other study-related costs, such as field trips, books, photocopying, private tutoring, or additional courses

Students from EUROSTUDENT countries (2021) who do not live with their parents allocate on average 35% of their total monthly expenses (including transfers) to accommodation, 23% to food, and 7% to transportation. Students often spend their money on meals, snacks, alcohol, and coffee.

Students from EUROSTUDENT countries also often spend their money on entertainment, electronic devices, and personal care products. Other students' costs are on computers, printers, e-readers, cell phones, internet, cable TV, and online movie subscriptions.

How do you feel about this? Could you relate? Student costs can often look alike. Where we all may differ is what would fall in the category of "my wants" and "my needs." What can represent "my wants" for one can represent "my needs" for another. And that is ok. What is important is to start asking yourself a question. "DO I really need this?" "Is there anything I should prioritize over this?" Once you start looking at things through your "needs" and "wants" glasses, things will get much clearer and easier to manage.

Benefits of Economic Security for Students' Well-being

Research shows (Kushlev et al., 2015) that wealth generates less discomfort but does not generate more happiness. The results of this study show that **financial independence actually really matters and increases our well-being**. Being rich does not.

Let me explain. Interesting results were revealed in a study on lottery winners and accident victims (Brickman et al., 1978). After one year of either winning or getting into an unfortunate accident, lottery winners were not happier than controls and lottery winners received even less pleasure from ordinary events of everyday life than controls. Accident victims were, on the contrary, after some time not as unhappy as we would expect. Is happiness really relative? This effect can be explained by adaptation level theory and leads to the surprising fact that lottery winners are not generally happier than people who didn't win the lottery after some time.

But what about financial security? Studies show that life satisfaction and perceived stress among university students are closely linked to **perceived financial security**. Economically secured students are **more likely to build and care for their well-being**. But studies also show that the majority of students don't feel economically secure. And I can only relate. In our studies (Koci et al., 2023), satisfactory investments, satisfactory savings, and good income always appear as the biggest insecurities of our students. And it is understandable. You often spend at school and studying together the same amount of the time the average adult spends at work. Looking at this from that perspective, your studies are often your full-time job. Instead of earning money, you invest your money and time into your future.

Even if money cannot buy you happiness, **economic security is a significant contributor to your well-being**. Take any opportunity to increase your financial literacy, manage your finances, set goals for satisfactory income, save money, invest once you feel like you can, and think of strategies on how to get access to quality health care. Let's assess your own economic security and let's learn some tips to increase your skills supporting your economic well-being among different areas of your economic security well-being building block.

Your Economic Security Flower Assessment

We have learned in Chapter 1 that economic security is one of the **nine essential building blocks** for generating well-being. One of the things that can be very useful is to reflect on and to think about your personal **economic security strengths**. Understanding the importance of economic security for your well-being, I would like to provide you with an opportunity to assess your economic security strengths!

In this exercise you will be asked to fill out your own **flower diagram**. You will be provided with a wheel that represents **six different strengths** for building your economic security. These go from good income, satisfactory savings, satisfactory investments, proper expense management, financial literacy, access to quality health care, and there is also a room for your own choice of another economic security strength you might feel needs to be reflected in your life as well.

Here is a **set of statements** that will help you assess how well you feel about each economic security strength. You might find it helpful to reflect by reading the descriptions of ideal states of all six of your strengths and assessing where you stand.

Good Income

I am **satisfied with my income**. I have an ideal **financial situation, vision,** and **plans** for my future income and I am doing well on working toward them.

Satisfactory Savings

I am **satisfied with my savings**. I save some **portion of my monthly income** regularly before any spending. I have saving **plans** that help me move toward my ideal economic security vision.

Satisfactory Investments

I am **satisfied with my investments**. I **invest regularly** and I keep up with my financial plans and visions.

Proper Expense Management

I **track** my earnings, savings, and spending. I have financial **goals** and I **plan** how to reach them. I **balance** my spending with my savings and I **prioritize** investments that are in line with my values.

Financial Literacy

I have satisfactory **knowledge** of how to manage my finances and how to **build** economic security for myself. I know where to **get more reliable information** about finances if needed. I am **aware** of my income plans and how to **reach** them and I feel **confident** with my investments.

Access to Quality Health Care

I have **access to quality health care**. I have **high-quality insurance** and **good health care** is always **accessible** to me physically if needed (I can **reach a doctor** if needed).

Other Economic Security Strengths

Are there any other economic security strengths on your mind you would like to assess? If yes, please scale them as you did the previous strengths.

So how do you actually assess your strengths? **Please imagine a ladder with steps numbered from 0 at the bottom to 10 at the top.**

The top of the ladder represents the best result (I feel very confident in this particular strength), while the bottom of the ladder represents the worst (I would like to build this particular strength better).

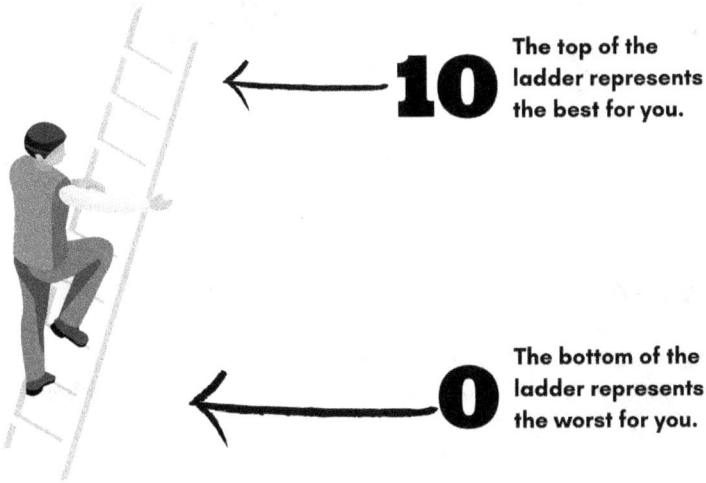

The top of the ladder represents the best for you.

The bottom of the ladder represents the worst for you.

Figure 10.1 Your well-being assessment ladder.

On which step of the ladder on a scale of 0–10 would you say you personally feel you stand at this time in terms of:

- good income
- satisfactory savings
- satisfactory investments
- proper expense management
- financial literacy
- access to quality health care
- other economic security strengths

After you assess all your economic security strengths, draw your very own economic security flower! Circle the resulting numbers of your strength on the economic security wheel ladders. Then draw the petal shape from the center of the wheel through all the numbers on each ladder to create your own flower (see Figure 10.2 for an example of the flower diagram).

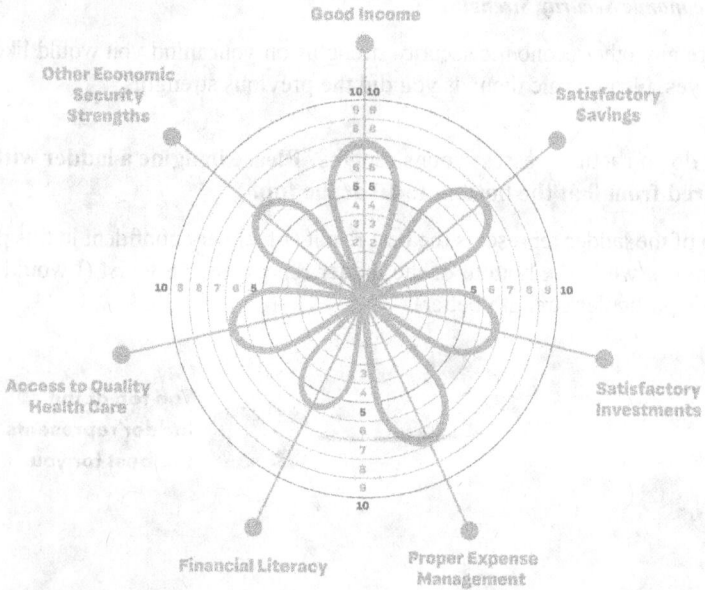

Figure 10.2 Example of your economic security flower diagram.

Let's assess your **economic security strengths** and later you can reflect on them and learn how to build particular strengths (if needed) in the upcoming chapter.

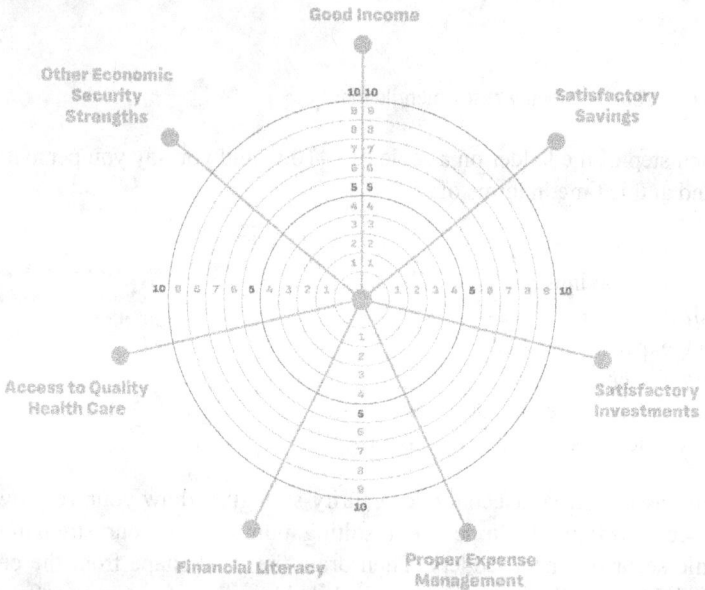

Figure 10.3 Your economic security flower assessment.

YOUR ECONOMIC SECURITY FLOWER REFLECTION

Great job! How do you feel?

Let's have a look at your personal **economic security flower**.

Remember, there is no judgment here; this is just an awareness exercise.

The goal of this exercise is to become **aware of your situation and decide what your next goal should be**. Then you will have a chance to think about what you can do to achieve said goal. This chapter will present some **evidence-based recommendations and activities** you can try right away to see if they fit your personality and lifestyle. It is fun to reflect on your flowers with your friends, but remember, the only one you can compare your flowers to is yourself. Enjoy checking on your flowers over time to track your progress or changes reflecting certain events in different stages of your life. The goal shouldn't be to have perfect, long petals in all your flowers – you should come to terms with imperfection. Invite the possibility of gradual growth of your flower petals rather than unhealthy overnight perfection.

Each flower reflects your **subjective perception**, rather than your objective state. You might rate your *Financial Literacy* petal lower while objectively your financial literacy is above average. Why do people do that? Our perception of ourselves is rarely objective. Sometimes, this can be caused by having a certain idea or vision of what our ideal *Financial Literacy* petal should look like. Sometimes, the *Financial Literacy* petal can be shaken by learning about new ways of investment that leave you feeling insecure. Hence, it can be reasonable to believe we still have room for growth. Rating your petals gives you **the opportunity to reflect on** your current state in certain areas of your life. It will also make you think about what strengths you are satisfied with for now and what strengths you might like to focus on. :-)

Let's see how you can **grow your economic security petals**.

Good Income

Working during university is a very common phenomenon. Students often have more than one job and with differences across majors, based on EUROSTUDENT (2021), approximately 60% of university students work at least part-time.

Students' jobs are often not our dream jobs but they help us make money for our expenses. They can build our experience portfolio, and they can also oftentimes be **great starting points for our future career**. To be satisfied with your income, it depends on whether you are able to cover your expenses or not. Your "elementary needs" and your "wants." So how can you find a suitable job for you?

Dream big but start small. Try to combine your job with something you already do or enjoy. If you love to bike, try food delivery in the city where you can bike to deliver your orders! If you love spending time around people and you enjoy talking to them, a waitress or barista at a coffee shop could be a good choice for you. If you enjoy driving in your car, consider becoming a driver for Uber. There are many options. But a great strategy is to choose a job that will let you use your strengths and that will also generate some joy in your life.

If you feel like you really need to focus on your school and studies and you choose not to work, scholarships can be a great way to get a little extra income. It is something worth trying. Check at your university what the rules are to apply for a scholarship. Whether the merit scholarship or the social scholarship. The truth oftentimes is that the applications are not overly competitive. Simply because many students don't believe they would get it. **Trying it literally costs you nothing!**

Satisfactory Savings

Building satisfactory savings definitely helps to create your economic security. But what are the steps to save money and to be satisfied with it? First, we need to become aware of our spending. We also need to set our financial goals and adapt our lifestyle so we can save what we would like to save. Reflecting on how we are doing is a valuable step as well. Then we only keep repeating the cycle. Until we do the whole process out of habit.

1   Track how much you earned and how much you spent.

   A student's budget is a type of list that clearly defines your income and expenses. It can be useful for you to help you manage your money in terms of spending and savings. The first important step to your money management is to track how much you make and how much you spend. This can be done by simply checking your bank account and writing down your income and spending in your phone notes. You can also download one of the existing apps to make your life easier! (Please check out the app Spendee and many more.)

2 Set your financial goals.

Many students make a budget for short-term goals, such as a vacation or to save money to buy something they wish for or want. While others may think of more long-term spending and savings plans. **Your choice!**

3 Adapt your lifestyle.

In the case of money management, many students' decisions should simply be based on budgets, and students may reduce or expand spending **according to their current situation, goals**, and **plans**. This simply might look like cutting your expenses on your wants in times of unexpected costs or, vice versa, you can start a savings account to save money for your future when you get a bonus at work.

4 Reflect on how you are doing.

Reflect every now and then on **how you are doing**. Are you ok with the way you are saving your money? How about your expenses? Aren't you limiting yourself too much? Or can you save just a little bit more? Be patient and kind to yourself. Reaching goals and desirable behavior takes a while.

5 Repeat.

Creating a habit can take a while. Keep going, keep learning, and keep acting in a new way. Sooner or later you will thank yourself for building a habit that **will actually serve you your whole life!**

Do It   **Reflect on good things**

Drozd et al. (2014) suggest practicing good things to generate our mental well-being. How can such an activity be implemented for university students' lifestyles, ideally also supporting our financial security? Make a list of good things in your student life that also support your economic security and implement them in your everyday life.

Write down a list of good things in your life. Analyze your list of good things and identify good things/activities from your everyday life that also support your current or future economic security. Those might be enjoying a coffee you make for yourself for breakfast. Running in the park after school costs you nothing. Or the ability to study and learn from books at the school library instead of buying them. Incorporate good things that are also economically healthy for you into your everyday life intentionally.

Satisfactory Investments

One way to increase our life satisfaction is through wise investments. But what is the best way to know where to invest our finances? Well, satisfactory investments are very specific to each and every one of us. There is not one way that would fit all of us. But knowing what is important to you in your life and trying to align your investments with what you appreciate in life the most can certainly increase your happiness.

First, identify your **life values**. Second, **align** your financial goals with your life goals. Third, **strategize** and **plan steps** to reach your life goals!

How to Identify Your Life Values?

Values are our personal judgments across all areas of life (people, objects, situations, and activities), reflecting on what is truly important to us. What is precious to us forms the basic component of our motivation.

Values are those life attitudes that tell us what we **value the most**, what we consider **most essential in life**, and what **motivates us most strongly** in achieving our goals. A synonym for values could be a *life priority*.

Every university student values something different. And you will probably also have a slightly different value hierarchy than your classmates or even your family members. Some students value success the most, thus studying to achieve good grades and recognition contributes to their well-being. Another student may be active during classes because they are eager for knowledge to increase their understanding. Gaining new experiences contributes to their well-being. Someone values pleasant events the most, such as quality time spent with friends, and will look for social contact at school to increase their well-being. Each student carries differently aligned life values, and as V. E. Frankl reminds us, *we are obliged to live according to these values until our last breath.*

For example, if you value learning, you might consider investing money in your education. If you value joy and fun, you might like to invest in your hobbies or in making new experiences. If you live for your friends and family, you might like to invest in high-quality time with them. Remember your values and your choices.

How Can You Reveal What Your Life Values Are?

Ask yourself, what is it you live for?
What gives your life meaning?
What would hurt you the most when losing it in your life?
What experiences do you value the most?

Don't think about it, and write down your answers. Circle your key words or even create some umbrella terms for your statements. And if you like, you can even determine your values from the most important ones. **Carry your values in your mind** and when making any decision, compare your decision outcomes to your values. No matter if the decision is related to money or not.

Proper Expense Management

Are you interested in fostering your financial well-being with proper expense management? David S. Rosenthal Center for Wellness and Health Promotion at Harvard University Health Services (2022) has many great tips for you. Check these:

- Track and review your spending by monitoring your bank account and keeping a list of all purchases in one week – it may be more than you think.
- Start with small changes that will add up over time (i.e. make your own coffee rather than buying it).
- Write a list and set a budget for yourself before going shopping.
- Ask yourself "do I really need this?" before an unplanned purchase.
- Start a savings account – add a small monthly automatic payment if possible.
- Ask for student discounts.

Potential benefits include achieving personal financial goals, reducing debt, decreasing financial stress, feeling in control of and secure in your finances, and increasing your savings for tomorrow. Needed assistance or help can be found through financial consultants at your university – ask for possibilities or even some financial aid.

Here are some additional tips for you to earn, save, and track your money:

- Save money on living expenses. Rent a place with a group of friends or even stay with your parents if this option is available.
- Spending after savings. Always put a bit of your income aside first before spending it.
- Track your finances on paper, in Excel, or on your phone through one of many available apps. This step might feel uncomfortable at first, but you will actually enjoy checking your finances sooner or later. Just start.
- Think before you spend! Be aware and be in charge. Do your math. Does your money management leave you in plus numbers or do you put yourself in minuses? Try to learn where your spending goes.
- Use your student's card and ask for sales. Study all your student benefits and don't hesitate to use them.
- Ask about scholarship possibilities. Search and study your options. Ask for help at student services.
- Get yourself a piggy bank. Save your change every now and then. Start small but plan big. You are creating the habit of setting something aside and it does not matter how much or how little you start with. Just start. You will thank yourself later in your life.

Also, check out these additional original tips that my awesome students put together in our well-being class:

- Unsubscribe from newsletters from your favorite stores – their messages about sales and promotions are only meant to make you spend more of your money on their products.
- Make your food and coffee at home. Making your own meals and coffee will help you save money and as a benefit, you can control the quality of what you eat as well. But also, buy yourself a fancy coffee once in a while please!
- Sign up for an economic security class. We all are lost. Not many of us got educated about finances!

Financial Literacy

The National Educators Council defines financial literacy as *possessing skills and knowledge on financial matters to confidently take effective action that best fulfills an individual's personal, family, and global community goals*. Taking a financial management class as my students suggest is actually a very good idea. In fact, not many of us really had an opportunity to learn about finances at school, nor was everyone lucky to be taught by their parents either. Read books. Think of someone who you consider inspiring in your circle and ask them openly what to do. But I would also like to provide you with some tips for online courses you might start taking to support your financial literacy right now.

Join the Course: Financial Planning for Young Adults

Financial Planning for Young Adults (FPYA) with Nicholas Paulson, developed in partnership with the CFP Board, is designed to provide an introduction to basic financial planning concepts for young adults. The FPYA course is organized across eight separate modules within a four-week window. Topics covered include financial goal setting, saving and investing, budgeting, financial risk, borrowing, and credit. Because financial planning is such a personal topic, you will be encouraged to define your own financial goals and objectives while we discuss concepts and provide tools which can be applied in helping you reach those goals.

Enroll in the course here: https://www.coursera.org/learn/financial-planning

---

Join the Course: Introduction to Finance and Accounting Specialization

Learn the basics of finance and accounting. Build a foundation of core business skills in finance and accounting.

Course begins with concepts and applications like time value of money, risk-return tradeoff, retirement savings, mortgage financing, auto leasing, asset valuation, and many others. The specialization uses Excel to make the experience more hands-on and help learners understand the concepts more directly. From valuing claims and making financing decisions to elements of a basic financial model, the coursework provides a solid foundation to corporate finance. Then the course moves to financial accounting, enabling learners to read financial statements and to understand the language and grammar of accounting. The coursework introduces bookkeeping fundamentals, accrual accounting, cash flow analysis, among much else! Finally, using the foundational knowledge of accounting, the specialization teaches learners how to understand and analyze key information that companies provide in their statements, including types of assets and liabilities and longer-term investments and debts, and finally the difference between tax reporting and financial reporting.

Enroll in the course here: https://www.coursera.org/specializations/finance-accounting

Join the Course: The Fundamentals of Personal Finance Specialization

Learn the Money Skills You Need with Brian Walsh. Gain a better understanding of personal finance topics and how to implement strategies to meet your financial goals.

This specialization is intended for anyone looking to take control of their finances. Through these five courses, you will cover a variety of personal finance topics, including budgets, investing, and managing risk. The readings, videos,

and activities will prepare you to understand the current state of your money as well as take actions to work toward your financial goals. This specialization is geared toward learners in the United States of America.

Enroll in the course here: https://www.coursera.org/specializations/personal-finance-fundamentals

Access to Quality Health Care

The World Health Organization (2022) defines quality of health care as *the degree to which health services for individuals and populations increase the likelihood of desired health outcomes.*

The World Health Organization states that quality health services should be effective (providing evidence-based health care services to those who need them), safe (avoiding harm to people for whom the care is intended), and people-centered (providing care that responds to individual preferences, needs, and values).

It is clear that access to quality health care is crucial for our well-being. **There are some options** on how to manage your health care strategy. You can be included on your parent's application, or the U.S. Centers for Medicare & Medicaid Services (2022) note that if your school offers a student health plan, it can be an easy and affordable way to get basic insurance coverage via your university. They point out that if you're enrolled in a student health plan, in most cases this can count as qualifying health coverage. This means you're considered covered under the health care law and won't have to pay the penalty for not having insurance. In any case, please check with the plan to be sure or contact your student health services to discuss your options with a professional. Many universities offer such consulting services, so please go and use them.

Ten Empowering Questions to Support My Economic Security Flower Growth

Do it

1   What are my core values I want to invest my energy, time, and money into?
2   What is my current economic security like and how is it different from my vision of ideal economic security?
3   What are the steps or actions I need to take to get closer to my ideal economic security?
4   What can I do to track my financial expenses better?

5   What can I do to secure my health care better?
6   What would I like to learn to increase my financial literacy?
7   Who can I learn from and who is my economic security inspiration?
8   Are there any possible ways for me to invest in my finances?
9   What would be the best strategy for me to save money?
10   How can I invest my finances to support my dreams coming true?

Do it   **Ten Tips to Build My Economic Security Flower**

1   Become your own financial management expert. Track your income and expenses. Watch where your money flows. Reflect on your financial situation regularly and strategize how to improve your economic security.
2   Decide to save some money and look for the best strategies that fit your personal lifestyle. Either buy a piggy bank or create a new savings account. Whatever will make it easier for you to put some money aside every month.
3   Educate yourself to increase your financial literacy. Read books, talk to people, and watch videos online from reliable sources. Use any way to get better at building your economic security for yourself.
4   Check the financial aid options with your health care at your school.
5   Make your financial income plans and visions. Put the numbers on paper. Write your dreams down. Think through what steps you need to take to work on your dreams.
6   Always have your student card on you. Ask for student sales in shops and actually use them.
7   Limit spending money on eating out and make your own food at home. Not only will you spend less, you will also probably eat much healthier.
8   Think the possibility of getting a part-time job (a side job) that would fit your strengths and hobbies preferences. For example, if your strength is organization and you love to do sports, of the possibility of applying for a bike food delivery job at the university recreational center.
9   Start a student bank account. Those are usually free and you can use them even after graduating. It will help you save some expenses.
10   Think of a possibility to combine your passion with your future career. Start developing a career you would love and where you would not mind to spend your time.

Tips to Economic Security Snacking

Building your economic security does not have to be complicated nor time demanding. Look at Figure 10.4 and try some of the tips right now.

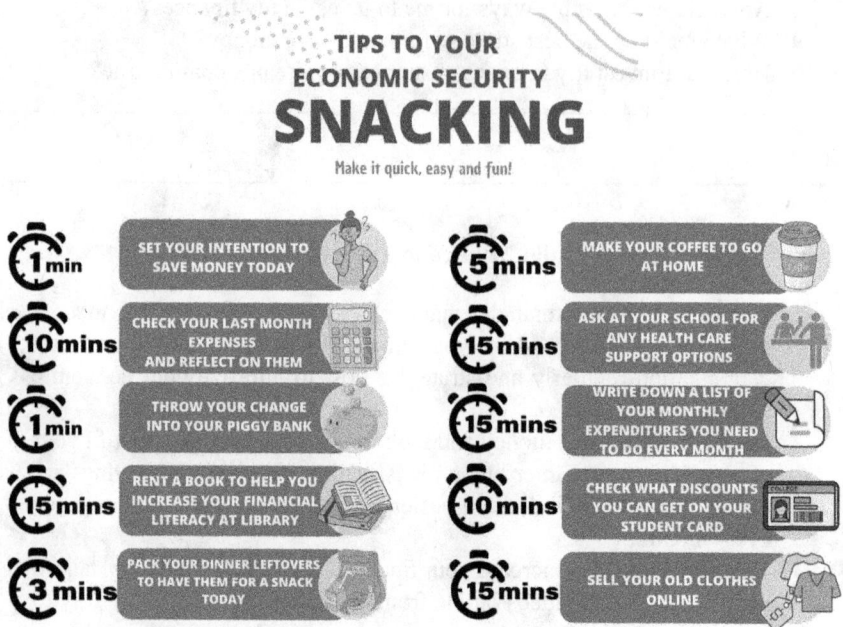

TIPS TO YOUR
ECONOMIC SECURITY
SNACKING

Make it quick, easy and fun!

1 min — SET YOUR INTENTION TO SAVE MONEY TODAY	**5 mins** — MAKE YOUR COFFEE TO GO AT HOME
10 mins — CHECK YOUR LAST MONTH EXPENSES AND REFLECT ON THEM	**15 mins** — ASK AT YOUR SCHOOL FOR ANY HEALTH CARE SUPPORT OPTIONS
1 min — THROW YOUR CHANGE INTO YOUR PIGGY BANK	**15 mins** — WRITE DOWN A LIST OF YOUR MONTHLY EXPENDITURES YOU NEED TO DO EVERY MONTH
15 mins — RENT A BOOK TO HELP YOU INCREASE YOUR FINANCIAL LITERACY AT LIBRARY	**10 mins** — CHECK WHAT DISCOUNTS YOU CAN GET ON YOUR STUDENT CARD
3 mins — PACK YOUR DINNER LEFTOVERS TO HAVE THEM FOR A SNACK TODAY	**15 mins** — SELL YOUR OLD CLOTHES ONLINE

Figure 10.4 Tips to economic security snacking.

Learning how to manage our finances can be hard, especially since we rarely had a chance to learn how to do this while growing up. But we can learn this as well as anything else in our lives. Tracking your finances can be scary at first, since we are afraid to reveal that we are making many transactions that can be eliminated. But take any opportunity to learn. Read some books, talk to people who inspire you, and ask them questions. Take some online classes. Support your economic security building block of well-being as much as you support the growth of other building blocks. This time investment will be paid back many times!

References

Brickman, P., Coates, D., & Janoff-Bulman, R. (1978). Lottery winners and accident victims: Is happiness relative? *Journal of Personality and Social Psychology*, 36(8), 917–927. https://doi.org/10.1037/0022-3514.36.8.917

David S. Rosenthal Center for Wellness and Health Promotion at Harvard University Health Services (2021). Your wellbeing, financial well-being. [November 25, 2022; online] Available at: https://wellness.huhs.harvard.edu/financial

Drozd, F., Mork, L., Nielsen, B., Raeder, S., & Bjørkli, C. A. (2014). Better days – A randomized controlled trial of an internet-based positive psychology intervention. *The Journal of Positive Psychology*, 9(5), 377–388.

EUROSTUDENT VII Synopsis of Indicators 2018–2021. *Social and Economic Conditions of Student Life in Europe*. German Centre for Higher Education Research.

Koci, J. (2023). *How to Build Well-being in University and College Students – Methodology of Academic Well-being Promotion*. Charles University, Prague. ISBN: 978-80-87489-38-3

Kushlev, K., Dunn, E., & Lucas, R. (2015). Higher income is associated with less daily sadness but not more daily happiness. *Social Psychological and Personality Science*, 6. https://doi.org/10.1177/1948550614568161

Social and Economic Conditions of Student Life in Europe: 2021. Germany. ISBN: 978-3-7639-6709-4 (Print) DOI: 10.3278/6001920dw

U.S. Centers for Medicare & Medicaid Services (2022). People under 30. Available at: https://www.healthcare.gov/young-adults/college-students/

World Health Organization (2022): Quality of care. Available at: https://www.who.int/health-topics/quality-of-care#tab=tab_1

Conclusion

First, let me please acknowledge your effort. I know you have a lot on your plate and I know you have stocks of other books you need to read for your classes. But you still managed to squeeze reading this book into your schedule. Second, I would like to thank you for doing this for yourself, for wanting to be well and success-ful in your life and for actually taking action on it. And third, thank you for trying the activites, exploring the tips, playing with them, and not giving up on adjusting your lifestyle. Not many changes happen overnight and making your life better for yourself is a journey. So please don't give up; continue cultivating your PERMA+4 building blocks of well-being and enjoy the process. Including taking it slow some-times. Be perceptive to your needs, desires, and the whole-being. Listen to your interests and try what excites you. Listen to your intuition and do what feels right for you. And pay attention to your body and mind and give yourself a break if you need to.

We humans are seasonal and our productive periods need to be compensated with time for rest. Life is a process and it flows in waves. Sometimes it flows faster, and sometimes it slows down a bit. Sometimes it is a roller coaster, and sometimes it is a much needed walk. Sometimes you will feel energized to make changes and to try new activities, and sometimes you will feel like resting and slowing things down. And that is important too. Deciding to give yourself grace, rest, and the op-tion to do nothing every now and then is a necessary part of it too. Remember roller coasters and sightseeing walks. They both take their own parts. So no matter where you are right now, whether you sit in the first carriage of a roller coaster about to ride the steep slope or you enjoy the slow walk looking around doing some sight-seeing in your life, I wish you from the bottom of my heart to enjoy it, to share it with people around you, and to live the way that feels right for you. Caring for your well-being is a beautiful lifelong job that never ends. We grow, we flourish, and we keep discovering ourselves over and over. You are motivated to care for yourself, skilled to really do so and knowledgeable about the main elements generating your well-being now. What activities did you enjoy the most? And what tips helped you to be well? What building block was your favorite? I am so curious how will your flowers change. Which one is the one you would like to focus on to make it grow next? You are welcome to come back to your flower assessments anytime to reflect on how your well-being feels at the moment. Go ahead and explore the activities

DOI: 10.4324/9781003378365-12

again and try new tools that support your well-being as much as you desire. You are the expert on your own well-being now, and you have the ability to do anything you want in your life. And if you ever feel alone on your journey, remember that this book will always be your companion.

May you feel safe, may you feel happy, may you feel passionate, may you feel fulfilled and complete, and may you feel loved on your well-being care adventure.

With deep appreciation,
Jana

Index

Note: *Italic* page numbers refer to figures.

academic: engagement 56; school 15;
    success 16–17; well-being 15–16
achievement 115–116; assessment ladder
    118; benefits 116; character
    strengths 123–129, *125*;
    flower assessment *120*; flower
    diagram *119*; flower growth
    136; flower reflection 146; grit
    132–133; passion for long-term
    goals 118, 133; perseverance
    for long-term goals 118, 133;
    personal superpowers 116–117;
    problem-solving *132*; recognition
    and enjoyment 117, 122–123;
    recognition and use 117, 123;
    responsibility 117, 129–132;
    satisfaction 117, 122; skills
    134–137; snacking 137–138, *138*;
    strengths 144, 120; subjective
    perception 121; superpowers 124;
    ten commandments *135*; tips to
    build 136–137; willpower 117, 132
active constructive listening 91, 95
active constructive responding 2, 21, 85
Adler, A. 20
anger 33, 90–91, 167
anxiety 6, 10, 20, 41, 43, 115, 130, 147,
    163, 165, 181–182
Authentic Happiness (Seligman) 17, 53
autonomy-supportive environment 44

Berkeley Well-being Institute 33
best self 21
big eight 186
binge-drinking 167
bio-behavioral synchrony 79
bravery 126, 137
broaden-and-build theory 35

caffeine 161
Centers for Disease Control and Prevention
    6, 167
character strengths 2, 21, 65, 86, 99, 110,
    116, 117, 123–129, 174, 204, 209
community environment 193, 196, 198,
    201, 208–209
creativity 58, 61, 126, 204, 208
critical thinking 21, 129, 196
Crum, A. 173
Csikszentmihalyi, M. 62, 66, 70, 88; *Good
    Business* 62

decision-making 21, 129
deep thinking 97
Dekker, I. 98
depression 10, 20, 147, 181
Donaldson, S.I. 18
dopamine 42
Duckworth, A.L. 133, 136
Dweck, C. 93, 187, 188

economic security 215–223; benefits 217;
    financial literacy 217, 226–228;
    flower assessment *220*; flower
    assessment 217–220; flower growth
    228–229; flower reflection 221;
    good income 218, 222; life values
    224; proper expense management
    218, 225–226; quality health care
    218, 228; satisfactory investments
    218, 223–224; satisfactory savings
    218, 222–223; snacking 213, *213*;
    strengths 219–220; tips to build 229
Ekman, P 33
Emmons, R. 41
emotional contagion 46
empathy training 21, 85

engagement 53–54; ability to focus 57, 59–60; alone time 57, 69–70; assessment ladder *58*; benefits 54–55; build flow 71–74; creativity 58; engagement flower diagram *59*; everyday life activities 57, 64; evidence-based tips 73–74; experiencing flow 58, 70; flower assessment *60*; flower assessment 56; flower growth 73; flower reflection 84; frequently engaged 55; hobbies 57, 68–69; other people 57, 69; outside your academic experiences 56; school 57, 64–65; set of statements 80; single tasking 62; snacking *74*; strengths 56, 58–60; student 54–55; subjective perception 61; work or part-time job 57, 66–68

environment 193–196, *194*; acts of kindness 205; assessment ladder *219*; benefits 2, 196; character strengths 208; community 198, 208–209; environmental strengths 198–199, *200*; family 197, 205; flower assessment 197; flower diagram *200*; flower growth 212; flower reflection 221; healthy *195*; home 197, 203–204; home and living environment 202–203; neighborhood 204; online 198, 210; personal character strengths 209; proximity *196*; school 197; school and study 206; snacking 213, *213*; spending time in nature 211; study achievement 207; subjective evaluation 195; time off(line) 210; time out in campus 207; time spent outdoors in nature 198; work and part-time job environment 198, 207–208

evidence-based activities 29, 32

fairness 95, 116, 126

family climate 205

family environment 193, 194, 197, 202, 204–205

fear 33, 55, 122, 126

financial capital 179

Flourishing (Seligman) 17, 53

flower reflection: achievement 120–121; economic security 220–221; engagement 61; environment 200–201; mindset 177–178; physical health 145–146; positive relationships 83–84; theory of meaning 120–121

forgiveness 126

Frankl, V.E. 224; *Man's Search for Meaning* 97

Fredrickson, B.L. 33, 34, 41, 63, 111

future orientation 175, 186–187

Gable, S. 91

Global Emotional Report, 2020 59, 7

goal-setting technique 97–98

Good Business (Csikszentmihalyi) 62

gratitude 126

gratitude visit 21, 86

Greater Good Magazine 90

Greater Good Science Center (GGSC) 41

Harvard Medical School 183

health: definition of 37; mental 37–6, 77; physical 24, 77, 138 (*see also* physical health); social 85, 99

Healthy Minds program 163, 164

heavy drinking 167

heightened stress 10

home environment 193, 194, 197, 203

honesty 116, 126

hope 41, 110, 126, 174, 180

human capital 179

humility 126

humor 87, 116, 126, 208

Ikigai 48, 108, *109*

imposter syndrome 10

integrative emotion regulation 44

kindness 86, 93, 116, 126, 205

leadership 126

life crafting 97, 98, 104, 111, 192

Littlefield, C. 42

living: core values 105; cost 216; engaged life 17; environment 193, 202; meaningful life 17; PERMA+4 19; pleasant life 17

longterm atmosphere 195

long-term goals 115, 117, 118, 133

love of learning 116, 126

Man's Search for Meaning (Frankl) 97

meditation 21, 63, 111, 163, 164

mental health 6, 15, 77, 163

mindfulness 21, 63, 111, 162, 165
mindset: assessment ladder *175*; benefits
    173–174; caring 183; confidence
    in yourself 174, 180–181; fixed
    traits *vs.* growth traits *188*; flower
    assessment *177*; flower diagram
    176; flower growth 190; flower
    reflection 201; future orientation
    175, 186–187; growth 175,
    187–189; HERO *186*; hope 174,
    180; optimism 174–175, 183–184,
    184; optimists and pessimistic
    184; psychological capital 179;
    resiliency 174, 181; school life 189;
    snacking 191–192, *191*; strengths
    198–199; stress management
    techniques *182*; subjective
    perception 178; tips to build
    190–191; unwinding and managing
    stress 181–182
mutually reinforcing activities 3

negative emotions 6, 33, 34
negative outcomes 20
nine building blocks 18, *18*, 23, 53
non-judgmental environment 44

objective dimension 16
optimism 54, 174–175, 183–184, *184*

PERMA 18, 53, 106
PERMA+4 *18*, 19, 22–23; achievement
    24; economic security 24–26;
    engagement 23; environment 24;
    flower diagram 23; meaning 23;
    mindset 24; nine different building
    blocks 23; physical health 24;
    positive emotions 23; relationships
    23; set of statements 23; subjective
    perception 27
personal: finance 227; goal-setting 97, 111,
    135; power 209; superpowers 116;
    traits 123
pessimistic 183, *184*
Peterson, C. 9, 123
physical health 3, 140–141; activities
    168; adequate body movement
    143, 147–149, *148*; assessment
    ladder *144*; avoidance of risky
    behavior 143; benefits 142; better
    and healthier sleep 161–163; body
    moving 151, *151*; body posture
    152; brain foods 158; complete

physical prosperity 141; definition
    141; empowering flower growth
    168–169; facilitating mindfulnes
    165; flower assessment *145*;
    flower assessment 142; flower
    diagram *145*; flower reflection
    146; healthy eating plate 156–158,
    157; high-quality sleep 143,
    160–161; mindful eating 159;
    mindfulness meditation 164;
    optimal nutrition 143, 156; physical
    activity snacking 149, *150*; power
    poses 154–155, *155*; proper body
    posture 143; proper breathing
    143, 165–166; proper sitting
    practice *153*, 153–154; proper
    standing practice *152*, 153; regular
    relaxation 143, 163–165; risky
    behavior 167–168; snacking 170,
    170; strengths 144–146; subjective
    perception 146; tips 150–151;
    tips to build 169; UCLA Mindful
    Awareness Research Center 164;
    yoga practice 152
Positive Education 13, *14*
positive emotions 33–34, *35*; assessment
    ladder *38*; benefits 35–36;
    enhanced health and fulfillment
    36; experience 36; experienced
    with other people 46; experiencing
    41–42; flower assessment *39*; flower
    assessment 36; flower diagram *39*;
    growing 41; hobbies and interests
    37, 45–46; hyper-focused 42; life
    satisfaction 37, 45; with other
    people 37; regulation styles 44; at
    school 37, 46; shared positivity 37,
    48–49; strengths 37–38; subjective
    perception 40; tips 49–51, *50*;
    useful skills 36; work or part-time
    job 37, 47–48
positive functioning 1, 17, 28, 35, 105, 142,
    179, 202
positive mindset 93, 172, 189
positive personality traits 87
positive psychology 8, 9, 13, 17, 70, 128
positive psychology interventions 15,
    19–20
positive relationships 76–78; assessment
    ladder *82*; benefits 78–80; boss/
    supervisor 80, 88; building
    blocks 80; classmates 80, 86–87;
    communicate openly 89; community

81, 92–93; co-workers 81, 88–89;
family members 81, 90–91; flower
assessment *83*; flower diagram
83; flower reflection 84; friends
81, 89–90; relationships flower
94–95; relationships strengths 82,
83; response to positive event *91*;
self-compassion 93; significant
other 91–92; significant other(s) 81,
91–92; snacking *95, 95*–96; social
skills 81, *85*; subjective perception
103; teachers 80, 87–88; yourself
81, 92–93
positivity resonance 78, 79, 87, 123
problem-solving 21, 131, *132*
prospection 186
prudence 126, 127, 137
PsyCap *see* psychological capital
psychological capital 24, 179–180

rapid eye movement (REM) 160
resiliency 149, 174, 181

Schippers, M.C. 97, 98, 111
school: academic well-being 15; life
        balance 15; traditional outcomes 13
self-compassion 85, 93, 94, 189–190
self-improvement 24, 29
self-regulation 126
Seligman, M.E.P. 8, 17, 18, 21, 53, 77,
        105, 106, 110, 123, 141, 183,
        186; *Authentic Happiness* 17, 53;
        Flourishing 17, 53
serotonin 42
shared positivity 36, 37, 79
single tasking 62
six basic emotions 33
SMART goal-setting 135
social capital 179
social clime 195
social intelligence 126
social problems 167
spirituality 100, 110, 126
stimulus 33
stress management techniques *182*
students: achievement 116; benefits of
        meaning 98; budget 222–223;
        economic security 217–218;
        engagement 54–55; environment
        196; EUROSTUDENT countries
        216; health services 34; mindsets
        173–174; physical health 142;

positive emotions 35; positive
        relationships 78–80; relaxation
        and meditation 163–164; scale 12;
        success 11; well-being of university
        12–14
subjective dimension 16
success 14–15, *15*; academic achievement
        14–17; internal factors 16

teamwork 126
theory of meaning: assessment ladder *100*;
        benefits 98; building relationships
        99, 109; everyday life activities 99,
        106–107; faith and spirituality 100,
        110; flower assessment *102*; flower
        assessment 98–99; flower diagram
        101; flower reflection 103–104;
        growing 122; Ikigai *109*; in life 99,
        105–106; life-crafting intervention
        104; mindfulness meditation 110;
        other strengths 100–101; personal
        goal-setting 111; purpose in life
        100, 109–110; school activities
        99, 107–108; serving others 99,
        108; snacking *113*, 113; subjective
        perception 103; tips to build 112;
        work activities 99, 108
translation 33

UCLA Mindful Awareness Research Center
        164, 165
unique moments 78–79
University of Pennsylvania 41
The UN World Happiness Report 7

Walker, M. 160, 161
well-being: activities 19–22; assessment
        ladder *25*; building blocks 2, 17–
        19; care 3–4, *4, 11*, 28–29; common
        words 11; five elements 18; flower
        diagram *26*; higher levels 10; long
        term 19–20; measuring 6–59;
        multiple components 20; negative
        outcomes 20; rate the best 12;
        skills *14*; state *6*; strengthening *22*;
        students success 11; success 14–15,
        15; tips 28; university students
        9–14
well-validated intervention practices 20
West, T.N. 41

zest 126

For Product Safety Concerns and Information please contact our EU
representative GPSR@taylorandfrancis.com
Taylor & Francis Verlag GmbH, Kaufingerstraße 24, 80331 München, Germany

9 781032 457208